FOUNDATIONS in SOCIOLINGUISTICS

An Ethnographic Approach

Dell Hymes

University of Pennsylvania Press
Philadelphia

Copyright © 1974 by
the University of Pennsylvania Press, Inc.

Library of Congress Catalog Card Number: 73-89288

ISBN (cloth): 0-8122-7675-2

ISBN (paper): 0-8122-1065-4

Printed in the United States of America. Editorial production and design by
Weidner Associates, Inc., Cinnaminson, NJ.

In memory of

Edward Sapir

Contents

Introduction

"Sociolinguistics" could be taken to refer to use of linguistic data and analyses in other disciplines, concerned with social life, and, conversely, to use of social data and analyses in linguistics. The word could also be taken to refer to correlations between languages and societies, and between particular linguistic and social phenomena. These worthwhile activities would not really require a special name. They leave linguistics and the other disciplines as they are. They presuppose a science of mankind among whose departments human life has been accurately and completely apportioned. But sociolinguistics merits our attention just insofar as it signals an effort to change the practice of linguistics and other disciplines, because their present practice perpetuates a fragmented, incomplete understanding of humanity. Sociolinguistics, so conceived, is an attempt to rethink received categories and assumptions as to the bases of linguistic work, and as to the place of language in human life.

The chapters of this book come together in the expression of three themes that I take to be fundamental to sociolinguistics: *first*, that there is a mode of organization of language that is a part of the organization of communicative conduct in a community, whose understanding requires a corresponding, new mode of description of language; *second*, that recognition of this mode of organization leads one to recognize that the study of language is a multidisciplinary field, a field to which ordinary linguistics is indispensable, but to which other disciplines, such as sociology, social anthropology, education, folklore, and poetics, are indispensable as well; *third,* that study of this mode of organization leads one to reconsider the bases of linguistics itself. One might say that the three themes have to do with the scope, the dependencies, and, ultimately, the foundations of linguistics.

The three themes are closely connected, and appear interwoven throughout the book. Still, each of them in turn provides the focus for a section. The first section, "Toward ethnographies of communication," presents the general standpoint to which recognition of speaking as a topic of ethnography brings one. It depicts the scope and goals of a sociolinguistic mode of description, first in the context of cultural patterning of communicative conduct generally (ch. 1), then specifically in terms of speech (ch. 2). The second section, "The status of linguistics as a science," takes up the concern and title of an essay by Sapir (1929). Toward the end of that essay, Sapir remarked:

> One can only hope that linguists will become increasingly aware of the significance of their subject in the general field of science and will not stand aloof behind a tradition that threatens to become scholastic when not vitalized by interests which lie beyond the formal interest in language itself. [SWES 16s]

In recent years the dominant vitalizing interest has linked linguistic inquiry with cognitive psychology, and has tended to reinforce, rather than transcend, a purely formal interest. The chapters in this second section show a running debate with that outlook, and stress the significance of several social and humanistic disciplines to the vitalization of linguistic inquiry. The third section of the book, "Linguistics as sociolinguistics," takes up technical questions within linguistics, in order to show that the perspective of the preceding chapters is not external to linguistics, but arises out of its own practice. The linguistic commandment, "capture generalizations," is applied to hitherto "marginal" aspects of language, and is shown to lead linguistics to new foundations. The final chapter takes up the major themes of the book in an overview, and addresses the social concerns of linguists directly. The scientific and social concerns of linguists are held to lead to a reconstruction of linguistics as sociolinguistics, that is, as a discipline which accepts the social constitution of its subject matter, and the social bases of its practice and theory.

In these chapters I sometimes speak of future directions for linguistics, as if the perspective set forth here should be considered the next stage in the development of the subject. Let me emphasize that I consider this perspective a desirable next stage, but do not think any particular development inevitable. Nor do I think that the construction of what seem to me necessary new foundations for linguistic theory and practice must eclipse all current lines of work, let alone entail scorn for such long-standing traditions as those of philology, comparative reconstruction, and the like. I continue to practice some of that sort of work myself, in connection with American Indian languages. It would be a healthy thing for linguistics if it could come to accept an advance in one direction without forgetting what it has learned and could still learn in others.

I say this with some feeling, and I hope, understanding, because some years ago I found myself with a mixed and troublesome intellectual and professional heritage—from anthropological philology, into which I had been willy nilly cast as a graduate student; from socialist aspirations, chosen in undergraduate years; from precedents and patterns in the development of anthropology, folklore, and Amerindian linguistics, for whose historiography I felt a steadily deepening affinity. With such a heritage the past decade or so has seemed one in which a generation of linguists talked of the same goals as those of the traditions I knew, if in sometimes different words, yet enthusiastically pursued a practice that appeared to deny them.

All these chapters share, then, the problem of coming to terms with an ostensible profession (my doctorate being in linguistics, although with a great deal of work in anthropology and folklore). Linguistics was veering from its roots in anthropology, and, as I felt, in human realities, already when I first encountered it; in a few years that direction was being pursued pell mell. Yet unresolved problems of the older traditions persisted, even came newly to awareness, and a certain logic, as to the bases of past advances, a certain pattern of advances, calling for completion, appeared as well. In a sense I could not help working out the ideas dealt with in these chapters. None of the original papers, in fact, represents a task set by an immediate research problem or technical issue; there have always been other things that might have been, perhaps should have been, worked on, or poems that might have got written. Thoughts on these problems have almost seemed to have taken up residence in my brain for meetings and purposes of their own, not asking my permission, but unpredictably popping up perhaps while I was drifting into sleep, or shaving, or listening to music. Often enough a bit of ethnographic data has turned out to conceal something problematic that had to be inspected, and fitted into something larger than itself.

It seems now that linguistics itself is moving into areas to which these ideas are pertinent, areas with which linguistics would be much better prepared to deal, had so much of earlier lines of work not been lost in the bliss of a revolutionary dawn and an atmosphere of contempt for all else. If these explorations in a border country prove central now, I shall be very glad indeed.

All these chapters were first written in response to an invitation or opportunity afforded by colleagues, and I want to thank them collectively here; most of this book might otherwise not have reached paper. In preparing this book, I have changed every paper to some degree, and most papers substantially. A good many bits of overlap and repetition have been excised, and I hope that those that remain are mutually clarifying and reinforcing, rather than tiring. In the most extended statements of approach (chs. 2, 4, and 6), the presentation of some essential terms and notions has been significantly revised. Thus this book is not an accurate source for the development of ideas, if any wish to trace that; and other versions of these papers are not an adequate portrait of what I take my ideas now to be.

This book does deal with ideas, more than with data; I hope that there is room in the study of language for both. The ideas I have most wrestled with, most kept coming back to, have been in work of Kenneth Burke, Ernst Cassirer, Noam Chomsky, Roman Jakobson, Karl Marx, and Edward Sapir. What I say here is not in strict agreement with any of them, indeed is critical or a crucial departure in one or another respect, but the saying has grown out of the wrestling. Linguists, I hope, will see in this book a contribution especially to the tradition of Sapir, whose work and whose family have touched on mine over the years in so many ways.

I owe a special debt to Erving Goffman; sociolinguistics is discovering that at its core lie concerns that have long been his, and this book would not exist without his intervention. The Center for Urban Ethnography, and its director, John Szwed, have been an ever present help these past few years; and it is no coincidence that the writing of the chapters in the book largely coincides with my participation in the Committee on Sociolinguistics of the Social Science Research Council. Let me also thank Al Romano and Iles Minoff for indispensable help in preparation of the manuscript. Iles Minoff prepared, and Sally Yerkovich typed, the index. Fred Wieck, Joel Sherzer, and Michael Silverstein objected successively to tentative titles; Virginia Hymes proposed the form and nouns of the third.

Dell Hymes
Mt. Hood National Forest
June 7, 1973

Part One

Toward Ethnographies
of Communication

To make a start
out of particulars
and make them general, rolling
up the sum, by defective means—
William Carlos Williams,
Paterson: Book I

Chapter 1

Toward Ethnographies
of Communication

The term "ethnography of communication" is intended to indicate the necessary scope, and to encourage the doing, of studies ethnographic in basis, and communicative in the range and kind of patterned complexity with which they deal.[1] That is, the term implies two characteristics that an adequate approach to language must have.

As to scope: one cannot simply take separate results from linguistics, psychology, sociology, ethnology, as given, and seek to correlate them, however partially useful such work may be, if one is to have a theory of language (not just a theory of grammar). One needs fresh kinds of data, one needs to investigate directly the use of language in contexts of situation, so as to discern patterns proper to speech activity, patterns that escape separate studies of

1. This chapter is based upon "Introduction: Toward Ethnographies of Communication," in *The Ethnography of Communication,* ed. by John J. Gumperz and Dell Hymes (Washington, D.C.: American Anthropological Association, 1964), pp. 1–34, issued as Part 2 of the *American Anthropologist* 66(6) (December). It comprises mainly sections VI and VII of that essay. To Susan Ervin-Tripp, John Gumperz, Michael Halliday, Sydney Lamb, Sheldon Sacks, and Dan Slobin, I am indebted for warm discussions of language and its social study; to Bob Scholte and Erving Goffman for pointed argument about the notion of communication; and to Harold C. Conklin, Charles Frake, Ward Goodenough, Floyd Lounsbury, and William C. Sturtevant, for discussion through several years of the nature of ethnography. To all much thanks and no blame.

3

grammar, of personality, of social structure, religion, and the like, each abstracting from the patterning of speech activity into some other frame of reference.

As to basis: one cannot take linguistic form, a given code, or even speech itself, as a limiting frame of reference. One must take as context a community, or network of persons, investigating its communicative activities as a whole, so that any use of channel and code takes its place as part of the resources upon which the members draw.

It is not that linguistics does not have a vital role. Analyzed linguistic materials are indispensable, and the logic of linguistic methodology is an influence in the ethnographic perspective. It is rather that it is not linguistics, but ethnography, not language, but communication, which must provide the frame of reference within which the place of language in culture and society is to be assessed. The boundaries of the community within which communication is possible; the boundaries of the situations within which communication occurs; the means and purposes and patterns of selection, their structure and hierarchy—all elements that constitute the communicative economy of a group, are conditioned, to be sure, by properties of the linguistic codes within the group, but are not controlled by them. The same linguistic means may be made to serve various ends; the same communicative ends may be served, linguistically, by various means. Facets of the cultural values and beliefs, social institutions and forms, roles and personalities, history and ecology of a community may have to be examined in their bearing on communicative events and patterns (just as any aspect of a community's life may come to bear selectively on the study of kinship, sex, or role conflict).

It will be found that much that has impinged upon linguistics as variation and deviation has an organization of its own. What seem variation and deviation from the standpoint of a linguist's analysis may emerge as structure and pattern from the standpoint of the communicative economy of the group among whom the analyzed form of speech exists. The structures and patterns that emerge will force reconsideration, moreover, of the analysis of linguistic codes themselves. Just as elements and relations of phonology appear partly in a new light when viewed from the organization of grammar, and just as elements and relations of the grammar appear in a new light when viewed from the organization of sememics (Lamb 1964), so elements and relations of the linguistic code as a whole will appear partly in a new light, viewed from the organization of the elements and relations of the speech act and speech event, themselves part of a system of communicative acts and events characteristic of a group.

To project the ethnography of communication in such a way

is tantamount to the belief that there awaits constitution a second descriptive science comprising language, in addition to, and ultimately comprehending, present linguistics—a science that would approach language neither as abstracted form nor as an abstract correlate of a community, but as situated in the flux and pattern of communicative events. It would study communicative form and function in integral relation to each other. In this it would contrast with long held views of linguistics and of what is within linguistics. Some divorce linguistic form from context and function. An old but apt illustration is found in Bloomfield's often cited remark that, if a beggar says "I'm hungry" to obtain food, and a child says "I'm hungry" to avoid going to bed, then linguistics is concerned just with what is the same in the two acts. It abstracts, in other words, from context. In contrast, an influential book has characterized pragmatics in a way exactly complementary as "all those aspects which serve to distinguish one communication event from any other where the sign types may be the same" (Cherry 1961: 225). It abstracts, in other words, from linguistic form.

Such views are not the only ones to be found, but they have been characteristic of linguistics, on the one hand, and social science, on the other, and most practice has exemplified one or the other. For ethnographies of communication, however, the aim must be not so to divide the communicative act or event, divorcing message-form (Cherry's sign-type) and context of use from one another. The aim must be to keep the multiple hierarchy of relations among messages and contexts in view (cf. Bateson, 1963). Studies of social contexts and functions of communication, if divorced from the means that serve them, are as little to the purpose as are studies of communicative means, if divorced from the contexts and functions they serve. Methodologically, of course, it is not a matter of limiting a structural perspective inspired by linguistics to a particular component of communication, but of extending it to the whole.

The ethnography of communication is indebted to the methodological gains from recent studies of linguistic form for its own sake, and to a climate of opinion created by arguments for the significance of formal linguistics. Its roots, however, are deeper and more pervasive. On the one hand, there is the long-term trend away from the study of sociocultural form and content as product toward their study as process—away from study of abstracted categories, departments of culture, toward study of situations, exchanges, and events (cf. Sapir 1933b). On the other hand, there is the continuing trend in linguistics itself toward study of the full complexity of language in terms of what the Prague Circle as long ago as 1929 (the year of Sapir's "The status of linguistics as a

science") called "functional and structural analysis," and which
Jakobson now designates as interwar efforts towards a "means-
ends model" (Jakobson 1963); there are parallels in the perspectives of J. R. Firth (1935—cf. ch. 4 of this volume) and of Sapir (cf.
chs. 3, 10 of this volume) in the same period. These traditions have
had their vicissitudes, but it is fair to see in the ethnography of
communication a renewal of them.

For many people, the place of the ethnography of communication will appear to be, not in relation to one or more traditions
in linguistics, but in relation to some general perspective on human
behavior. For many, the name of this perspective will be social
anthropology, or sociology, or psychology, or some other disciplinary category. The work required does fall somewhere into
place within the purview of each such discipline, and there can be
no quarrel with any, except to say that the division of the study of
man into departmentalized disciplines seems itself often arbitrary
and an obstacle. What is essential, in any case, is that the distinctive focus of concern advanced here be recognized and cultivated,
whatever the disciplinary label. One way to state the need is to
remark that there are anthropological, sociological, and psychological studies of many kinds, but of ethnographic analyses of
communicative conduct, and of comparative studies based upon
them, there are still few to find. (Chs. 3 and 4 take up relationships
with sociology and social anthropology further.)

These remarks apply as well to the field of interest under
which others would subsume the concerns represented here,
namely, semiotics. De Saussure had proposed semiology as a field
more general than linguistics, and Levi-Strauss has characterized
it as the study of the life of signs in the bosom of social life, subsuming both linguistics and social anthropology within it (1960).
Despite the broad interpretation given the term, however, semiotics (semiology) has continued to suggest most readily logical
analysis, and the study of systems of signs as codes alone. The
empirical study of systems of signs within systems of use in actual
communities seems secondary, when not lost from sight.

Here a division of semiotics in the tripartite formulation of
Morris (1946) might serve. Pragmatics, concerned with the use of
signs by an interpreter, might be the bridge between the present
area of concern and linguistics proper, and stand as name for the
cultivation of theory of the use of language (and other codes),
alongside theory of their formal and semantic structure (Morris'
syntagmatics and semantics). Such a usage of the term 'pragmatics'
indeed seems to be gaining vogue in German-language research.
Some characterizations of pragmatics, to be sure, would not be
adequate, as has been noted above. A conception of pragmatics as

concerned with what varies in import, while message-form remains constant, allows for but one of the two relationships between structures of action and structures of communicative form. The relations between means and ends are multiple in both directions, the same means serving sometimes varied ends, and the ends being served by sometimes varied means.

In terms of the criteria systematized by Lamb (1964), we can indeed see a natural extension of grammar to features of action, a pragmemic level if one wishes to call it that. Lamb distinguishes linguistic strata by the twin criteria of "diversification" and "neutralization" (see further ch. 4). Diversification is illustrated by such facts as that one element of meaning can occur in diverse representations (as in *dog house* : *kennel*, or *cat house* : *whore house*); neutralization is illustrated by such facts as that the same representation may serve diverse elements of meaning (as *dog* in *dog house, dog fight, dognap*, or *cat* in *cat house, cat fight, catnap*). One might well recognize a stratum involving the "pragmeme" as an element or feature of action, since the same feature of action can occur in diverse semantic representations, and the same semantic representations can serve diverse features of action. To use an example from Susan Ervin-Tripp, the same feature of request may be encoded in "Would you get me my coat?" and "Don't you think it's getting cold?"; and conversely, to complete the example, "Don't you think it's getting cold?" may express (among other things) features of literal question or demand for action ("Get me my coat," "Take me inside").

Invaluable as a structural pragmemics would be, it would not suffice for the whole of the subject. Nor, as ordinarily conceived, would communication theory or cybernetics. What is sometimes specifically meant by each of the latter terms would seem to fit, quite importantly indeed, as parts of a general strategy for ethnographic research into communication.

In general, experience suggests that work contributing to study of communication in an ethnographic spirit is likely not to duplicate work under another aegis. Each of the other general notions seems in practice to lose sight of concrete communication, in the sense of actual communities of persons. Forms of formalization, the abstract possibilities of systems, hoped-for keys to mankind as a whole, seem to overshadow the dogged work of making sense of real communities and lives. I find in this a political as well as a scientific liability. In any case, the long-standing, close ties between ethnography and linguistic description; the ethnographic practice of participant observation; and the values placed on the specifics of cultural life and the viewpoint of the other participants in the communication that is ethnography—

such traits tend to ensure two characteristics. First, there is likely
to be a more egalitarian distribution of detailed interest among
the several components of communicative events. Not only the
participants and the contents of messages, but also the structures,
degrees of elaboration, distinctiveness, values and genres associated with channels, codes, message-forms and settings attract
attention partly in their own right—the linguistic codes, of course,
as most explicit, and as indispensable, if not wholly adequate,
avenues of access to other codes, and to the meanings of other
components—but also specialized subcodes and marginal systems,
techniques of speech disguise, languages of concealment, drum-
languages, ceremonial speech and oratory; the channels, especially
when complexly elaborated as in West Africa, or distinctively
specialized, as writing for lovers' messages among the Hanunoo of
the Philippines; the forms of poetry, ritual speech, and dramatic
enactment; and so forth. Such aspects of communication are less
likely to receive full due in studies whose concern with communication is not so much with an activity of people, but with fodder
for models, or not so much with realization of the purposes of
others, as with a way of achieving purposes of one's own. The
ethnographer is likely to have, or come to have, the view that
models are for people, not people for models; and that there are
no masses, only ways of regarding people as masses; that one
man's mass is another's public, or community, and that to speak
of mass communications is already to express a separateness from
the portion of humanity concerned that prejudices the result (see
Williams 1960: 315–58). The ethnographer is likely to look at
communication from the standpoint and interests of a community
itself, and to see its members as sources of shared knowledge and
insight. I believe that the only worthwhile future for the sciences
of man lies in the realization of such an approach (cf. Hymes
1972c).

The linguistics that can contribute to the ethnography of communication is now generally known as sociolinguistics, and it is
here that my own training and experience lie. Such a sociolinguistics, however, is not identical with everything that currently
comes under that name. The sociolinguistics with which we are
concerned here contributes to the general study of communication
through the study of the organization of verbal means and the
ends they serve, while bearing in mind the ultimate integration of
these means and ends with communicative means and ends generally. Such an approach within sociolinguistics can be called, in
keeping with the general term, ethnography of communication,
the study of the "ethnography of speaking." (Cf. Hymes 1962, and
ch. 4). For the contribution of the ethnography of speaking to be

realized, there must be change with respect to a number of orientations toward language. Seven can be singled out as the Pleiades,
pointing to the North Star, of this firmament. Primacy must go to
(1) the structure, or system of speech (*la parole*); (2) function as
prior to and warranting structure; (3) language as organized in
terms of a plurality of functions, the different functions themselves warranting different perspectives and organizations; (4) the
appropriateness of linguistic elements and messages; (5) diversity
of the functions of diverse languages and other communicative
means; (6) the community or other social context as starting point
of analysis and understanding; (7) functions themselves to be war-
ranted in context, and in general the place, boundaries, and organization of language and of other communicative means in a community to be taken as problematic. In short, primacy of speech
to code, function to structure, context to message, the appropriate
to the arbitrary or simply possible; but the interrelations always
essential, so that one cannot only generalize the particularities, but
also particularize the generalities.

It remains that sociolinguistics, conceived in terms of the
ethnography of speaking, is ultimately part of the study of communication as a whole. To further establish this context, I shall
sketch a general framework in terms of communication proper.
The other chapters of this book should be read with the communicative framework in mind.

There are four aspects to the framework, concerned, respectively, with (1) the components of communicative events; (2) the
relations among components; (3) the capacity and state of components; and (4) the activity of the whole so constituted. It is
with respect to the third and fourth aspects that two topics promi-
nently associated with the topic of communication, communication
theory (in the sense of information theory), and cybernetics, find
a place.

THE COMPONENTS OF COMMUNICATIVE EVENTS

The starting point is the ethnographic analysis of the communicative conduct of a community. One must determine what
can count as a communicative event, and as a component of one,
and admit no behavior as communicative that is not framed by
some setting and implicit question. The communicative event thus is
central. (In terms of language the speech event, and speech act,
are correspondingly central; see ch. 2).

Some frame of reference is needed for consideration of the
several kinds of components copresent in a communicative event.
The logical or other superiority of one classification over another

is not at issue. What is at issue is the provision of a useful guide
in terms of which relevant features can be discerned—a provi-
sional phonetics, as it were, not an a priori phonemics, of the
communicative event.

For what has to be inventoried and related in an ethnographic
account, a somewhat elaborated version of factors identified in
communications theory, and adapted to linguistics by Roman Jakobson (1953;1960), can serve. Briefly put, (1) the various kinds of
participants in communicative events—senders and receivers,
addressors and addressees, interpreters and spokesmen, and the
like; (2) the various available *channels,* and their modes of use,
speaking, writing, printing, drumming, blowing, whistling, singing,
face and body motion as visually perceived, smelling, tasting, and
tactile sensation; (3) the various *codes* shared by various participants, linguistic, paralinguistic, kinesic, musical, interpretative,
interactional, and other; (4) the *settings* (including other communication) in which communication is permitted, enjoined, encouraged, abridged; (5) the *forms of messages,* and their *genres,*
ranging verbally from single-morpheme sentences to the patterns
and diacritics of sonnets, sermons, salesmen's pitches, and any
other organized routines and styles; (6) the *attitudes and contents*
that a message may convey and be about; (7) the *events* themselves, their kinds and characters as wholes—all these must be
identified in an adequate way.

Ethnography here is conceived in reference to the various
efforts of Conklin, Frake, Goodenough, Metzger, Romney, and
others to advance the techniques of ethnographic work and to
conceptualize its goal, such that the structural analysis of cultural
behavior generally is viewed as the development of theories adequate to concrete cases, just as the structural analysis of behavior
as manifestation of a linguistic code is so viewed. One way to
phrase the underlying outlook is as a question of validity. Just as
analysis of phonological capabilities must determine what set of
phonological features is to be taken as relevant to identification
and distinction of phonological sound on the part of the possessors
of those capabilities, so analysis of cultural capabilities generally
must determine what sets of features are to be taken as relevant
to identification and contrast of cultural behavior on the part of
the participants. (Sapir's "Sound Patterns in Language" [1925],
seen as implying a general statement about the cultural aspect of
behavior, remains classic and crucial to the development of
anthropological thought in this regard, although it has taken a
generation for its ethnographic import to become salient.) Another
way to phrase the underlying outlook is as a question of the common element in the situation of ethnographer and person-in-the-

culture. Each must formulate from finite experience theories adequate to predict and judge as appropriate or inappropriate what is, in principle, an infinite amount of cultural behavior. (Judgments of grammaticality are a special case.)

Mere observation, however systematic and repeated, can obviously never suffice to meet such high standards of objectivity and validity. As Sapir once observed regarding a rule of avoidance among the Wishram Chinook:

> Incidentally there is a lesson here for the theoretical ethnologist. If the avoidance of man and woman here were known only objectively it would present a situation resembling that, say, in Melanesia. One might suppose then the explanation to be that women were set apart from the man's social fabric because of the low esteem in which they were held, or that men avoided them because of their periodic impure state. Either guess would be a shot far wide of the mark. The moral is that it is as necessary to discover what the native sentiment is as well as to record the behavior.[2]

The point is essentially the same as that of "Sound Patterns in Language," from which stems the current distinction of "etic" and "emic." An "emic" account is one in terms of features relevant in the behavior in question; an etic account, however useful as a preliminary grid and input to an emic (structural) account, and as a framework for comparing different emic accounts, lacks the emic account's validity. The point is an old one in anthropology, only made more trenchant by the clarity with which the point can be made in terms of the contrast between phonetics and phonemics. (See Pike 1954 for coinage of the terms, and conscious development of the perspective from a linguistic basis beyond linguistics, under inspiration from Sapir.) Ethnographic objectivity is intersubjective objectivity, but in the first instance, the intersubjective objectivity in question is that of the participants in the culture. No amount of acoustic apparatus and sound spectrography can crack the phonemic code of a language, and a phonemic analysis, based on the intersubjective objectivity in the behavior of those who share the code, is the necessary basis for other studies, experimental and otherwise. (Cf. Hockett 1955:210–11; Lisker, Cooper, and Liberman 1962.) The same is true for the shared codes which constitute the mutual intelligibility of the rest of cultural behavior. The advantages of such an approach in providing a criterion against which to appraise participants' own explanations and con-

2. Spier and Sapir (1930: 217, n. 97). The point and the language indicate that the comment is due particularly to Sapir. The Wishram avoidance is due to the severe punishment, even death, visited for constructive adultery, which offense may be attributed in some circumstances even for private conversation or physical contact. Cf. the last section of Hymes (1966b).

ceptualizations of their behavior, their "homemade models," should be obvious, as should the advantages in providing a basis for controlled comparison, study of diffusion, and any other generalizing or analyzing approach that depends in the last analysis on the adequacy and precision of ethnographic records of cultural behavior. (Ethnographic records, of course, may be of other things: censuses, for example.)

In a discussion of genealogical method, Conklin (1964:25–26), observing that all kinship data derive from ethnographic contexts, makes explicit his assumptions regarding the nature and purpose of ethnography (citing also Goodenough 1956, and noting Frake 1962b, 1964, and a previous article of his own [1962]). The statement applies to communicative data as well as to kinship data, and can be adopted here:

> An adequate ethnography is here considered to include the culturally significant arrangement of productive statements about the relevant relationships obtaining among locally defined categories and contexts (of objects and events) within a given social matrix. These nonarbitrarily ordered statements should comprise, essentially, a cultural grammar (Goodenough 1957a; Frake 1962a). In such an ethnography, the emphasis is placed on the interpretation, evaluation, and selection of alternative statements about a particular set of cultural activities within a given range of social contexts. This in turn leads to the critical examination of intracultural relations and ethnotheoretical models (Conklin 1955; Goodenough ms.). Demonstrable intracultural validity for statements of covert and abstracted relationships should be based on prior analysis of particular and generalized occurrences in the ethnographic record (Lounsbury 1955:163-164, 1956; cf. Morris 1946). Criteria for evaluating the adequacy of ethnographic statements with reference to the cultural phenomena described, include: (1) productivity (in terms of appropriate anticipation if not actual prediction); (2) replicability or testability; and (3) economy. In actual field situations, recording activities, analytic operations, and evaluative procedures (in short, the application of ethnographic technique, method, and theory) can, and I think should, be combined. The improvement and constant adjustment of field recording is, in fact, dependent upon simultaneous analysis and evaluation.

Notice that strict conception of ethnography constrains the conception of communication that is admissible. Just as what counts as phonemic feature or religious act cannot be identified in advance, so with what counts as a communicative event. There are, of course, general criteria for phonemic and for communicative status; it is a question of the phenomena by which they are satisfied in a given case. If one examines the writings of anthropologists and linguists, one finds that general conceptions of communicative status vary, sometimes in ways at variance with the conception of ethnography adopted here.

The concept of message would seem to suffice as starting point for any conception, if one grants two kinds of things. The first is that the concept of message implies the sharing (real or imputed) of (1) a code or codes in terms of which the message is intelligible to (2) participants, minimally an addressor and addressee (who may be the same person), in (3) an event constituted by its transmission and characterized by (4) a channel or channels, (5) a setting or context, (6) a definite form or shape to the message, and (7) a topic and comment, i.e., that it says something about something—in other words, that the concept of message implies the array of components previously given. The second is that what can count as instances of messages, and as instances of the components of the event constituted by the transmission of a message, must be determined in the given case along the lines of the ethnographic approach just discussed and just characterized by Conklin.

If one accepts the latter point, then some anthropological conceptions of communication must be judged to exclude too much, or to include too much, or, occasionally, both. To take first the problem of excluding too much, one cannot a priori define the sound of approaching footsteps (Sapir 1921:3) or the setting of the sun (Hockett 1958:574) as not communicative. Their status is entirely a question of their construal by a receiver. In general, no phenomenon can be defined in advance as never to be counted as constituting a message. Consider a case related by Hallowell:

> An informant told me that many years before he was sitting in a tent one afternoon during a storm, together with an old man and his wife. There was one clap of thunder after another. Suddenly the old man turned to his wife and asked, "Did you hear what was said?" "No," she replied, "I didn't catch it." My informant, an acculturated Indian, told me he did not at first know what the old man and his wife referred to. It was, of course, the thunder. The old man thought that one of the Thunder Birds had said something to him. He was reacting to this sound in the same way as he would respond to a human being, whose words he did not understand. The casualness of the remark and even the trivial character of the anecdote demonstrate the psychological depth of the "social relations" with other-than-human beings that becomes explicit in the behavior of the Ojibwa as a consequence of the cognitive "set" induced by their culture. [1964:64]

There are manifold instances from cultures around the world, e.g., to take a recent report, the drinking, questioning and answering in which Amahuaca men are joined by the class of supernaturals known as *yoshi* associated interestingly enough with a specific form of chant and use of the vocal channel (vocal chords tightly constricted) (Carneiro 1964:8). Hallowell's account of the Ojibwa concept of person shows with particular depth the implications of

cultural values and world view for occurrences of communicative
behavior. As indication of the contribution a conscious ethnography of communication, focused on occurrences of activity such
as speech, might make to such anthropological concerns as world
view, let me cite one other Ojibwa instance and Hallowell's inter-
polated regret: having discussed the fact that stones are classified
grammatically as animate in gender, and are conceived as potentially capable of animate behavior, especially in ceremonially-
linked circumstances, Hallowell records:

> A white trader, digging in his potato patch, unearthed a large
> stone similar to the one just referred to. He sent for John Duck, an
> Indian who was the leader of the *wabano*, a contemporary cere-
> mony that is held in a structure something like that used for the
> Midewiwin (a major ceremony during which stones occasionally
> had animate properties such as movement and opening of a mouth).
> ·The trader called his attention to the stone, saying that it must
> belong to his pavilion. John Duck did not seem pleased at this. He
> bent down and spoke to the boulder in a low voice, inquiring
> whether it had ever been in his pavilion. According to John the
> stone replied in the negative.
> It is obvious that John Duck spontaneously structured the sit-
> uation in terms that are intelligible within the context of Ojibwa
> language and culture. . . . I regret that my field notes contain no
> information about the use of direct verbal address in the other
> cases mentioned (movement of stone, opening of a mouth). But it
> may well have taken place. In the anecdote describing John Duck's
> behavior, however, his use of speech as a mode of communication
> raises the animate status of the boulder to the level of social inter-
> action common to human beings. Simply as a matter of observa-
> tion we can say that the stone was treated *as if* it were a "person,"
> not a "thing," without inferring that objects of this class are, for
> the Ojibwa, necessarily conceptualized as persons. [1964:56]

Again, within the aboriginal culture of the Wishram and
Wasco Chinook of the Columbia River, one must recognize not
one but three communicative networks within a community,
defined by distinct shared codes. One consisted of normal adults,
and children past infancy; a second comprised babies, dogs, coyotes, and the guardian spirits Dog and Coyote, and, possibly old
people possessing those guardian spirits; a third comprised those
whose guardian spirit experience had granted them the power of
being able to interpret the language of the spirits.[3]

If the strict ethnographic approach requires us to extend the
concept of communication to the boundaries granted it by partici-

3. With regard to the first and second networks, babyhood lasted "until
they could talk clearly" (Spier and Sapir 1930: 218)—in Wishram, of course.
With regard to the second, "Such guardian spirits could understand the language of babies. They maintain that a dog, a coyote, and an infant can understand each other, but the baby loses his language when he grows old enough
to speak and understand the tongue of his parents" (*ibid.*: 255). With regard

pants of a culture, it also makes it necessary to restrict it to those boundaries. To define communication as the triggering of a response (as Hockett [1958:573] has done, and Kluckhohn [1961: 895] has accepted), is to make the term so nearly equivalent to behavior and interaction in general as to lose its specific value as a scientific and moral conception. There are many illustrations possible of actions that trigger response and are not taken as communicative by one or both participants. As an act clearly based on the triggering of response (in another or oneself), sexual intercourse would be an ideal event to test this point; what part, less than all, of triggering of response is sent or received as communication? Again, it is desirable to treat the transmission or receipt of information as not the same as, but a more general category than, communication, the latter being treated as a more specific sphere, necessarily either participated in or constituted by persons (cf. Cherry 1961:247 n). The sound of footsteps or the setting of the sun may be taken as a source of information without being taken as a message (although in either case a receiver may interpret the event as a message).

From this standpoint, genes may transmit information, but the process is communicative only from the standpoint of, and as reported by, an observer and interpreter. For the human observer to report and treat the process experienced or inferred as a communicative one is of course a right not to be challenged, for, formally, it is the same right that the ethnographer accepts when acted upon by an Ojibwa, Wishram, or other participant in a culture. The formal feature is that the evidence for the communicative event is a report by one who did not participate in it as either addressor or addressee. Such reported events (E", or narrated events, in Roman Jakobson's symbolization [1957] for the constituents of speech events) are common in myth, for example, and are of course of considerable importance, as when the origin of the world is so described by the ancient Hebrews, or the origin of death explained by the Wishram in a narrative culminating (as is typical for their myths) in an announcement ordaining how that aspect of cultural life is to be and what people will say in its regard.

We deal here, in short, with the fact that the communicative

---

ot the third, the group may have been individuated into various dyadic relationships between particular persons and spirits, for the example is given as "For instance, one who had gained the protection of Coyote could tell, on hearing a coyote's howl, what person was going to die" (ibid.: 239); but men still living, who make no claim to having had guardian spirit experience, recall having been able to understand the import of howls of coyotes (Mr. Hiram Smith, pers. comm.).

event is the metaphor, or perspective, basic to rendering experience intelligible. It is likely to be employed at any turn, if with varying modes of imputation of reality (believed, supposed, entertained in jest, etc.). It is this fact that underlies the apparently central role of language in cultural life. Of codes available to human beings, language, as the one more than any other capable at once of being explicitly detailed and transcendent of single contexts, is the chief beneficiary under many circumstances of the primary centrality of communication. Under some circumstances, of course, it is not.

In general, any and all of the components of a communicative event, and the occurrence of a message itself, can be imputed by one who adopts the standpoint of an addressor, addressee, or receiver as observer. One consequence is the point already made, but the ethnographic observer must do more than observe to prevent his own habits of imputation from interfering with recognition of where and what participants in another culture impute. Another consequence, since persons can impute either an addressor and intent or an addressee and attention, is to make heuristically useful for ethnographic purposes a characterization of a communicative event as one in which to the observer one at least of the participants is real.

The identification of communicative events and their components has been dwelt on, because it is seldom treated, except incidentally, in most writing relevant to ethnography. The discussion so far has been concerned with gross identification of events as such and of components individually. In point of fact, adequate determination usually will involve more than inventory of channels, setting, etc. The structures of relations among different events, and their components; the capabilities and states of the components; the activity of the system which is the event; all will be involved. Explication of genres of verbal art, once such have been identified (e.g., Ssukung Tu 1963),[4] commonly involves appeal at least to relations among components, and often to their states and activity. Such questions comprise the other aspects of the frame of reference being sketched, and to these we now turn.

4. The classical Chinese writer Ssukung Tu discriminated 24 modes, translated as Grand, Unemphatic, Ornate, Grave, Lofty, Polished, Refined, Vigorous, Exquisite, Spontaneous, Pregnant, Untrammeled, Evocative, Well-knit Artless, Distinctive, Devious, Natural, Poignant, Vivid, Transcendent, Ethereal, Light-hearted, Flowing (Ssukung Tu, as translated [1963] with accompanying discussion by Wu Tiao-kung, "Ssukung Tu's Poetic Criticism," 78–83). Such modes would entail considering the relevant components of the event constituted by the composing or performance of a poem from the standpoint of what is labelled "key" in ch. 2.

RELATIONS AMONG COMPONENTS

In one sense, the focus of the present approach is on communities organized as systems of communicative events. Such an object of study can be regarded as part of, but not identical with, an ethnography as a whole.[5] One way in which to indicate that there is a system, either in the community or in the particular event, is to observe that there is not complete freedom of cooccurrence among components. Not all imaginably possible combinations of participants, channels, codes, topics, etc., can occur.

It is to the structure of relations among components that much of the surge of work in sociolinguistics is directed. (Notice that focus on relations among components more readily invites description and comparative analysis of the variety of such marginal systems than does focus on the code alone. Also, more generally, it leads into description and comparison of whatever may characterize such an event or relationship, e.g., talk to babies, whether or not special features characterize it from the standpoint of the code as such. It is equally important to know the characteristics of talk to babies in societies where "baby talk" is eschewed. With regard to message-form, there is much to be discovered and described in the sequential patterning of speech as routines, specialized to certain relationships.)

Ervin-Tripp (1964) suggests that the structures of relations with respect to language will prove to be specific in some ways, to be more than illustration of more general sociological or psychological or cultural notions. The same is likely to prove true for each of the kinds of codes employed in a community. The heuristic assumption is that their separate maintenance implies some specific role for each which is not wholly duplicated by any other (including language). On the other hand, studies focused on the relations among components of communicative events are likely to discern patterns general to them, but partly independent of, and cutting across, the other departments of study into which the events might be cast ethnographically. Once looked for, areal styles, in the use of specific codes, and areal communicative styles generally, are likely to be found. Lomax (1959) has suggested such for musical performance, and Melville Jacobs (1958) has suggested such may be the case for the dramatic performances that enact myths.

5. Notice Conklin (1962: 199): "An adequate ethnographic description of the culture (Goodenough 1957a) of a particular society presupposes a detailed analysis of the communications system and of the culturally defined situations in which all relevant distinctions in that system occur."

It is especially important to notice that delineations of communities in these respects are crucial to understanding of the place of language in culture, and to understanding of the particular place of language in culture signalled by what is commonly called the Sapir-Whorf hypothesis. To assume that differences in language shape or interact with differences in world view is to assume that the functional role of language in relation to world view is everywhere the same. Indeed, anthropological thought quite generally has tended to assume identity or equivalence of function for language throughout the world (see discussion in Hymes 1961: 1962; 1966b).

When a particular code is considered but one component of communicative events, the studies of the structure of communicative events in a society will provide detailed evidence on the differential ways in which the code enters into communicative purposes and cultural life. The different ways and stages in which a language enters into enculturation, transmission of adult roles and skills, interaction with the supernatural, personal satisfactions, and the like will appear. Languages, like other cultural traits, will be found to vary in the degree and nature of their integration into the societies and cultures in which they occur. It will be possible to focus on the consequences of such differences for acculturation and adaptation of both languages and peoples. Such information has been brought to attention in studies of acculturation, bilingualism, and standard languages. What is necessary is to realize that the functional relativity of languages is general, applying to monolingual situations too.

With particular regard to the Sapir-Whorf hypothesis, it is essential to notice that Whorf's sort of linguistic relativity is secondary, and dependent upon a primary sociolinguistic relativity, that of differential engagement of languages in social life. For example, description of a language may show that it expresses a certain cognitive style, perhaps implicit metaphysical assumptions. but what chance the language has to make an impress upon individuals and behavior will depend upon the degree and pattern of its admission into communicative events. The case is clear in bilingualism; we do not expect a Bengali using English as a fourth language for certain purposes of commerce to be influenced deeply in world view by its syntax. What is necessary is to realize that the monolingual situation is problematic as well. Peoples do not all everywhere use language to the same degree, in the same situations, or for the same things; some peoples focus upon language more than others. Such differences in the place of a language in the communicative system of a people cannot be assumed to be without influence on the depth of a language's influence on such things as world view.

More particularly, if a language is taken as a device for categorizing experience, it is not such a device in the abstract. There remains the question of what may be the set of events in which categorizing dependent upon the language occurs. (The set includes events in which a single person is using a language excogitatively.) Although anthropologists have sometimes talked of the use of language "merely" as a tool of communication, and of the categorizing of experience as if it were a superior category (cf. Hymes 1967c), the role of a language as a device for categorizing experience and its role as an instrument of communication cannot be so separated, and indeed, the latter includes the former. This is the more true when a language, as is often the case, affords alternative ways of categorizing the same experience, so that the patterns of selection among such alternatives must be determined in actual contexts of use—as must also, indeed, the degree to which a language is being used as a full-fledged semantic instrument (as distinct from its use as an expressive, directive, etc., instrument) at all in a given case.

Such considerations broach the third aspect of our frame of reference.

CAPACITY AND STATE OF COMPONENTS

So far we have considered the identification of events and components, and the structures of relations among them. Now we must consider their capacities, or capabilities, and states. It is here that "communication theory," in the sense in which the term is equivalent to "information theory," enters, with its concern for the measurement of capacity. Although associated primarily with the capacity of channels and codes, the underlying notion extends equally to all components of a communicative event, and to the events of a system.

Questions of capability can be broached in terms of focus upon some one of the components of an event (or the event itself) in relation to all other components in turn. Some topics of long-standing anthropological interest find a place here. The relation of language to environment, both natural and social, in the sense of elaboration of a code's capacity, especially via vocabulary, to deal with snow, cattle, status, etc., as topics, is one. Another is the relationship between the capability of a code, and the capabilities of its users, in the sense of the Whorfian concern with habitual behavior and fashions of speaking. In both cases there must be reference from the start to the distribution in use of the portion of the code in question, both among communicative events and in relation to their other components. (The necessity of this has been argued for the Whorfian problem above; on cultural focus, elaboration of vocabulary, and folk-taxonomy of semantic domains, cf. the views on dependence on context of situation of Brown [1958:255–58], Frake [1961:121–22], Gluckman [1959], Meillet [1906], and Service [1960].)

With regard to participants, differential competence and performance are salient concerns (cf. Gross 1972 mss. a and b; Hymes 1973b). Often this level and the preceding one are but faces of the same coin, the formal structure of relations being grounded culturally in judgments (and facts) as to capability, and circumstances as to capability being dependent upon the structures of relations.

The ethnography of communication deals in an empirical and comparative way with many notions that underlie linguistic theory proper. This is particularly so when linguistic theory depends upon notions such as those of "speech community," "speech act," and "fluent speaker." How varied the capabilities of speakers can be in even a small and presumably homogeneous tribe is sketched incisively by Bloomfield (1927) in a paper that deserves to be classic for its showing that such variation, including possibilities of grammatical mistake, is universal. The range and kind of abilities speakers and hearers show is an area largely unexplored by ethnographers and linguists, but one of great import both to cultural and linguistic theory. (I have tried to draw some implications of a focus on the concept of speakers' abilities in Hymes 1964a and ch. 3.)[6]

6. The term "capability" is used with conscious reference to Tylor's definition of culture (or civilization) as all those capabilities acquired by man in society (1873: 1). I subscribe to the view that what is distinctively cultural, as an aspect of behavior or of things, is a question of capabilities acquired or elicited in social life, rather than a question of the extent to which the behavior or things themselves are shared. The point is like that made by Sapir (1916: 425) with regard to similarity among cultures due to diffusion, namely, that the difference between similarity due to diffusion and similarity due to independent retention of a common heritage is one of degree, rather than of kind. The currency of a cultural element in a community is already an instance of diffusion that has radiated from an individual.

Sapir's point converges with the focus of grammatical theory on an individual's ability to produce and interpret novel, yet acceptable, utterances. The frequency and degree of spread of a trait is important, but secondary, so far as concerns the criterion for its being a product of cultural behavior, as having a cultural aspect. A sonnet, for example, is such a product, whether or not it goes beyond a desk drawer, or even survives the moment of completion. In the course of the conduct of much cultural behavior, including verbal behavior, it will not be known, or will be problematic to the participants, whether or not some of what occurs and is accepted as cultural, has in fact ever previously occurred. (cf. Hymes 1964a: 33–41). For many problems, it is essential to single out for study phenomena shared to the limits of a community, or as nearly so as possible. For other problems, a group, family, person, or the ad hoc productivity of adaptation to an event, will be the desired focus. To restrict the concept of the cultural to something shared to the limits of a community is an arbitrary limitation on understanding, of both human beings and the cultural.

Capacity varies with event, and with the states in which participants, channels, etc., may be in the event, including the values and beliefs of participants, as properties of their states that help constitute events as communicative, and that determine other properties. In part the question is one not of what a language does for and to participants, their personalities, culture, and the like, but of what participants, their personalities, and the like, do for and to a language.

Only by reference to the state of participants, moreover, does it seem possible to introduce in a natural way the various types of functions which communicative events may serve for them.

There has been a bias in American linguistics, and in American extensions of linguistic methodology, favoring a "surface-level" approach that stresses identification and segmentation of overt material, and hesitates to venture far into inner structural relations and ascription of purpose. (The bias perhaps reflects the favoring of visual over acoustic space, the trust of the eye, not the ear, that Carpenter and McLuhan [1960:65–70] find characteristic of our society.) In Kenneth Burke's terms, there has been a tendency to treat language and its use as matters of "motion" (as if of the purely physical world), rather than as matters of "action" (as matters of the human, dramatistic world of symbolic agency and purpose) (cf. ch. 7). With all the difficulties that notions of purpose and function entail, there seems no way for the structural study of language and communication to engage its subject in social life in any adequate, useful way, except by taking this particular bull by the horns. The purposes, conscious and unconscious, the functions, intended and unintended, perceived and unperceived, of communicative events for their participants are here treated as questions of the states in which they engage in them, and of the norms by which they judge them. (Those aspects of purpose and function that have to do with feedback, exchange, response to violations of norms, and the

---

The perspective sketched here has the same fulcrum as Sapir's "Why cultural anthropology needs the psychiatrist" (1938) (cf. ch. 3). Sapir's insights do not imply reduction of cultural behavior to psychiatric subject matter; he himself explained ([1939] 1949: 579, n. 1):

As some of my readers have from time to time expressed their difficulty with my non-medical use of the terms 'psychiatry' and 'psychiatric,' I must explain that I use these terms in lieu of a possible use of 'psychology' and 'psychological' with explicit stress on the total personality as the central point of reference in all problems of behavior and in all problems of 'culture' (analysis of socialized behavior). . . . 'Personology' and 'personalistic' would be adequate terms but are too uncouth for practical use.

Sapir and Chomsky perhaps agree in considering linguistics to be ultimately a branch of psychology, but clearly the kind of psychology each has in mind is different.

like, are considered with the fourth aspect of the present frame of reference, that of the activity of the system.)

For ethnographic purposes, an initial "etic grid" for delineating and "notating" possible types of functions is needed, and it does seem possible to provide one, by considering the possibilities of focus upon each component in turn in relation to each of the others. The grid so derived has proven adequate to accommodate the various schemes of functions, and of functional types of messages, which have come to my attention. Ethnographic work will of course test and probably enlarge and revise it, just as experience of additional languages has enlarged and revised phonetic charts. Literary, philosophical, and other schemes of functions, and of functional types of messages, are also useful as sources of insight and details. (It may prove desirable to undertake a comparative and historical analysis of such schemes, as "home-made models" from our own culture. Among reviews, note Schaff 1962, Part 2, and Stern 1931, ch. 2.)

It must be kept in mind that functions may prove specific to individuals and cultures, and that they require specific identification and labelling in any case, even when subsumable under broad types. The "etic grid" serves only to help perceive kinds of functions that may be present, and possibly to facilitate comparison.

Focus on the addressor or sender in relation to other components entails such types of function as identification of the source, expression of attitude toward one or another component or toward the event as a whole, excogitation (thinking aloud), etc. Such function may be of course intended, attributed, conscious, unconscious. *Focus on the addressee* or other receiver entails such types of function as identification of the destination, and the ways in which the message and event may be governed by anticipation of the attitude of the destination. Persuasion, appeal, rhetoric, and direction enter here, including as well the sense in which the characteristics of the addressee govern the other aspects of the event as a matter of protocol. Effects on receivers may be of course intended, attributed, conscious, unconscious, achieved, frustrated. *Focus on channels* in relation to other components entails such functions as have to do with maintenance of contact and control of noise, both physical and psychological in both cases. *Focus on codes* in relation to other components entails such functions as are involved in learning, analysis, devising of writing systems, checking on the identity of an element of the code use in conversation, and the like. *Focus on settings* in relation to other components entails all that is considered contextual, apart from the event itself, in that any and all components may be taken as defining the setting of the event, not just its location in time and space. Such context has two aspects, verbal and nonverbal from the standpoint of speech, kinesic and nonkinesic from the standpoint of body motion, and, generally, for any one code or modality, context constituted for a message by other messages within the same code or modality, as distinct from context constituted by all other facets of the event. *Focus on message-form* in relation to other components entails such functions as proofreading, mimicry, aspects of emendation and editing, and poetic and stylistic concerns. *Focus on topic* in relation to other components entails functions having to do with reference (in the sense both of linguistic meaning proper and denotation) and content. *Focus on the event* itself entails whatever is comprised under metacommunicative types of function. If the message is taken as subsuming all, or all the immediately relevant, other components, then focus on the message as surrogate of the whole event may be taken as entailing metacommunicative functions ("the message 'this is play'"; Russell's types, etc.; see Bateson 1963 on the importance of this function).

Common broad types of functions associated with each type of focus can be variously labelled: expressive, directive, contact (phatic), metalinguistic, contextual, poetic (stylistic), referential, and metacommunicative are useful. The etic framework implied here can be handled with pencil and paper for visual purposes (and expanded also) by two devices, one of horizontal placement, one of vertical placement, of components relative to each other. In handling the five broad types of components of action used in his analysis (Scene, Act, Agent, Agency, Purpose), Burke devises various "ratios"; thus, the relation of Scene to Act is the Scene-Act ratio, and can be represented as if a numerator over a denominator: Scene/Act (Burke 1945). In explicating grammatical categories in terms of the components of speech events, Jakobson (1957) discriminates speech events (E^s) and narrated events (E^n), and participants in each (P^s, P^n), expressing relations with a diagonal; thus, the relation of the narrated event to the speech event (involved in verbal categories) is expressed E^n/E^s. Either device could be used to express all the possible combinations and permutations of focus upon the relation of one component of a communicative event to each of the others. Either device is useful in explicating other logical and empirical schemes of functions and functional types of messages in terms of a common denominator, a problem which is a converse in effect of the usual problem of componential analysis. (There one proceeds from etic grid to discover an emic system, here one is concerned to proceed from a possibly emic system to discover an etic grid.)

Most of the functions and components noted above have been discussed with examples of Jakobson 1960 and Hymes 1962.

ACTIVITY OF THE SYSTEM

Information theory is one topic notably associated with communication; cybernetics is the other. Having taken information theory in its quantitative sense as pertaining to the third aspect of the present frame of reference, we take cybernetics as pertaining to the fourth. Studies concerned with the information theory aspect of ethnographic systems of communication are almost nonexistent, and the case is the same for studies concerned with the cybernetic aspect. One can think in both respects of unpublished work by John Roberts and of a few celebrated and isolated examples in the work of Levi-Strauss (1953) and Bateson (1949; 1958) where sybernetic notions are applied.[7]

The activity of the system is the most general aspect of the four, and ultimately the one in terms of which it is necessary to view the rest. For particular purposes, of course, any one aspect, or part of one, can be segregated for analysis, and there is much to be done in the ethnographic and comparative study of every aspect and component. To take the channel component as an illustration, there are few if any ethnographic studies to compare with Herzog's multifaceted account of the system of channels elaborated among the Jabo of Liberia, considering, as it does, the structure of the code in each, the relation of code and messages in each to base messages in speech, native categories and conceptions, social correlates, and circumstances of use (Herzog 1945). There is a fair variety of reports of specialized uses of the vocal channel, but the account of Mazateco whistle talk by Cowan (1948) again is almost unique in providing a technical linguistic base and ethnographic context that could support controlled comparison. We have noted that paralinguistic and kinesic investigations have but begun to be extended cross-culturally, and attention to the sociopsychological context of attitude toward use of a channel, or modality, for instance the voice and gesture, such as Devereux (1949, 1951) has shown in work with the Mohave, is far to seek. Two general comparative studies (May 1956, Stern 1957) look toward historical interpretation in terms of distribution and origins, but not toward controlled comparison of structures and functions, perhaps because the available data

7. Goodenough (1957b) introduces communication theory in the Shannon sense into his critical review of an anthropological book on communication (Keesing and Keesing 1956) that does not itself make use of such theory.

offers little encouragement. Stern's classification of speech surrogates, derived from notions of communication theory, needs
clarification and extension to include writing systems, which
are logically comprised by the categories. As for the structural
and functional aspects of writing and literacy, empirical studies
of the diversity of the patterns that occur are few, and as for
contrastive studies of their absence, that of Bloomfield (1927) is
the only one known to me. Interpretations of the determinism of
particular channels, such as those of McLuhan (1962) and of
Goody and Watt (1963), and interpretations of the determinism
of media (channels) generally, such as are expressed in the
orientation of Carpenter and McLuhan (1960) and McLuhan
(1964), interesting as they are, seem oversimplified, where not
simply wrong, in the light of what little ethnographic base we
have. There is a tendency to take the value of a channel as given
across cultures, but here, as with every aspect and component
of communication, the value is problematic and requires investigation. (Consider for example the specialization of writing to
courtship among young people by the Hanunoo, and to a bor-
rowed religion among the Aleut; and the complex and diverse
profiles with regard to the role of writing in society, and in individual communicative events, for traditional Chinese, Korean,
and Japanese cultures, with regard both to the Chinese texts
shared by all and to the materials specific to each.) To provide
a better ethnographic basis for the understanding of the place of
alternative channels and modalities in communication is indeed
one of the greatest challenges to studies of the sort we seek to
encourage. At the same time, such work, whether on channels or
some other aspect and component, profits from taking into account the complete context of the activity of the system of communication of the community as a whole.

It is with this aspect that the ethnographic study of communication makes closest contact with the social, political, and
moral concerns with communication, conceived as value and a
determinant in society and in personal lives.

The frame of reference just sketched can be summed up as
asking a series of questions: What are the communicative events,
and their components, in a community? What are the relationships among them? What capabilities and states do they have, in
general, and in particular cases? How do they work?

Some of the variety of current lines of work that can contribute to, and benefit from, ethnographic study of communication can be briefly mentioned.

Linguistic investigation of the abilities and judgments of appropriateness of speakers, when pursued in a thoroughgoing way, must lead into study of the full range of factors conditioning the exercise of judgment and ability. The potential richness of studies of socialization, enculturation, and child development in this regard is manifest. The situation here is parallel to that with regard to the abilities and judgments of adults. Work focused on the linguistic code needs to be extended into concern with the whole of the child's induction into the communicative economy of its community. (Some notes and queries on this are advanced in Hymes 1961b, 1962, 1964e; cf. ch. 3). The importance of concern with the child is partly that it offers a favorable vantage point for discovering the adult system, and that is poses neatly one way in which the ethnography of communication is a distinctive enterprise, i.e., an enterprise concerned with the abilities the child must acquire, beyond those of producing and interpreting grammatical sentences, in order to be a competent member of its community, knowing not only what may possibly be said, but also what should and should not be said.

These studies bear importantly on work in fundamental education and literacy, which raises problems of particular interest; it can be a source of data and insight, and ethnographic studies of communication can contribute to it. The various purposes of educators, workers in literacy, translators, missionaries, and applied anthropologists may be facilitated by prior ethnographic study of the communicative economy with which they are engaged; the same of course applies to teachers and schools in our own society (cf. ch. 5).

Ethnographic work not concerned primarily with communication may make a contribution through precision of focus and detail. Thus one of the accounts of Metzger and Williams (1963: 218–19, 227–28) permits one to determine something of the place of speech, as one communicative modality among others, in a hierarchy of ritual means.[8] With more such analyses one could begin to have controlled comparisons. The study of folk taxonomies, and of ethnographic semantics generally, needs specification of communicative contexts if it is to achieve the implicit goal of discovering the structures of whole vocabularies (cf. Hymes 1964d, and ch. 4). The methods of ethnographic semantics, in turn, are helpful in discovering kinds and components of communicative events.

There is a somewhat different relation to the interest of

8. Verbal means are more pervasive than tactile means, but a tactile means, pulsing, holds the highest level alone; and where the two types of means are combined, it is the verbal type, prayer, that a master curer may delegate.

analytic philosophers in speech acts and modes of language use. Studies in the ethnography of communication afford a necessary ground for empirical testing of the adequacy beyond our own society, or some portion of it, of logical and intuitive analyses of types of act, such as promising, of conversational assumptions, and the like. In turn, ethnography cannot but benefit from additional precision of concepts for etic and typological purposes.

A similar relationship holds with work in paralinguistics, kinesics, and other aspects of codes circumjacent to language in communication. Ethnographic and comparative studies in the context of communication are needed to extend the etic frameworks, and to ascertain emic relevance amidst the wealth of data that even a few minutes of observation can supply. In turn, these investigations are needed to delimit the place and interrelations of modalities, spoken language being but one, in the communicative hierarchy of a community, and as a basis for interpreting the evolution of communication.

The problems of the study of primate communication are in principle the same as those of the ethnographic study of communication in human communities. The importance of studies of primate and other animal communication to help determine, by comparison and contrast, the specific properties of human language, and to help picture its evolutionary emergence, is well known. Ethnographies of communication here play a complementary role, which has yet to gain recognition, since it tends to be assumed that the functions and uses of human language are constant and already known. Empirical questions, such as the minimum role that language can play in the communicative system of a small hunting and gathering community, and of the adequacy of very minimal derived codes in closeknit communities, are not taken into account. Extrapolations as to the relations between code and communicative context at stages of human evolution need a basis in comparative ethnography as well as in formal comparison of codes. Not codes alone, but whole systems of communication, involving particular needs and alternative modalities, must be considered and compared. In general, to the evolutionary approach to culture, ethnographic studies of communication can contribute a framework within which languages can be treated adaptively in ways which articulate with the study of sociocultural evolution as a whole, and with microevolutionary studies (cf. Hymes 1961a, 1964d, 1971d).

What can be sketched now is but an outline of a future in which, one can hope, ethnographic studies of communication will be commonplace, and an ethnographic perspective on the engagement of language in human life the standard from which more specialized studies of language will depart.

Chapter 2

Studying the Interaction
of Language and Social Life

Diversity of speech has been singled out as the hallmark of sociolinguistics. Of this two things should be said. Underlying the diversity of speech within communities and in the conduct of individuals are systematic relations, relations that, just as social and grammatical structure, can be the object of qualitative inquiry.[1]

Diversity of speech presents itself as a problem in many sectors of life—education, national development, transcultural communication. When those concerned with such problems seek scientific cooperation, they must often be disappointed. There is as yet no body of systematic knowledge and theory. There is not even agreement on a mode of description of language in interac-

1. This chapter is adapted from "Models of the Interaction of Language and Social Life," in *Directions in Sociolinguistics: The Ethnography of Communciation*, ed. by John J. Gumperz and Dell Hymes (New York: Holt, Rinehart, and Winston, 1972), 38–71. Many of the examples come from an examination of ethnographic data undertaken with support of the Culture of Schools program of the Office of Education in 1966–67. I am greatly indebted to Regna Darnell, Helen Hogan, Elinor Keenan, Susan Philips, Sheila Seitel, Joel Sherzer, K. M. Tiwary, and my wife, Virginia, for their participation in that work, and to Robert Conrad, Howard Hanson, Louis Kemnitzer, Robert Litteral, Elmer Miller, J. David Sapir, and David and Dorothy Thomas, for discussion of examples from their field experiences. My work on the general problem benefited also from a small grant in spring 1968 from the National Institute of Mental Health; I want to thank Philip Sapir for his interest.

tion with social life, one which, being explicit and of standard form, could facilitate development of knowledge and theory through studies that are full and comparable. There is not even agreement on the desirability or necessity of such a mode of description.

Bilingual or bidialectal phenomena have been the main focus of the interest that has been shown. Yet bilingualism is not in itself an adequate basis for a model or theory of the interaction of language and social life. From the standpoint of such a model or theory, bilingualism is neither a unitary phenomenon nor autonomous. The fact that two languages are present in a community or are part of a person's communicative repertoire underlain by a variety of different relationships may be of meaning and use. Conversely, distinct languages need not be present for the underlying relationships to find expression through linguistic means (cf. chs. 4, 8).

Bilingualism par excellence (e.g., French and English in Canada, Welsh and English in North Wales, Russian and French among prerevolutionary Russian nobility) is a salient, special case of the general phenomenon of linguistic repertoire. No normal person, and no normal community, is limited to a single style of speech, to an unchanging monotony that would preclude indication of respect, insolence, mock seriousness, humor, role distance, and intimacy by switching from one mode of speech to another.

Given the universality of linguistic repertoires, and of choices among the forms of speech they comprise, it is not necessary that the forms be distinct languages. Relationships of social intimacy or of social distance may be signaled by switching between distinct languages [Spanish: Guarani in Paraguay (Rubin 1962, 1968)]; between varieties of a single language (standard German; dialect), or between pronouns within a single variety (German Du:Sie). Segregation of religious activity may be marked linguistically by a variety whose general unintelligibility depends on being of foreign provenance (e.g., Latin, Arabic in many communities), on being a derived variety of the common language [Zuni (Newman 1955)], or on being a manifestation not identifiable at all (some glossolalia). Conversely, shift between varieties may mark a shift between distinct spheres of activity [e.g., standard Norwegian: Hemnes dialect (see Blom and Gumperz 1972) or the formal status of talk within a single integral activity [e.g., Siane in New Guinea (Salisbury 1962)], Latin in a contemporary Cambridge University degree ceremony (e.g., *Cambridge University Reporter* 1969).

A general theory of the interaction of language and social life must encompass the multiple relations between linguistic means and social meaning. The relations within a particular community or personal repertoire are an empirical problem, calling for a mode of description that is jointly ethnographic and linguistic, conceiving ways of speaking as one among the community's set of symbolic forms (cf. Cassirer 1944).

If the community's own theory of linguistic repertoire and speech is considered (as it must in any serious ethnographic account), matters become all the more complex and interesting. Some peoples, such as the Wishram Chinook of the Columbia River in what is now the state of Washington, or the Ashanti of Ghana, have considered infants' vocalizations to manifest a special language (on the Wishram, see Hymes 1966b: on the Ashanti, Hogan 1972—cf. ch. 4). For the Wishram, this language was interpretable only by men having certain guardian spirits. In such cases, the native language is in native theory a second language to everyone. Again, one community may strain to maintain mutual intelligibility with a second in the face of great differentiation of dialect, while another may declare intelligibility impossible, although the objective linguistic differences are minor. Cases indistinguishable by linguistic criteria may thus be now monolingual, now bilingual, depending on local social relationships and attitudes (discussed more fully in Hymes 1968b).

It is common in a bilingual situation to look for specialization in the function, elaboration, and valuation of a language. Such specialization is only an instance of a universal phenomenon, one that must be studied in situations dominantly monolingual as well. Language as such is not everywhere equivalent in role and value; speech may have different scope and functional load in the communicative economies of different societies. In our society sung and spoken communication intersect in song; pure speaking and instrumental music are separate kinds of communication. Among the Flathead Indians of Montana, speech and songs without text are separate, while songs with text, and instrumental music as an aspect of songs with text, form the intersection. Among the Maori of New Zealand instrumental music is a part of song, and both are ultimately conceived as speech. It is interesting to note that among both the Flathead and Maori it is supernatural context that draws speech and music together, and makes of both (and of animal sounds as well among the Flathead) forms of linguistic communication. These examples draw on a study by Judith Temkin Irvine (1968). With regard to speaking itself, while Malinowski has made us familiar with the importance of phatic communication, talk for the sake of something being said, the ethnographic record suggests that it is far from universally an important or even accepted motive (see Sapir 1933, SWES 16, 11). The Paliyans of south India "communicate very little at all times and become almost silent by the age of 40. Verbal, communicative persons are regarded as abnormal and often as offensive" (Gardner 1966:398). The distribution of required and preferred silence, indeed, perhaps most immediately reveals in outline form a community's structure of speaking (see Samarin 1965; Basso 1970). Finally, the role of language in thought and culture (Whorf's query) obviously cannot be assessed for bilinguals until the role of each of their languages is assessed; but the same is true for monolinguals since in different societies language enters differentially into educational experience, transmission of beliefs, knowledge, values, practices, and conduct (see Hymes 1966b). Such differences may obtain even between different groups within a single society with a single language.

What is needed, then, is a general theory and body of knowledge within which diversity of speech, repertoires, ways of speaking, and choosing among them find a natural place. Such a theory and body of knowledge are only now beginning to be built in a sustained way. It is not necessary to think of sociolinguistics as a novel discipline. If linguistics comes to accept fully the sociocultural dimensions, social science the linguistic dimensions, of their subject matters and theoretical bases, "sociolinguistics" will simply identify a mode of research in adjacent sectors of each. As disciplines, one will speak simply of linguistics, anthropology, and the like (see ch. 4). But, as just implied, the linguistics, anthropology, etc., of which one speaks will have changed. Social scientists asking relevant functional questions have usually not had the training and insight to deal adequately with the linguistic face of the problem. Linguistics, the discipline central to the study of speech, has been occupied almost wholly with developing analysis of the structure of language as a referential code.

In order to develop models, or theories, of the interaction of language and social life, there must be adequate descriptions of that interaction, and such descriptions call for an approach that partly links, but partly cuts across, partly builds between the ordinary practices of the disciplines to answer new questions and give familiar questions a novel focus. Such work is the essence of what may be called the ethnography (and ethnology) of speaking and communication, as an approach within the general field of sociolinguistics. (On the relation between the approach and the field, see the footnotes to ch. 4).

THE CASE FOR DESCRIPTION AND TAXONOMY

For some of the most brilliant students of language in its social setting, the proper strategy is to select problems that contribute directly to current linguistic and social theory. A primary concern is relevance to particular problems already perceived as such in the existing disciplines, although the modes of work of those disciplines must often be transformed for the problems to find solutions. Field studies in societies exotic to the investigator, where strong control over data and hypothesis testing cannot easily be maintained, are not much valued. A concern to secure reports from such societies is thought pointless since it suggests a prospect of endless descriptions which, whatever their quantity and quality, would not as such contribute to theoretical discovery.

My own view is different. I accept an intellectual tradition, adumbrated in antiquity, and articulated in the course of the Enlightenment, which holds that mankind cannot be understood apart from the evolution and maintenance of its ethnographic diversity. A satisfactory understanding of the nature and unity of men must encompass and organize, not abstract from, the diversity. In this tradition, a theory, whatever its logic and insight, is inadequate if divorced from, if unilluminating as to, the ways of life of mankind as a whole. The concern is consonant with that of Kroeber, reflecting upon Darwin:

> anthropologists . . . do not yet clearly recognize the fundamental value of the humble but indispensable task of classifying—that is, structuring, our body of knowledge, as biologists did begin to recognize it two hundred years ago. [1960:14]

Even the ethnographies that we have, though almost never focused on speaking, show us that communities differ significantly in ways of speaking, in patterns of repertoire and switching, in the roles and meanings of speech. They indicate differences with regard to beliefs, values, reference groups, norms, and the like, as these enter into the ongoing system of language use and its acquisition by children. Individual accounts that individually pass without notice, as familiar possibilities, leap out when juxtaposed, as contrasts that require explanation. The Gbeya around the town of Bossangoa in the western Central African Republic, for example, are extremely democratic, and relatively unconcerned with speech. There is no one considered verbally excellent even with regard to traditional folklore. Moreover,

> Gbeya parents and other adults focus little attention on the speech of children. No serious attempt is made to improve their language. In fact, a child only uncommonly takes part in a dyadic speech

event with an adult. . . . Among the Gbeya "children are seen and not heard." Finally, there appears to be very little interest in reporting *how* a person speaks. [Samarin 1969]

The Anang (Nigeria) received their name from neighboring Ibo, the term meaning "ability to speak wittily yet meaningfully upon any occasion."

> The Anang take great pride in their eloquence, and youth are trained from early childhood to develop verbal skills. This proverb riddle [not quoted here, but see discussion] instructs young people to assume adult duties and responsibilities as early as possible, even if doing so is difficult and unpleasant at times. As the vine must struggle to escape growing into the pit [the riddle], so must the child strive to overcome his shyness and insecurity and learn to speak publicly [the proverbial answer], as well as perform other adult roles. [Messenger 1960:229]

Or, to consider the word and the sword, among the Araucanians of Chile the head of a band was its best orator, and his power depended upon his ability to sway others through oratory. Among the Abipon of Argentina no desired role or status depended upon skill in speaking; chiefs and members of the one prestigious men's group were selected solely on the basis of success in battle. The Iroquois value eloquence in chiefs and orators as much as bravery in war; the two are usually mentioned together and with equal status. A chief could rise equally quickly by either.

Since there is no systematic understanding of the ways in which communities differ in these respects, and of the deeper relationships such differences may disclose, we have it to create. We need taxonomies of speaking and descriptions adequate to support and test them.

Such description and taxonomy will share in the work of providing an adequate classification of languages. If the task of language classification is taken to be to place languages in terms of their common features and differences, and if we consider the task from the standpoint of similarities, then four classifications are required. Languages are classified according to features descended from a common ancestor (genetic classification), features diffused within a common area (areal classification), features manifesting a common structure or structures, irrespective of origin or area (typological classification), and features of common use or social role, as koine, standard language, pidgin, etc. (functional classification—see Hymes 1968c; Greenburg 1968: 133–35). The processes underlying the classifications (various kinds of retention, divergence, convergence) all can be viewed in terms of the adaption of languages to social contexts, but the forms of classification in which the dependence on social processes can be most readily excluded (genetic, typological) are the forms that have been most developed. Sociolinguistic research reinforces the intermittent interest that areal classification has received, and can properly claim the most neglected sector, functional classification, the interaction between social role and features of languages, for its own. The natural unit for sociolinguistic taxonomy (and description), however, is not the language but the speech community.

Of course, sociolinguistic taxonomy is not an end in itself, any more than is language classification. A taxonomy is not in itself a theory or explanation, though it may conceal or suggest one. There will indeed be a variety of taxonomies, answering to a variety of significant dimensions, as well as taxonomies of whole communities, societies, and social fields. (For a step in the latter direction, see Ferguson 1966.) The work of taxonomy is a necessary part of progress toward models (structural and generative) of sociolinguistic description, formulation of universal sets of features and relations, and explanatory theories. (I shall say something about each of these later.) Just the demonstration that the phenomena of speaking are subject to comparative study may help end the obscuring of actual problems by descant on the function of language in general, as in the recent examples of uncritical praise and intransigent indictment of language, respectively from Hertzler 1965 and Parain 1969. On "high and low evaluations of language" as an integral part of the history of philosophy and human culture, see Urban 1939:12, 23–32.

AN ILLUSTRATION

As an indication of what can be done, as well as of how much there is to be done, let me briefly consider the grossest, and most likely to be reported, aspect of speech, quantity. Contrasts were drawn already in antiquity, although amounting only to folk characterization, as when the Athenian says to his Spartan and Cretan interlocutors,

> But first let me make an apology. The Athenian citizen is reputed among all the Hellenes to be a great talker, whereas Sparta is renowned for brevity, and the Cretans have more wit than words. Now I am afraid of appearing to elicit a very long discourse out of very small matter. [Plato, Laws 641E:423][2]

2. According to Sandys (1920, vol. 1:4), the noun philologia is first found in Plato, and its adjective, philologia, is used in this passage to contrast "lover of discourse" with "hater of discourse."

One could extract a dimension with three points of contrast, naming the types according to the dialogue (as kinship systems are named after societies in which they are identified, Crow, Omaha, and the like):

i
Dimension: *verbose*   *laconic*   *pithy*
Type: ATHENIAN   SPARTAN   CRETAN

A number of analytically different dimensions are probably confounded within gross observations as to quantity of speech, length and frequency of speech, and the like; and there are qualitative characteristics vital to the interaction of language with social life in the particular societies. Something of this appears in the quotation from Plato, and becomes explicit in the following contrast:

ii
Dimension: *voluble*   *reserved, reticent*   *taciturn*
Type: BELLA COOLA   ARITAMA   PALIYAN

BELLA COOLA (British Columbia). Fluent, interesting speech is valued, and a common, if not a requisite, part of social life. Essential roles in ceremonial activity, and an important spirit impersonated in the Kusiut initiation, had to have the ability to talk constantly, keeping up a flow of witty and insulting remarks. The ethnographer McIlwraith found that if he could not joke with them constantly, people lost interest. When groups talked, one was sure to hear bursts of laughter every few minutes.

ARITAMA (Colombia). People in Aritama are not much given to friendly chatting and visiting. They are controlled and taciturn,[3] evasive and monosyllabic.... This reserve ... is not only displayed toward strangers, but characterizes their own interpersonal contacts as well. There is a font of ready answers and expressions, of standard affirmations and opinions, and there is always, in the last resort, the blank stare, the deaf ear or the sullen *no se*.... Such behavior ... leads frequently to a highly patterned type of confabulation. [Reichel-Dolmatoff 1961:xvii]

PALIYAN (south India). See previous quotation from Gardner (1966). According to Gardner, the many hunting-and-gathering societies of the world should be divided into two types; of one the Paliyans are a perhaps extreme representative.

3. Although the Reichel-Dolmatoffs use "taciturn" here of the Aritama, the subsequent term "reserved" characterizes them well, while "taciturn" is specifically apt for the Paliyans. As taxonomy and description develop, careful explication of technical terms will be increasingly important. Note that the three groups are also respectively "now-coding," "then-coding," and "non-coding" (cf. n. 5).

The dimensions may, of course, apply within, as well as between, societies, as to groups, cultural content, verbal style, and situations. As to groups,

iiia

Dimension:	voluble		taciturn
Type:		ARAUCANIAN	
Subcategory:	Men		Women

ARAUCANIAN (Chile). The ideal Araucanian man is a good orator, with good memory, general conversationalist, expected to speak well and often. Men are encouraged to talk on all occasions, speaking being a sign of masculine intelligence and leadership. The ideal woman is submissive and quiet, silent in her husband's presence. At gatherings where men do much talking, women sit together listlessly, communicating only in whispers or not at all. On first arriving in her husband's home, a wife is expected to sit silently facing the wall, not looking anyone directly in the face. Only after several months is she permitted to speak, and then, only a little. Sisters-in-law do not speak much to each other. The one means by which women can express their situation is a form of social singing (ulkantun) in which mistreatment, disregard, and distress can be expressed. The one approved role for a woman to be verbally prominent is as shamanistic intermediary of a spirit (Hilger 1957). (Silence is expected of a bride in her new home in a number of cultures, e.g., traditional Korea. The restriction of women's expression of grievances to certain occasions and a musical use of voice also is widespread, as in Bihar, India.)

As to situations,

iiib

Dimension:	discursive	reticent
	disclosure	quotation
Type:	WISHRAM-WASCO CHINOOK	
Scene: (See discussion)		

WISHRAM-WASCO CHINOOK (Washington, Oregon). Recitation of myths in winter, public conferral of personal name, and disclosure of an adolescent guardian spirit experience upon approaching death are three major communicative events. In each event, discursive disclosure (of the myth as a whole, the identification of name and person, or the verbal message of the vision) comes only when an implicit relationship (of culture to nature, person to reincarnated kin-linked "title," or persons to personal spirit) has been validated. Each is part of a cycle—the annual round of society, a cycle of reinstituting names of deceased kin, an individual life cycle from adolescence to death. At other times during the cycle there may be quotations (of a detail in a myth, a

name in address, a song from one's vision in a winter spirit dance),
but the substance of the relationship must not be explicitly
stated. In each case of discursive disclosure the speaker is a
spokesman, repeating words previously said, this being one rule
that constitutes formal speech events. (See Hymes 1966b.)

As to cultural content,

iv

Dimension: *verbal elaboration   verbal sparseness*
Type: HIDATSA   CROW

HIDATSA (North Dakota). CROW (Montana). According to
Lowie (1917:87–88), "The culture of the Hidatsa differs from that
of the Crow not merely by the greater number and elaboration of
discrete features but also in a marked trait of their social psychology—the tendency towards rationalization and systematization."
Lowie illustrates the contrast in four domains: formal instruction;
accounting for cultural phenomena; individual interpretation and
conception of names, myths, and prayer; and kinship nomen-
clature. In each domain the Hidatsa use language to systematize
and stabilize the cultural universe to an extent greatly in contrast
to the Crow. (It was the Crow that Lowie knew more intimately;
hence his sense of greater Hidatsa elaboration is trustworthy). Of
particular interest here is the following:

> The Crow child . . . seems to have grown up largely without
> formal instruction. Even on so vital a matter as the securing of
> supernatural favor, the adolescent Crow was not urged by his
> elders but came more or less automatically to imitate his associ-
> ates. . . . With the Hidatsa everything seems to have been ordered
> and prearranged by parental guidance; the father repeatedly
> admonished his sons, at the same time giving them specific instruc-
> tions.[4]

As to verbal style:

v

Dimension: *elaborate, profuse   restrained, sparse*
Type: ENGLISH   YOKUTS

ENGLISH, YOKUTS (California). A contrast with regard to
the limits of acceptable use of syntactic possibilities has been

4. As the initial quotation indicates, Lowie did not relate the contrast
explicitly to the role of language in social life. A major task and methodological challenge is to go beyond superficial presence or absence of overt mention of speech, in order to restate existing ethnographic analyses, wherever
possible, in terms of speaking, just as it is often possible to find in earlier
accounts of languages evidence permitting restatement in terms of contemporary phonological and grammatical models. Such restatement is more than
an exercise; it contributes to the range of cases for comparative studies.

drawn by Newman, who views each language from the standpoint of the other. Sparseness and restraint are found to characterize Yokuts narrative style as well (Gayton and Newman 1940).

Work in societies, with the goals of taxonomy and descriptive models in mind, is interdependent with detailed work in one's own society. Each provides insight and a test of universality and adequacy for the other. It has been suggested, for example, that there is only a class-linked British relevance to Bernstein's sociological model of elaborated vs. restricted coding, governed by personal vs. positional types of social control.[5] While some Americans indeed have misapplied Bernstein's two types to ethnic and class differences in the United States, from the standpoint of taxonomy and description, the model takes on a new scope. It suggests a set of universal dimensions, and possibly polar ideal types, isolable and applicable to the description and comparison of situations and whole communities, as well as particular groups.

Thus Margaret Mead has analyzed the Arapesh and Iatmul of New Guinea as contrasting types of society in which the adult patterns seem appropriately interpreted as *personal* and *positional,* respectively. In the ARAPESH type (which includes the Andamanese, Ojibwa, and Eskimo), societies depend, for impetus to or inhibition of community action in public situations, upon the continuing response of individuals. The point of communication is to excite interest and bring together persons who will then respond with emotion to whatever event has occurred. In the IATMUI type the societies depend upon formal alignments of individuals, who react not in terms of personal opinions but in terms of defined position in a formal sociopolitical structure.

At the same time the comparative perspective extends the model. Mead identifies a third type of society, such as that of BALI, which does not depend on situations in which individuals express or can be called upon to express themselves for or against something, so as to affect the outcome regarding it, but which functions by invoking participation in and respect for known impersonal patterns or codes, and in which communicators act as if the audience were already in a state of suspended, unemotional attention, and only in need of a small precise triggering of words to set them off into appropriate activity. Mead interprets the differences as ones in which political feeling depends on "How do

5. Elaborated codes are largely *now-coding,* and adaptive in lexicon and syntax to the ad hoc elaboration of subjective intent, while restricted codes are largely *then-coding,* and adaptive to the reinforcement of group solidarity through use of preformulated expressions. Personal social control appeals to individual characteristics, role discretion, and motivation; positional social control bases itself on membership in categories of age, sex, class, and the like. See Bernstein 1972; cf. n. 3).

I (and A, B, and C) feel about it?" (Arapesh); "How does my group (their group) feel about it?" (Iatmul); and "How does this fit in?" (Bali). Such a type as Bali seems appropriately labeled one of *traditional* social control and communication. (Obviously, only a subset of the societies lumped together as "traditional" by some social scientists can be said to be so in a useful way.) (See Mead 1937, 1948; the latter article discusses Manus as well.) Keesing and Keesing (1956:258) suggest Samoa as a type combining Iatmul and Bali characteristics, but distinctive [Mead (1937) places it also as a type intermediate between Iatmul and Bali], so that one might have:

vi

Dimension:	*personal*	*positional*	*traditional*	*positional,*
				traditional
Type:	ARAPESH	IATMUL	BALI	SAMOA
				ZUNI

Comparative ethnographic examples show the need to separate sometimes the dimensions joined together in Bernstein's model. Iatmul is a society with important development of oratory, which might seem an instance of elaboration which should go with personal control. If the oratory is then-coding, employing largely preformulated expressions, there is, in fact, no discrepancy. Positional and personal social control do, however, crosscut then-coding to define four types of cases, not just two. Cat Harbour, Newfoundland, as described by Faris (1966, 1968), shows positional social control and restriction of personal expression in speech and other normally scheduled activities. As in most societies, there are certain situations marked as reversals of normal conduct (e.g., legitimated stealing of food); and, as if to compensate for plainness of life and to satisfy the great interest in "news" of any kind, while remaining within normal restraints, there has arisen a genre known as the "cuffer." A "cuffer" may arise spontaneously, or someone may be asked to start one. It consists of developing an intense argument over an unimportant detail (such as how many men actually were lost in a boatwreck some decades back); but to show personal emotional involvement brings shame and exclusion. We thus find elaborated now-coding, indeed, extensive invention, in a positional setting. There can be then-coding in a situation of ad hoc subjective intent as well, as when Ponapeans arrive at the status of mutual lovers through manipulating a long sequence of verbal formulas which allow for role discretion at each step (Paul Garvin, pers. comm.), or when a traditional saying is used precisely because its impersonal, preformulated character grants role discretion to another that direct rebuke would not (e.g., the Chaga of Central Africa use proverbs to children in this way).

RELEVANT FEATURES AND TYPES

The examples just presented show that it is essential to isolate the dimensions and features underlying taxonomic categories. These features and dimensions, more than particular constellations of them, will be found to be universal, and hence elementary to descriptive and comparative frames of reference. This is not to consider universal features and dimensions the only goal. Explanation faces two ways, toward the generic possibilities and general constraints, on the one hand (Chomsky's "essentialist" form of explanatory adequacy), and toward the types that are historically realized and their causes (an "existential" or "experiential" form of explanatory adequacy), on the other. The heuristics of description require an etics of types as well as of elements, for insight into the organization intrinsic to a case, as against a priori or mechanical structuring of it.

By both defining some universal dimensions of speaking and proposing explanation within social theory of certain constellations of them, Bernstein has shown the goal toward which work must proceed. The total range of dimensions and of kinds of explanation, to be sure, will be more varied. Indeed, the fact that present taxonomic dimensions consist so largely of dichotomies—restricted vs. elaborated codes, transactional vs. metaphorical switching, referential vs. expressive meaning, standard vs. non-standard speech, formal vs. informal scenes, literacy vs. illiteracy—shows how preliminary is the stage at which we work. With regard to ways of speaking, we are at a stage rather like that of the study of human culture, as a whole, a century ago, when Tyler, Morgan, and others had to segregate relevant sets of data, and give definiteness and name to some of the elementary categories on which subsequent work could be built (on Tylor, see Lowie 1937: 70–71; Tylor 1871, ch. 1).

Like Tylor and Morgan, we need to establish elementary categories and names. Among the Bella Coola of British Columbia, for instance, there is a discourse style such that at the investiture of an inheritor of a privilege validated by a myth, someone tells a public audience kept outside just enough of the recited myth to be convincing as to the validation, but not so much as to give it away (knowledge of the myth itself being part of the privilege) (McIlwraith 1948). Among the Iatmul of New Guinea knowledge of the correct version of a myth may also be proof of a claim, in this instance to land and group membership. In public debate a speaker refers to his myth in clichés that fragment the plot. In this way "he demonstrates his membership in a group and at the same time keeps outsiders in the dark as to the esoteric matrix of the story" (Mead 1964b:74). We lack a name for this recurrent style. Identifying it would increase the chances that others will notice and report it in ways that will lead to knowledge of the conditions under which it occurs in various parts of the world.

Anthropological contributions to this branch of comparative research are almost nonexistent. Even a list of terms lacking careful definition is to be noted (Keesing and Keesing 1956); careful description and analysis of named concepts is remarkable (Calame-Griaule 1965; Abrahams and Bauman 1971). There are no books on comparative speaking to put beside those on comparative religion, comparative politics, and the like. In the major anthropological collection of data for comparative studies, the Human Relations Area Files, information on ways of speaking is only sporadically included and is scattered among several categories. Existing manuals and guides for ethnography, or for specific aspects, such as socialization, largely neglect speech.

The first break in this neglect is the pioneering field manual prepared by a group at Berkeley (Slobin 1967). The manual has already contributed to (and benefited from) the research of a number of fieldworkers. It is important to note that it is *acquisition* of the *structure* of language with regard to which the manual can be most detailed. The linguistic code takes pride of place as to topics, procedures, and specific questions and hypotheses, even though the acquisition of linguistic codes is in principle recognized as but part of the acquisition of communicative competence as a whole. It is recognized that "before a description of the child's language acquisition can be undertaken, the conventions of the adult members of the group must be described" (Slobin 1967:161), but it has not been found possible to make such description the initial matrix of research, nor to show what such description would be like, beyond sketching a conceptual framework with illustrations.

An ethnographic guide to the acquisition of speaking as a whole has been drafted by a group initially at the University of Pennsylvania, and an outline has been published (Sherzer and Darnell 1972).

The need for etics (Pike 1967, ch. 2) of terms and types, as an input to description, is clear from the frequency with which fieldworkers have let observations of great interest lie fallow, lacking precedent and format for their presentation. There is need to show ethnographers and linguists a way to see data as ways of speaking. At this juncture we are still attempting to achieve "observational adequacy" in the sense of being able adequately to record what is there in acts of speech.

For an adequate etics we of course most need field studies of the sort the manual and guide just cited encourage. We can also make use of ethnographic accounts not obtained with analysis of speaking in mind, by a procedure that can be called "socio-linguistic restatement" (see Hymes 1966b; Hogan 1972; Sherzer 1970). We must draw as well on the accumulated insight of all the fields that deal with speech, rhetoric, literary criticism, and the like. To be sure, the terminologies of rhetoric and literary criticism fall short of the range to be encompassed. Terminology for ways of speaking seems not to have developed much since the heyday of rhetorical education in the Renaissance—the recent revival of interest in rhetorical analysis indeed returns to the starting pont (see Joseph 1962; Lanham 1968; Sonnino 1968). But treatments of verbal art of necessity draw distinctions and make assumptions as to notions with which a descriptive model of speaking must deal, as does much work in philosophy, most notably in recent years "ordinary language" philosophy and the work of J. L. Austin, John Searle, and others on "illocutionary acts," or performatives. Several philosophers, psychologists, and literary critics, as well as linguists, have proposed classifications of the components of the functions served in them (Karl Bühler, Kenneth Burke, Roman Jakobson, Bronislaw Malinowski, Charles Morris, C. K. Ogden and I. A. Richards, B. F. Skinner, William Soskin, and Vera John). Much is to be hoped from the growing interests of folklorists in the analysis of verbal performance (see ch. 6). A systematic explication of these contributions is greatly to be desired. These lines of work provide concepts and insights from which much can be learned, and for which a comparative ethnography of speaking can perform anthropology's traditional scientific role, testing of universality and empirical adequacy.

In sum, just as a theory of grammar must have its universal terms, so must a theory of language use. It can indeed be argued that the notions of such a theory are foundational to linguistics proper—see Hymes 1964a, where the theory is called "(ethno)-linguistic." The fundamental problem—to discover and explicate the competence that enables members of a community to conduct and interpret speech—cuts deeper than any schema any of us have so far developed.

The primary concern now must be with descriptive analyses from a variety of communities. Only in relation to actual analysis will it be possible to conduct arguments analogous to those now possible in the study of grammar as to the adequacy, necessity, generality, etc., of concepts and terms. Yet some initial heuristic schema is needed if the descriptive task is to proceed. What is presented here is quite preliminary—if English and its grammarians permitted, one might call it "toward toward a theory." Some of it may survive the empirical and analytical work of the decade ahead.

Only a specific, explicit mode of description can guarantee the maintenance and success of the current interest in sociolinguistics. Such interest is prompted more by practical and theoretical needs, perhaps, than by accomplishment. It was the development of a specific mode of description that ensured the success of linguistics as an autonomous discipline in the United States in the twentieth century, and the lack of it (for motif and tale types are a form of indexing, distributional inference a procedure common to the human sciences) that led to the until recently peripheral status of folklore, although both had started from a similar base, the converging interest of anthropologists, and English scholars, in language and in verbal tradition.

The goal of sociolinguistic description can be put in terms of the disciplines whose interests converge in sociolinguistics. Whatever his questions about language, it is clear to a linguist that there is an enterprise, description of languages, which is central and known. Whatever his questions about society and culture, it is clear to a sociologist or an anthropologist that there is a form of inquiry (survey or ethnography) on which the answers depend. In both cases, one understands what it means to describe a language, the social relations, or culture of a community. We need to be able to say the same thing about the sociolinguistic system of a community.

Such a goal is of concern to practical work as well as to scientific theory. In a study of bilingual education, for example, certain components of speaking will be taken into account, and the choice will presuppose a model, implicit if not explicit, of the interaction of language with social life. The significance attached to what is found will depend on understanding what is possible, what universal, what rare, what linked, in comparative perspective. What survey researchers need to know linguistically about a community, in selecting a language variety, and in conducting interviews, is in effect an application of the community's sociolinguistic description (see Hymes 1970a). In turn, practical work, if undertaken with its relevance to theory in mind, can make a contribution, for it must deal directly with the interaction of language and social life, and so provides a testing ground and source of new insight.

Sociolinguistic systems may be treated at the level of national states, and indeed, of an emerging world society. My concern here is with the level of individual communities and groups. The interaction of language with social life is viewed as first of all a matter of human action, based on a knowledge, sometimes conscious, often unconscious, that enables persons to use language. Speech events and larger systems indeed have properties not reducible to those of the speaking competence of persons. Such competence, however, underlies communicative conduct, not only within communities but also in encounters between them. The speaking competence of persons may be seen as entering into a series of systems of encounter at levels of different scope.

An adequate descriptive theory would provide for the analysis of individual communities by specifying technical concepts required for such analysis, and by characterizing the forms that analysis should take. Those forms would, as much as possible, be formal, i.e., explicit, general (in the sense of observing general constraints and conventions as to content, order, interrelationship, etc.), economical, and congruent with linguistic modes of statement. Only a good deal of empirical work and experimentation will show what forms of description are required, and of those, which preferable. As with grammar, approximation to a theory for the explicit, standard analysis of individual systems will also be an approximation to part of a theory of explanation.

FUNDAMENTAL NOTIONS

Among the notions with which a theory must deal are those of ways of speaking, fluent speaker, speech situation, speech event, speech act, components of speech events and acts, rules (relations) of speaking, and functions of speech.

Ways of Speaking

Ways of speaking is used as the most general, indeed, as a primitive term. The point of it is the heuristic, or regulative, idea, that communicative conduct within a community comprises determinate patterns of speech activity, such that the communicative competence of persons comprises knowledge with regard to such patterns. (Speech is taken here as surrogate for all manifestations and derivations of language, including writing, song, speech-linked whistling, drumming, horn-calling, etc.)

Ways of speaking can be taken to refer to the relationships among speech events, acts, and styles, on the one hand, and personal abilities and roles, contexts and institutions, and beliefs, values, and attitudes, on the other. The vantage point taken here is that of the first series of considerations (events, acts, styles).

An alternative focus on the whole of a community's ways of speaking is possible from the vantage point of the second series of considerations, or of some one part of the series. In effect, one could consider the whole from the standpoint of persons, a vantage point which would most closely fit Sapir's 'psychiatric' perspective (cf. chs. 3, 10); from the standpoint of beliefs, values, and attitudes, a vantage point which might bring out most saliently the respect in which ways of speaking constitute symbolic forms; or from the standpoint of contexts and institutions. This last vantage point could support an alternative conception and name for the focus of the descriptive enterprise, which might be expressed as the study of the *speech economy* of a community (cf. Hymes 1961a; I am indebted to my wife and to Richard Bauman for discussion of this point).

Fluent Speaker

The aspect of ability that grammars are intended to model presumably is connected with fluency; the kind of person whose abilities are most closely approximated is presumably the fluent speaker. Of course a person may have grammatical knowledge and be unable to use it; but the thrust of linguistics has been toward an image of a person who both has the knowledge and is unimpeded in its use (cf. Chomsky 1965: 3). The difficulty for an ethographer is that persons differ in ability, in life, if not in grammars (cf. ch. 3). Even if one abstracts from individual differences, community differences remain. "Fluency" would appear to mean different profiles of ability in different communities, and indeed would seem not to be the most appropriate label everywhere for the abilities considered those of an ideal speaker (-hearer). We know too little about community ideals for speakers —the lack is great with regard to the complex makeup of American society itself—and too little about the role of such conceptions in acquistion of speech, in what goes on in schools and jobs, in linguistic change. As illustrations earlier in this chapter have shown, communities may hold differing ideals of speaking for different statuses and roles and situations. Moreover, the dimensions of ideal speaking may differ—"knowledge that" such and such is the case in a language vs. "knowledge how" to accomplish something verbally; memorization vs. improvisation; vocal carrying power and endurance vs. certain qualities of voice; etc. Thus, normative notions of ability, as embodied in kinds of speakers, must be part of ethnography. Knowledge of them is of course indispensable background to study of actual abilities.

Speech Community

Speech community is a necessary, primary concept in that, if taken seriously, it postulates the unit of description as a social, rather than linguistic, entity. One starts with a social group and considers the entire organization of linguistic means within it, rather than start with some one partial, named organization of linguistic means, called a "language." This is vital because the notion of "a language" can carry with it a confusion of several notions and attributes that in fact have to be sorted out.

The first confusion is between the notions of a speech community and a language. Bloomfield (1933), Chomsky (1965) and others have in effect reduced the notion of speech community to that of a language, by equating the two. The result is to make "speech community" itself a redundant concept, having no part to play in research, beyond honoring its definitional foundations with its nominal presence. Definition of a speech community in terms of a language is inadequate to the bounding of communities, either externally or internally. Externally, the linguistic and communicative boundaries between communities cannot be defined by linguistic features alone (cf. Hymes 1968b). Forms of speech of the same degree of linguistic difference may be counted as dialects of the same language in one region, and as distinct languages in another, depending on the political, not linguistic, history of the regions. This is so in parts of Africa (Jan Voorhoeve, pers. comm.), for example, and lies beneath the appearance of linguistic neatness in Europe. Were the standard languages removed from above them, a mapping of Europe's linguistic units would look much more like native North America. With regard to internal bounding of a community, two different conceptions have been advanced. Many have implicitly assumed a "natural" unity among members of a community, in virtue solely of identity, or commonality, of linguistic knowledge; but no real community can be accounted for as produced by merely mechanical "replication of uniformity" (cf. Wallace 1961, and discussion of Marx on Feuerbach in ch. 5). Bloomfield, and some others following him, have postulated a quantitative measure of frequency of interaction as defining a community. It is clear from work of Barth (1969), Gumperz, Labov, Le Page, and others that definition of situations in which, and identities through which, interaction occurs is decisive. (Sociolinguistics here makes contact with the shift in rhetorical theory to identification as key concept—(see Burke 1950: 19–37, 55–59).

This first and worst confusion is essentially a confusion

between a linguistic entity and a functional role, between an object defined for purposes of linguistic inquiry and various attributes of the counterpart of that object in social life. The basic confusion as between a speech community and a language manifests itself with regard to three attributes frequently associated with a "language," having to do with *provenance of content, intelligibility*, and *use*.

Sometimes different forms of speech are called by the same language name (and a single speech community implied to exist) because their historical provenance is seen to be substantially the same. One speaks normally of the English language, and of dialects of English, wherever forms of speech are found whose contents, or resources, are basically derived from the line of linguistic tradition called "English." Sometimes communities are said to have the same, or to have different, languages on the grounds of mutual intelligibility between their principal forms of speech, or lack thereof. Sometimes a form of speech is said to be the "language" of a community, because it is the primary mode of interaction (the "vernacular").

One may unreflectingly associate all of these attributes with, say, the "English" that is analyzed in current "linguistic theory." Yet these three attributes do not necessarily coincide; taken seriously as dimensions of forms of speech, they are found to sort separately. Not all forms of speech derived from a common English source (a more or less common source, since the earlier dialect diversity of English must not be overlooked) are mutually intelligible; cf. Yorkshire and Indian English. Their uses vary considerably around the world, from childhood vernacular to language of aviation to bureaucratic lingua franca. Not all mutually unintelligible forms of speech are distinct languages. Pig Latin, for example, derives from English by one or two operations; Hanunoo and Tagalog speech disguise derive from ordinary Hanunoo and Tagalog in more complex ways. Sometimes a derived form remains intelligible within its community of origin, but reduces explicit signalling to a point that conceals messages from others (Mazateco whistle-talk, Jabo drum-signalling). Finally, not all primary forms of speech are easily assigned to a single tradition, so far as at least some groups are concerned—cf. the French-suffused speech of prerevolutionary Russian aristocracy, or the mixed Latin-German of Luther's table talk. In general, forms of speech defined in terms of use in a social role cannot be assumed to consist of the resources of a single linguistic tradition. Thus the "language of the demons" among Sinhalese conflates (a) Sanskrit, (b) Pali, (c) Classical Sinhalese, nad (d) a polyglot mixture, according as to whether (a) Hindu or (b) Buddhist deities are invoked or mentioned, or (c) origin myths are narrated, or (d) demons are directly addressed and commanded (Tambiah 1968:177).

Put another way, entities defined in terms of provenance are distinct in crucial ways from questions of the content of linguistic competence in a community. Consider further the dimension of intelligibility. Sharing of grammatical knowledge of a form of speech is not sufficient. There may be persons whose English I could grammatically identify, but whose messages escape me. I may be ignorant of what counts as a coherent sequence, request, statement requiring an answer, situation requiring a greeting or making a greeting anomalous, requisite or forbidden topic, marking of emphasis or irony, normal duration of silence, normal level of voice, etc.; native American communities in which English means of speech serve Indian modes of conduct afford many instances. I may have no metacommunicative means or opportunity for discovering such things. Within our own community or habitual group, the nonequivalence of knowledge of a form of speech and knowledge of a way of speaking may not become apparent, the two having been acquired and maintained together. Communities indeed often merge a linguist's grammaticality with an ethnographer's cultural appropriateness. Among the Cochiti of New Mexico J. R. Fox was unable to elicit the first person singular possessive form of "wings," on the grounds that the speaker, not being a bird, could not say "my wings," but became himself the only person in Cochiti able to say it, on the grounds, his informant explained, that "your name is Robin."

The nonequivalence of the two kinds of knowledge is more likely to be noticed when a shared form of speech is a second one for one or both parties. Sentences that translate each other grammatically may be mistakenly taken as equivalent culturally, as having the same status as speech acts, just as words that translate each other may be taken as having the same semantic function. There may be substratum influence, or interference (Weinreich 1953), in the one as in the other. J. Neustupný has coined the term *Sprechbund* 'speech area' (parallel to *Sprachbund* 'language area') for the phenomenon of shared features of speaking across language boundaries. Thus, Czechoslovakia, Hungary, Australia and southern Germany may be found to share norms of greeting, acceptable topics of inquiry, what is said next, etc.

If sharing of grammatical knowledge of a form of speech is not sufficient, neither is sharing of knowledge of rules of speaking. A Czech who knows no German may belong to the same *Sprechbund* (and get by in it with a certain tolerance and goodwill), but not the same speech community, as an Austrian.

The notions of *Sprachbund* and *Sprechbund* are oriented

toward cultural patterns as attributes of communities. When we consider corresponding phenomena from the standpoint of persons, we see even more clearly that provenance and the dimension of use are quite distinct. Persons often command more than a single form of speech, of course, and may command knowledge of more than one set of norms as to speaking. The range of languages within which a person's knowledge of forms of speech enables him to move may be called his *language field*. The range of communities within which a person's knowledge of ways of speaking enables him to move communicatively may be called his *speech field.* Notice that the two are distinct. A scholar's language field may not entail communicative participation for some of his languages (the great French linguist Meillet is said to have spoken and written no language other than French, although he read many); the kind of participation might be said to be in cultural worlds, rather than, or only indirectly, in communities. Again, one's command of a certain language (so identified by provenance of its resources) may be particular to one's local community, so that the command does not permit easy access to other communities in which the same "language" is known. On the other hand, the knowledge of speaking rules required to move within a field larger than one's own community may be complemented by quite minimal command of another form of speech, far less than would be required for normal participation in the other communities.

Within the speech field must be distinguished the *speech network,* a specific linkage of persons through shared knowledge of forms of speech and ways of speaking. Thus in northern Queensland, Australia, different speakers of the same language (e.g., Yir Yoront) may have quite different networks along geographically different circuits of travel, based on clan memberships, and involving different multilingual repertoires. In Vitiaz Strait, New Guinea, the Bilibili islanders (a group of about 200–250 traders and potmakers in Astrolabe Bay) have collectively a knowledge of the languages of all the communities with which they have had economic relations, a few men knowing the language of each particular community in which they have trading partners. In sum, a personal language field will be delimited by a repertoire of forms of speech; a personal speech field by a repertoire of patterns of speaking; and a personal speech network will be the effective union of these two. In virtue of such a union, one may be able to participate in more than one speech community.

To participate in a speech community is not quite the same as to be a member of it. Here we encounter the limitation of any conception of speech community in terms of knowledge alone, even knowledge of patterns of speaking as well as of grammar, and of course, of any definition in terms of interaction alone. Just the matter of accent may erect a barrier between participation and membership in one case, although be ignored in another. Obviously membership in a community depends upon criteria which in the given case may not even saliently involve language and speaking, as when birthright is considered indelible. The analysis of such criteria is beyond our scope here—in other words, I duck it, except to acknowledge the problem, and to acknowledge the difficulty of the notion of community itself. Social scientists are far from agreed as to its use. For our purposes it appears most useful to reserve the notion of community for a local unit, characterized for its members by common locality and primary interaction (Gumperz 1962:30–32), and to admit exceptions cautiously.

A speech community is defined, then, tautologically but radically, as a community sharing knowledge of rules for the conduct and interpretation of speech. Such sharing comprises knowledge of at least one form of speech, and knowledge also of its patterns of use. Both conditions are necessary. Since both kinds of knowledge may be shared apart from common membership in a community, an adequate theory of language requires additional notions, such as *language field, speech field*, and *speech network*, and requires the contribution of social science in characterising the notions of community, and of membership in a community.

In effect, we have drawn distinctions of scale and kind of linkage with regard to what Gumperz (1962) termed the *linguistic community* (any distinguishable intercommunicating group). Descriptions will make it possible to refine a useful typology and to discover the causes and consequences of the various types.

Speech Situation

Within a community one readily detects many situations associated with (or marked by the absence of) speech. Such contexts of situation will often be naturally described as ceremonies, fights, hunts, meals, lovemaking, and the like. It would not be profitable to convert such situations en masse into parts of a sociolinguistic description by the simple expedient of relabelling them in terms of speech. (Notice that the distinctions made with regard to speech community are not identical with the concepts of a general communicative approach, which must note the differential range of communication by speech, film, art object, music.) Such situations may enter as contexts into the statement of rules of speaking as aspects of setting (or of genre). In contrast to speech events, they are not in themselves governed by such rules, or one set of such rules throughout. A hunt, e.g., may comprise both verbal and nonverbal events, and the verbal events may be of more than one type.

In a sociolinguistic description, then, it is necessary to deal with activities which are in some recognizable way bounded or integral. From the standpoint of general social description they may be registered as ceremonies, fishing trips, and the like; from particular standpoints they may be regarded as political, esthetic, etc., situations, which serve as contexts for the manifestation of political, esthetic, etc., activity. From the sociolinguistic standpoint they may be regarded as speech situations.

Speech Event

The term *speech event* will be restricted to activities, or aspects of activities, that are directly governed by rules or norms for the use of speech. An event may consist of a single speech act, but will often comprise several. Just as an occurrence of a noun may at the same time be the whole of a noun phrase and the whole of a sentence (e.g., "Fire!"), so a speech act may be the whole of a speech event, and of a speech situation (say, a rite consisting of a single prayer, itself a single invocation). More often, however, one will find a difference in magnitude: a party (speech situation), a conversation during the party (speech event), a joke within the conversation (speech act). It is of speech events and speech acts that one writes formal rules for their occurrence and characteristics. Notice that the same type of speech act may recur in different types of speech event, and the same type of speech event in different contexts of situation. Thus, a joke (speech act) may be embedded in a private conversation, a lecture, a formal introduction. A private conversation may occur in the context of a party, a memorial service, a pause in changing sides in a tennis match.

Speech Act

The *speech act* is the minimal term of the set just discussed, as the remarks on speech events have indicated. It represents a level distinct from the sentence, and not identifiable with any single portion of other levels of grammar, nor with segments of any particular size defined in terms of other levels of grammar. That an utterance has the status of a command may depend upon a conventional formula ("I hereby order you to leave this building"), intonation ("Go!" vs. "Go?"), position in a conversational exchange ("Hello" as initiating greeting or as response, as when answering the telephone), and the social relationship obtaining between the parties (as when an utterance that is in form a polite question is in effect a command, when made by a superior to a subordinate). In general the relation between sentence forms and speech acts is of the kind just mentioned: a sentence interrogative in form may be now a request, now a command, now a statement; a request may be mainfested by a sentence that is now interroga- tive, now declarative, now imperative in form; and one and the same sentence may be taken as a promise or as a threat, depend- ing on the norm of interpretation applied to it (cf. ch. 9).

To some extent speech acts may be analyzable by extensions of syntactic and semantic structure, as commonly analyzed in lin- guistics, but much of the knowledge that speakers share about the status of utterances as acts is immediate and abstract, and having to do with features of interaction and context as well as of gram- mar.

In terms of speech acts discourse may be viewed both para- digmatically and syntagmatically; i.e., both in terms of sets of speech acts among which choice can be considered to have been made at given points, and as a sequence of such choices, or such sets of possible choices. When the entirety of discourse is an- alyzed in terms of speech acts as minimal unit, it becomes necessary to recognize each sequential unit as complex, as per- haps a bundle of features. It is not enough to place an act as, say, a promise or a threat; one will need to specify a speech act in terms of several functional foci (see ch. 1), or several components (see below in this chapter). Perhaps the minimum number of foci or components needing to be specified will be always at least three. In terms of functional foci, for example, that an act is (referentially) a threat, but (expressively) a mock threat, and (rhetorically, or in contact function within the course of an utter- ance) also a summons; in terms of components, that an act is in message content (topic), a threat; in key, mock; and in norm of interaction, a summons.

Components of Speech

A descriptive theory requires some schema of the compon- ents of speech acts. At present such a schema can be only an etic, heuristic input to descriptions. Later it may assume the status of a theory of universal features and dimensions.

Long traditional in our culture is the threefold division be- tween speaker, hearer, and something spoken about. It has been elaborated in information theory, linguistics, semiotics, literary criticism, and sociology in various ways. In the hands of some investigators various of these models have proven productive, but their productivity has depended upon not taking them literally, let alone using them precisely. All such schemes, e.g., appear to agree either in taking the standpoint of an individual speaker or in postulating a dyad, speaker-hearer (or source-destination, sender-receiver, addressor-addressee). Even if such a scheme is intended to be a model, for descriptive work it cannot be. Some rules of speaking require specification of *three* participants—addressor, addressee, hearer (audience), source, spokesman, addressees, etc.; some of but *one*, indifferent as to role in the speech event; some of *two*, but of speaker and audience (e.g., a child); and so on. In short, serious ethnographic work shows that there is one general, or universal, dimension to be postulated, that of *participant*. The common dyadic model of speaker-hearer specifies sometimes too many, sometimes too few, sometimes the wrong participants. Further ethnographic work will enable us to state the range of actual types of participant relations and to see in differential occurrence something to be explained.

Ethnographic material so far investigated indicates that some sixteen or seventeen components have sometimes to be distinguished. No rule has been found that requires specification of all simultaneously. There are always redundancies, and sometimes a rule requires explicit mention of a relation between only two, message form and some other. (It is a general principle that all rules involve message form, if not by affecting its shape, then by governing its interpretation.) Since each of the components may sometimes be a factor, however, each has to be recognized in the general grid.

1. *Message form.* The form of the message is fundamental, as has just been indicated. The most common, and most serious, defect in most reports of speaking probably is that the message form, and, hence, the rules governing it, cannot be recaptured. A concern for the details of actual form strikes some as picayune, as removed from humanistic or scientific importance. Such a view betrays an impatience that is a disservice to both humanistic and scientific purposes. It is precisely the failure to unite form and content in the scope of a single focus of study that has retarded understanding of the human ability to speak, and that vitiates many attempts to analyze the significance of behavior. Content categories, interpretive categories, alone do not suffice. It is a truism, but one frequently ignored in research, that *how* something is said is part of *what* is said. Nor can one prescribe in advance the gross size of the signal that will be crucial to content and skill. The more a way of speaking has become shared and

meaningful within a group, the more likely that crucial cues will be efficient, i.e., slight in scale. If one balks at such detail, perhaps because it requires technical skills in linguistics, musicology, or the like that are hard to command, one should face the fact that the human meaning of one's object of study, and the scientific claims of one's field of inquiry, are not being taken seriously.

Especially when competence, the ability of persons, is of concern, one must recognize that shared ways of speaking acquire a partial autonomy, developing in part in terms of an inner logic of their means of expression. The means of expression condition and sometimes control content. For members of the community, then, "freedom is the recognition of necessity"; mastery of the way of speaking is prerequisite to personal expression. Serious concern for both scientific analysis and human meaning requires one to go beyond content to the explicit statement of rules and features of form.

While such an approach may seem to apply first of all to genres conventionally recognized as esthetic, it also applies to conversation in daily life. Only painstaking analysis of message form—how things are said—of a sort that indeed parallels and can learn from the intensity of literary criticism can disclose the depth and adequacy of the elliptical art that is talk.

2. *Message content.* One context for distinguishing message form from message content would be: "He prayed, saying '. . .' " (quoting message form) vs. "He prayed that he would get well" (reporting content only).

Content enters analysis first of all perhaps as a question of *topic*, and of change of topic. Members of a group know what is being talked about, and when what is talked about has changed, and manage maintenance, and change, of topic. These abilities are parts of their communicative competence of particular importance to study of the coherence of discourse.

Message form and message content are central to the speech act and the focus of its "syntactic structure"; they are also tightly interdependent. Thus they can be dubbed jointly as components of "act sequence" (mnemonically, A).

3. *Setting.* Setting refers to the time and place of a speech act and, in general, to the physical circumstances.

4. *Scene.* Scene, which is distinct from setting, designates the "psychological setting," or the cultural definition of an occasion as a certain type of scene. Within a play on the same stage with the same stage set the dramatic time may shift: "ten years later." In daily life the same persons in the same setting may redefine their interaction as a changed type of scene, say, from formal to informal, serious to festive, or the like. (For an example of the

importance of types of scene to analysis of speech genres, see Frake's (1972) contrast of the Subanun and Yakan. Speech acts frequently are used to define scenes, and also frequently judged as appropriate or inappropriate in relation to scenes. Settings and scenes themselves, of course, may be judged as appropriate or inappropriate, happy or unhappy, in relation to each other, from the level of complaint about the weather to that of dramatic irony.

Setting and scene may be linked as components of act situation (mnemonically, S). Since "scene" implies always an analysis of cultural definitions, "setting" probably is to be preferred as the informal, unmarked term for the two.

5. *Speaker,* or *sender.*
6. *Addressor.*
7. *Hearer,* or *receiver,* or *audience.*
8. *Addressee.*

These four components were discussed in introducing the subject of components of speech. Here are a few illustrations. Among the Abipon of Argentina *-in* is added to the end of each word if any participant (whatever his role) is a member of the Hocheri (warrior class). Among the Wishram Chinook, formal scenes are defined by the relationship between a source (e.g., a chief, or sponsor of a ceremony), a spokesman who repeats the source's words, and others who constitute an audience or public. The source whose words are repeated sometimes is not present; the addressees sometimes are spirits of the surrounding environment. In the presence of a child, adults in Germany often use the term of address which would be appropriate for the child. Sometimes rules for participants are internal to a genre and independent of the participants in the embedding event. Thus male and female actors in Yana myths use the appropriate men's and women's forms of speech, respectively, irrespective of the sex of the narrator. Use of men's speech itself is required when both addressor and addressee are both adult and male, "women's" speech otherwise. Groups differ in their definitions of the participants in speech events in revealing ways, particularly in defining absence (e. g., children, maids) and presence (e.g., supernaturals) of participation. Much of religious conduct can be interpreted as part of a native theory of communication. The various components may be grouped together as participants (mnemonically, P).

9. *Purposes—outcomes.* Conventionally recognized and expected outcomes often enter into the definition of speech events, as among the Waiwai of Venezuela, where the central speech event of the society, the *oho-chant,* has several varieties, according to whether the purpose to be accomplished is a marriage contract,

a trade, a communal work task, an invitation to a feast, or a composing of social peace after a death. The rules for participants and settings vary accordingly (Fock 1965). A taxonomy of speech events among the Yakan of the Philippines (analyzed by Frake 1972) is differentiated into levels according jointly to topic (any topic, an issue, a disagreement, a dispute) and outcome (no particular outcome, a decision, a settlement, a legal ruling).

10. *Purposes—goals.* The purpose of an event from a community standpoint, of course, need not be identical to the purposes of those engaged in it. Presumably, both sides to a Yakan litigation wish to win. In a negotiation the purpose of some may be to obtain a favorable settlement, of others simply that there be a settlement. Among the Waiwai the prospective father-in-law and son-in-law have opposing goals in arriving at a marriage contract. The strategies of participants are an essential determinant of the form of speech events, indeed, to their being performed at all (see Blom and Gumperz 1972).

With respect both to outcomes and goals, the conventionally expected or ascribed must be distinguished from the purely situational or personal, and from the latent and unintended. The interactions of a particular speech event may determine its particular equality and whether or not the expected outcome is reached. The actual motives, or some portion of them, of participants may be quite varied. In the first instance, descriptions of speech events seek to describe customary or culturally appropriate behavior. Such description is essential and prerequisite to understanding events in all their individual richness; but the two kinds of account should not be confused (see Sapir 1927a, SWES: 534, 543).

Many approaches to communication and the analysis of speech have not provided a place for either kind of purpose, perhaps because of a conscious or unconsciously lingering behaviorism. Kenneth Burke's (1945) approach is a notable exception. Yet communication itself must be differentiated from interaction as a whole in terms of purposiveness (see Hymes 1964). The two aspects of purpose can be grouped together by exploiting an English homonymy, *ends* in view (goals) and *ends* as outcomes (mnemonically, E).

11. *Key.* Key is introduced to provide for the tone, manner, or spirit in which an act is done. It corresponds roughly to modality among grammatical categories. Acts otherwise the same as regards setting, participants, message form, and the like may differ in key, as e.g., between *mock: serious* or *perfunctory: painstaking* (cf. chs. 7, 9).

Key is often conventionally ascribed to an instance of some other component as its attribute; seriousness, for example, may be the expected concomitant of a scene, participant, act, code, or genre (say, a church, a judge, a vow, use of Latin, obsequies). Yet there is always the possibility that there is a conventionally understood way of substituting an alternative key. (This possibility corresponds to the general possibility of choosing one speech style or register as against another.) In this respect, ritual remains always informative. Knowing what should happen next, one still can attend to the way in which it happens. (Consider, for example, critics reviewing performances of the classical repertoire for the piano.)

The significance of key is underlined by the fact that, when it is in conflict with the overt content of an act, it often overrides the latter (as in sarcasm). The signalling of key may be nonverbal, as with a wink, gesture, posture, style of dress, musical accompaniment, but it also commonly involves conventional units of speech too often disregarded in ordinary linguistic analysis, such as English aspiration and vowel length to signal emphasis. Such features are often termed *expressive,* but are better dubbed *stylistic* since they need not at all depend on the mood of their user. Revill (1966:251) reports, for instance, that "some forms have been found which *cannot* [emphasis mine] be described as reflecting feelings on the part of the speaker, but they will be used in certain social situations" e.g., for emphasis, clarity, politeness (mnemonically, K).

12. *Channels.* By choice of channel is understood choice of oral, written, telegraphic, semaphore, or other medium of transmission of speech. With regard to channels, one must further distinguish modes of use. The oral channel, e.g., may be used to sing, hum, whistle, or chant features of speech as well as to speak them. Among the San Blas Cuna of Panama, different poetic or ceremonial genres involve different uses of the voice: the historical-political-religious genres and some varieties of curing are chanted; the *kantule* or chiche festival variety is yelled or shouted; the interpretations of the chief's spokesman, animal stories, some curing, "advice" to newly married couples and to individuals who have misbehaved, and *sekrettos*, are spoken (Sherzer and Sherzer 1972: 189; *sekrettos* are usually extremely short, meaningless combinations of words, combining Cuna and other languages, such as Choco, English, and/or Spanish). Two goals of description are accounts of the allocation of channels in respect to genres and events (cf. Sherzer and Sherzer 1972: 194–95), of their interdependence in interaction (cf. Sherzer 1973), and of possible relative hierarchy among them (cf. ch. 1, n. 8).

13. *Forms of Speech.* Earlier discussion of the speech community dealt with the distinction between the provenance of lin-

guistic resources, and the mutual intelligibility, and the use, of
some organized set of them. Where common provenance of a stock
of lexical and grammatical materials is in question, one can easily
continue to speak of *languages* and *dialects*. Where mutual intelligibility is in question, whether due to different provenance or to
derivation by addition, deletion, substitution, permutation from a
common set of resources, the term *code* is most appropriate; it
suggests decoding and intelligibility. Where use is in question, the
term *variety* has become fairly well established (Ferguson and
Gumperz 1960), especially for community-wide uses or use in
relation to broad domains; for situation-specific use, the British
term *register* has gained acceptance.

The notion of register broaches a perspective that may be
called that of *speech styles*. We can understand the perspective
as applying to any and all organization of linguistic features, of
verbal means, in relation to a social context. The perspective is
general indeed, for while a grammar is usually referred to a "language," a language may itself be considered from the standpoint
of style, as an expression of a historically continuous community
(of. the Yokuts illustration earlier in this chapter, and Hymes
1961c, 1966b). The term "style" implies selection of alternatives
with reference to a common frame or purpose, and so can be
applied at any level of analysis. Having identified codes, varieties,
registers, or even community styles, one could still speak of personal styles with regard to any of them. It is not yet possible to
know whether some one level of choice will prove to be the most
appropriate and useful for ordinary unmarked use of the term
"style," and it may always be necessary to keep context of application clear. The great value of the notion is that it does insist that
modes of organization of linguistic features, including the level of a
"language," are not simply given, but are to be determined in
relation to a community or other social context.

A wholly general methodological approach to styles has been
developed by Ervin-Tripp (1972), building on work of John Gumperz. In brief, speech styles are defined by rules of co-occurrence
(at whatever degree of delicacy), and are themselves subject to
choice in terms of rules of alternation (see further in chs. 8 and
10).

"Forms of speech" suggests more readily organizations of
linguistic means at the scale of languages, dialects, and widely
used varieties [cf. Greenberg (1968:36) for use of "speech forms"
in this sense], while "speech styles" more readily suggests an aspect of persons, situations and genres. Both terms are capable of
wholly general application, and "speech styles" has now a methodological basis as well. Still, "forms of speech" seems less likely

to be misconstrued at the present time, and has been adopted here.

Channels and forms of speech can be joined together as means or agencies of speaking, and labeled *instrumentalities* (mnemonically, I).

14. *Norms of Interaction.* All rules governing speaking, of course, have a normative character. What is intended here are the specific behaviors and proprieties that attach—that one must not interrupt, for example, or that one may freely do so; that normal voice should not be used, except when scheduled, in a church service (whisper otherwise); that turns in speaking are to be allocated in a certain way. Norms of interaction obviously implicate analysis of social structure, and social relationships generally, in a community (cf. chs. 3, 9). Little can be said, until a number of ethnographic descriptions of communities in terms of such patterns are available, since communities differ significantly in this regard. Putative universals, whether logical or substantive, would be specious, vacuous or too remote from conduct to be of use at this point—thus, the conversational postulates associated with the philosopher Grice do not fit Madagascar (E. Keenan, pers. comm.).

As an illustration of a norm regarding topic:

> The next morning during tea with Jikjitsu, a college professor who rents rooms in one of the Sodo buildings came in and talked of koans. "When you understand Zen, you know that the tree is really *there*."—The only time anyone said anything of Zen philosophy or experience the whole week. Zenbos never discuss koans or sanzen experience with each other. [Snyder 1969:52]

15. *Norms of interpretation.* An account of norms of interaction may still leave open the interpretation to be placed upon them, especially when members of different communities are in communication. Thus it is clear that Arabic and American students differ on a series of interactional norms: Arabs confront each other more directly (face to face) when conversing, sit closer to each other, are more likely to touch each other, look each other more squarely in the eye, and converse more loudly (Watson and Graves 1966: 976-7). The investigators who report these findings themselves leave open the meanings of these norms to the participants (p.984).

The problem of *norms of interpretation* is familiar from the assessment of communications from other governments and national leaders. One often looks for friendliness in lessened degree of overt hostility. Relations between groups within a country are often affected by misunderstandings on this score. For white middle-class Americans, for example, normal hesitation behavior involves "fillers" at the point of hesitation ("uh," etc.). For many blacks, a normal pattern is to recycle to the beginning of the utterance (perhaps more than once). This black norm may be interpreted by whites not as a different norm but as a defect. (I owe this example to David Dalby.)

Norms of interpretation implicate the belief system of a community. The classic precedent in the ethnographic analysis of a language is Malinowski's (1935) treatment of Trobriand magical formulas and ritual under the heading of *dogmatic context*. (Malinowski's other rubrics are roughly related to these presented here in the following way: His *sociological context* and *ritual context* subsume information as to setting, participants, ends in view and outcome, norms of interaction, and higher level aspects of genre; *structure* reports salient patterning of the verbal form of the act or event; *mode of recitation* reports salient characteristics of the vocal aspect of channel use and message form.)

The processes of interpretation discussed by a Garfinkel (1972) including "ad hocing" generally, would belong in this category. These two kinds of norms may be grouped together (mnemonically, N).

16. *Genres.* By genres are meant categories such as poem, myth, tale, proverb, riddle, curse, prayer, oration, lecture, commercial, form letter, editorial, etc. From one standpoint the analysis of speech into acts is an analysis of speech into instances of genres. The notion of genre implies the possibility of identifying formal characteristics traditionally recognized. It is heuristically important to proceed as though all speech has formal characteristics of some sort as manifestation of genres; and it may well be true (on genres, see Ben-Amos 1969). The common notion of "casual" or unmarked speech, however, points up the fact that there is a great range among genres in the number of and explicitness of formal markers. At least there is a great range in the ease with which such markers have been identified. It remains that "unmarked" casual speech can be recognized as such in a context where it is not expected or where it is being exploited for particular effect. Its lesser visibility may be a function of our own orientations and use of it: its profile may be as sharp as any other, once we succeed in seeing it as strange.

Genres often coincide with speech events, but must be treated as analytically independent of them. They may occur in (or as) different events. The sermon as a genre is typically identical with a certain place in a church service, but its properties may be invoked, for serious or humorous effect, in other situations. Often enough a genre recurs in several events, such as a genre of chanting employed by women in Bihar state in India; it is the prescribed form for a related set of acts, recurring in weddings, family visits, and complaints to one's husband (K. M. Tiwary, pers. comm.). A great deal of empirical work will be needed to clarify the interrelations of genres, styles, events, acts, and other components (mnemonically, G) (cf. Bauman 1972, Bricker 1973, 1974a, 1974b, Tedlock ms.).

Psycholinguistic work has indicated that human memory works best with classifications of the magnitude of seven, plus or minus two (Miller 1956). To make the set of components mnemonically convenient, at least in English, the letters of the term SPEAKING can be used. The components can be grouped together in relation to the eight letters without great difficulty. Clearly, the use of SPEAKING as a mnemonic code word has nothing to do with the form of an eventual model and theory. That the code word is not wholly ethnocentric appears from the possibility of relabeling and regrouping the necessary components in terms of the French PARLANT: *participants, actes, raison (resultat), locale, agents (instrumentalities), normes, to (key), types (genres)*.

Rules(Relations) of Speaking

In discovering the local system of speaking, certain familiar guidelines are, of course, to be used. One must determine the local taxonomy of terms as an essential, though never perfect, guide. A shift in any of the components of speaking may mark the presence of a rule (or structured relation), e.g., from normal tone of voice to whisper, from formal English to slang, correction, praise, embarrassment, withdrawal, and other evaluative responses to speech may indicate the violation or accomplishment of a rule. In general, one can think of any change in a component as a potential locus for application for a "sociolinguistic" commutation test: What relevant contrast, if any, is present?

The heuristic set of components should be used negatively as well as positively, i.e., if a component seems irrelevant to certain acts or genres, that should be asserted, and the consequences of the assertion checked. In just this way Arewa and Dundes (1964) discovered additional aspects of the use of proverbs among the Yoruba: channel had seemed irrelevant (or rather, always spoken). Pressing the point led to recognition of a change in the form of proverbs when drummed, in keeping with a pattern of partial repetition particular to drumming. Again, the status of participant (user) as adult seemed invariant. Pressing the point by stating it as a rule led to discovery of a formulaic apology by which a child could make use of proverbs.

Many generalizations about rules of speaking will take the form of statements of relationship among components. It is not yet clear that there is any priority to be assigned to particular components in such statements. So far as one can tell at present, any component may be taken as starting point, and the others viewed in relation to it. When individual societies have been well analyzed, hierarchies of precedence among components will very likely appear and be found to differ from case to case. Such differences in hierarchy of components will then be an important part of the taxonomy of sociolinguistic systems. For one group, rules of speaking will be heavily bound to setting; for another primarily to participants; for a third, perhaps to topic.

We must bear in mind that the defining level may not be at the detailed, fine-grained "micro" level of the texture of discourse itself, but at the broad, "macro" level of major groups of components. Thus, Bauman (1972), seeking to discover what sector of speaking in a Nova Scotian community is esthetically marked by people themselves, found that no specific linguistic or symbolic features, genres, or performance skills or styles, were defining, but rather a specific scene (340–41):

> What is apparently going on in the culture of the La Have Islanders is that within the whole range of speech situations making up the speech economy of the islanders, the session at the store is singled out as special, isolated from the others and enjoyed for its own sake, because talking there may be enjoyed for its own sake and not as part of another activity or for some instrumental purpose. In other words, the fact that this situation is set aside for *sociability* [my emphasis], pure and simple, makes it special.

One seems to have here an instance of poetic function, not in the textural sense of Jakobson and others (cf. ch. 1), but in the dramatistic or dialectical sense of Burke (cf. ch. 7), the enjoyment of symbolic resources for their own sake. One could state the defining relationship in terms of members of Burke's pentad (again cf. ch. 1), here "Scene/Purpose" ratio, with the agency, talk, subordinate. Of course one would still expect that some features of the discourse in the general store would be specific and recognizable, enabling a member of the community to identify a stretch of it as the kind of talk that goes on there, and not elsewhere. The features might not be consciously known, and might have to do with turn-taking, pausing, pacing, responding, and other interactional norms, more than with verbal detail, except insofar as (Bauman suggests) the interactional basis of the setting may possibly induce fuller performance realizations of yarns, which themselves are told in a number of other places as well.

Experimentation with the detailed formal statement of rules of speaking has only recently begun. (An example is found in Sherzer 1970.) When prose descriptions of events are so restated, there can be a considerable gain in understanding of structure; or, one might say, a considerable clarification of what one understood to be the structure. The form of the event is disengaged, as it were, from the verbal foliage obligatory in prose sentences, and can be more readily seen. In order to compare events within a society, and across societies, some concise and standard formats are needed. Comparison cannot depend upon memorization or shuffling of prose paragraphs vastly different in verbal style. And it is through some form of formal statement that one can commit oneself to a precise claim as to what it is a member of a society knows in knowing how to participate in a speech act.

It was explicit analysis of more formally defined events that led Sherzer (1970) to notice features of the same sort in casual mention by the source of an informal use of speech. More than one mode of formal (explicit) statement obviously might be attempted. The point is that to put analysis in such a format forces one to confront what prose may let escape: Just exactly what does one's information specify, and what does it fail to specify? Sherzer's analysis is from the "syntactic" standpoint of act sequence. Analysis is also possible from the standpoint of categories of acts. Instances of types of acts can be seen somewhat as subcategorizations in the context of the event or participant. The meanings of acts can also be seen as entries in a communicative lexicon, where the familiar formulation X → (is rewritten, or realized, as) Y/ (in the context) W—Z, can be adapted to read, X (has the value) Y/ (in the context) W—Z.

Functions of Speech

Such a mode of analysis permits formal treatment of many of the acts of speech. The conventional means of many such functions can indeed be analyzed as relations among components, e.g., message form, genre, and key in the case of the –y form of the accusative plural of masculine nouns in Polish, which has the value "solemn" in the genre of poetry, and the value "ironic, pejorative" in the genres of nonpoetic speech. Functions themselves may be statable in terms of relations among components, such that poetic function, e.g., may require a certain relationship among choice of code, choice of topic, and message form in a given period or society.

It would be misleading, however, to think that the definition of functions can be reduced to or derived from other components.

Such a thought would be a disabling residue of behavior ideology. Ultimately, the functions served in speech must be derived directly from the purposes and needs of human persons engaged in social action, and are what they are: talking to seduce, to stay awake, to avoid a war. The formal analysis of speaking is a means to the understanding of human purposes and needs, and their satisfaction; it is an indispensable means, but only a means, and not that understanding itself.

EXPLANATION

Beyond description is the task of devising models of explanation. The many kinds of act and genre of speech are not all universal; each has a history, and a set of conditions for its origin, maintenance, change, and loss. All the questions that attach to explanation in social science—questions of primacy of factors (technology, social structure, values, and the like), considerations of areal patterning, diffusion, independent development, and evolution, will impinge. If the kind of explanatory adequacy discussed by Chomsky (1965) is recognized as "essential," i.e., as concerned with what is internal to language, and beyond that, internal to human nature, we can see the need for an "existential" or "experiential" explanatory adequacy, a kind of explanation that will link speaking with human history and praxis (Petrovich 1967:111–18, 126–27, 171–72; LeFebvre 1968:34, 45–46). To do this is not only to see languages as part of systems of speaking but also to see systems of speaking from the standpoint of the central question of the nature of sociocultural order—a theory of the maintenance of order being understood as implying a corresponding theory of change, and conversely.[6]

Each case, or each type of case, to be sure, may be valued in its own right as an expression of mankind. My own work stems

6. See Cohen 1968. His cogent, penetrating account takes explanation as fundamental to theory and social order as central to what is to be explained (pp. x, 16, ch. 2). Cohen speaks simply of "social order." I use "sociocultural order" to make explicit the inclusion of symbolic or cognitive order (see Berger 1967). On the relevance of sociolinguistics, note the introduction by Donald MacRae (center p. x). On an adquate theory of linguistic change, see Weinreich, Labov and Herzog 1968, especially pp. 100–101: "The key to a rational conception of language change—indeed, of language itself—is the possibility of describing orderly differentiation in a language serving a community . . . native like command of heterogeneous structures is not a matter of multidialectalism or "mere" performance, but is part of unilingual linguistic competence . . . in a language serving a complex (i.e., real) community, it is *absence* of structured heterogeneity that would be dysfunctional" (101). The conclusions (187–188) make clear that an adequate theory must be sociolinguistic and be based on sociolinguistic description.

in part from a desire to understand the meanings of language in individual lives, and to work toward ending the frequent alienation from human beings of something human beings have created (see Berger 1967, ch. 1, especially pp. 12–13, and nn. 1, 2 and 11; Lefebvre 1966: ch. 8, and 1968:72–74; and Merleau-Ponty 1967). Individuating, interpretive, and phenomenological motives are consistent with a concern for general, causal explanation. Each case and type is valuable, enlarging and testing general knowledge, and it is only with a general view of conditions and possibilities that the value of individual ways of speaking can be accurately assessed. Each case is an instance of the way in which universal and particular functions of speech have taken life and form, among the set of symbolic forms through which the members of a community interpret and make their history.

We require a widely ranging series of descriptions, whatever the motives that severally produce them. Neither a descriptive model nor an explanatory theory is convincing if it has not met the test of diverse situations, of a general body of data. Recall that Darwin's exposition of natural selection, and Tylor's (1871, ch. 1) exposition of a science of culture, were convincing in part for such a reason. We require some initial ordering of the diversity, although the ordering need not be conceived as either historical or unique. Sociolinguistic description and taxonomy are joint conditions of success for understanding and explaining the interaction of language and social life.

Part Two

The Status of Linguistics
as a Science

Cooperating in this competition
Until our naming
Gives voice correctly,
And how things are
And how we say things are
Are one.

Kenneth Burke,
Dialectician's Prayer

Chapter 3

Why Linguistics Needs
the Sociologist

I

Sociolinguistics identifies an area of research, one whose problems can be studied by members of a variety of disciplines.[1] Nevertheless, the term "sociolinguistics" does pose the special question of the relation between linguistics and sociology. It is to that question that this paper is addressed.

My title is adapted from Sapir (1938), as are some of my words. A generation ago Sapir saw in another discipline a reference point from which to highlight certain limitations of cultural anthropology. He wished to transcend a mode of analysis that abstracted from variation and persons. Today sociology is a reference point from which one can highlight certain limitations of linguistics, if one wishes to transcend again a mode of analysis that fails in "taking account of the actual interrelationships of

1. This chapter is adapted from the paper of the same title published in *Social Research* 34 (4): 632–47 (1967), and I thank Peter Berger, then the editor, for inviting me to submit it. The essay was written on the invitation of Everett Hughes for session 67, "Sociolinguistics," of the 61st annual meeting of the American Sociological Association, Miami Beach, Florida, September 1, 1966, and presented there; I am grateful to Murray Wax and Michael Micklin for their discussion at that time, and to Immanuel Wallerstein for comment later. The last paragraph of the original essay has been integrated with the last paragraph of ch. 10 of this volume; the last paragraph of the present chapter is based on that of Hymes 1969, together with a former n. 3.

human beings" (Sapir 1938: 575). Sapir chose an example from an earler scholar (Dorsey), that of the Omaha Indian, Two Crows; I have followed him in using a similar example, that of the Menomini, White-Thunder.

II

Until recently linguistics and sociology seemed miles apart in the United States. Structural linguistics was conceived as a discipline which concerned itself little, if at all, with society. Its province was rather to analyze those aspects of language which belonged to the realm of form as such. There was little need to ask questions which demanded a more intimate knowledge of users of a language, speech acts, and speech communities, than could be assumed on the basis of common experience or common assumption. The whole temper of linguistics was impersonal and formal to a degree. In this earlier period of the American science it seemed indeed almost intellectually indecent, or wrong in principle, to obtrude observations that smacked of heterogeneity in descriptive result, through appeal to the users and uses of a language. The assumption was that in some way not in the least clearly defined as to method it was possible for the linguist to arrive at conclusive statements which would hold for a given "language" and its entire community as such. One was rarely in a position to say whether such an inclusive analysis reflected in fact a particular informant, perhaps a particular type of context, topic, or style, or was a carefully tested generalization from study of a full range of users and occasions of use.

Perhaps it is just as well that no strict questioning of such method arose. It must then (as it might now) discourage the invaluable work of rescuing what one can of the structures of obsolescent languages from one or a handful of survivors. It might have impeded the development of the methods of formal analysis that are indispensable to any study dealing with linguistic structure, whatever its social referent. Perhaps, indeed, the entire complex of assumptions characteristic of the formative period of American structural linguistics was necessary to its success. By isolating linguistic form as object of study; by implicitly picturing a simple relation of one language uniform throughout a single community, as basis for theory as to structure and function; by restricting attention to the referential function upon which linguistic form in the usual sense is based; by positing the functional equivalence and essential equality of all languages—one rejected mistaken evolutionary stereotypes, guaranteed the worth of the many unwritten and obsolescent languages whose diversity was capital for scientific advance, and made for a time unthinkable the many sociological questions that might have distracted from the conquest of structure. (Here indeed is a first use for sociology in linguistics: the sociology of knowledge applied to the development of the profession and the ideological aspect of its theoretical assumptions. For some notes on the subject, see Hymes (1966 ms., 1970a).

From such a standpoint, what would one make of Bloomfield's early sketches of individual differences in competence among Menomini Indians of Wisconsin? Consider in particular the sketch of White-Thunder (Bloomfield 1928: 395):

> White-Thunder, a man around forty, speaks less English than Menomini, and that is a strong indictment, for his Menomini is atrocious. His vocabulary is small; his inflections are often barbarous; he constructs sentences of a few threadbare models. He may be said to speak no language tolerably.

Probably the case would be set aside as a perhaps interesting but isolated observation; such cases were in fact never taken up as a basis for theoretical concern.

This is not the place to introduce anything like a complete analysis of the meaning of such cases. The only thing that we need to be clear about is whether an approach to language which implicity assumes the irrelevance of such a case is in the long run truly possible. There has been so much emphasis on the autonomy of linguistic form, and, recently, on the image of the native abilities of a child gaining for it a fluent knowledge of its language almost spontaneously, that we should not blink at this problem.

Let us consider White-Thunder first as an individual case. Some evidence of personality difficulty or unusual personal history, such as having survived in quasi-feral circumstances as a child, might be invoked. One would then be regarding the case as analogous to that of someone mute or deaf, whose linguistic abilities had been affected by the fact. There might even be evidence of a comprehension of the language, an intuitive knowledge of it, that surpasses the poor performance which White-Thunder displays in speaking. All such considerations have the effect of taking the qualities of White-Thunder's use of Menomini as accidental, so far as the language itself is concerned. Obviously one would not choose White-Thunder as an informant, if at all possible; but his limitations, however unfortunate, are a personal misfortune; they say nothing about the language called Menomini.

Bloomfield goes on to say of White-Thunder, however, that "His case is not uncommon among younger men, even when they speak but little English." In effect, then, White-Thunder's case could become that of a generation, a generation that might go on to become the sole users of Menomini. What would it mean for a later investigator to report, "Menomini is a language no one speaks tolerably?" Or, since there might me left no internal standard of comparison, simply that Menomini is a language of small vocabulary and of sentences constructed of a few threadbare models?

Such a possibility goes against the grain of the common assumptions of American linguists that languages are immune to inadequacy, that their historical evolutions do not affect the essential equality and functional equivalence of all languages in their communities; yet the possibility cannot be dismissed. Indeed, it is likely the common case of the first generation or more of users of a newly creolizing pidgin; and a Peruvian sociologist is now investigating Indians who, so to speak, give up Quechua before they learn Spanish (John Murra, pers. comm.).

White-Thunder forces us to face the fact that for both the individual and the community, a language in some sense *is* what those who have it can do with it—what they have made of it, and do make of it; and that in consequence, notable differences in facility and adequacy may be encountered that are not accidental, but integral, to the langauge as it exists for those in question. In short, one must sharply distinguish between the potential infiniteness and equivalence of languages as formal devices and the degree of finiteness and inequality, actual and existential, that characterizes them among their users in the real world.

To say this is not to reduce the actuality of White-Thunder's Menomini to a mere list of what he may have been observed actually to say. No doubt his linguistic competence was deeper than any particular set of sentences he had uttered; no doubt his vocabulary and sentence models allowed him to say novel things, and were capable of many sentences that may be considered to have been unattested only accidentally. This sort of openness is universal for normal use of language. There is an openness, an infinite potentiality of larger size, so to speak, however, that comprises novel things that a Menomini of White-Thunder's type could *not* have said, even though the formal mechanism of Menomini might have been brought to express them. Their absence from a corpus would be a matter, not of accident, but of inability. *There is a fundamental difference, in other words, between what is not said because there is no occasion to say it, and what is not said because one has not and does not find a way to say it.* For the language to be used to say such things, the language must change.

There is thus no inherent impossibility in an entire community for whom a language, or language as such, is an instrument inadequate or restricted in respect to communicative needs. In cases such as White-Thunder's generation ways of saying things have been lost. The changes in capacity, however, need not at all be in such a direction. The history of many languages in recent centuries or generations is one of change in respects that have markedly enhanced the capacity of the languages and of groups of their users. Notice also that drastic social change need not be involved. Bloomfield refers the case of White-Thunder's generation to acculturation, suggesting that "Perhaps it is due, in some indirect way, to the impact of the conquering language." It is entirely possible, however, that in the ordinary course of their history communities will come to differ in the degree and direction in which they develop their linguistic means, and in the place assigned such means in their communicative life.

In sum, the competencies of users of a language, and thus their language itself, may change, even though the differences may not appear in the structure of the language within the limits of the usual description. The same formal linguistic system, as usually described, may be part of different, let us say, *sociolinguistic* systems, whose natures cannot be assumed, but must be investigated.

III

What would one have needed to know about White-Thunder's generation in order to describe the sociolinguistic system of which it was part, in order to explain the process by which the change of system came about? Bloomfield's sketches (pp. 394–96) give us some clues. One must obviously begin, not with the Menomini language, but with the speech community which comprises it, English, and occasionally other languages. Social positions must be specified, for the Menomini (like other communities) pervasively evaluate pronunciations, lexicon and grammar, and the judgments of "good" and "bad" are dependent (according to Bloomfield) ultimately on which persons are taken as models of conduct, including speech. Types of use must be specified, for Bird-Hawk (who spoke only Menomini, possibly also a little Ojibwa) "spoke with bad syntax and meagre, often inept vocabulary, yet with occasional archaisms" once he departed from ordinary conversation. Styles of speech—overelegant, archaic, emphatic or rhetorical, can be distinguished. One can guess that Menomini was perhaps being compartmentalized to certain domains of use, as has been the case with the surviving Indian languages of the American southwest.

Such observations are incidental in Bloomfield's account. An

adequate understanding of the nature and changes of sociolinguistic systems must have a systematic basis. The usual theory of
language and linguistics has not provided such a basis. The practice, method, and conceptualization needed is beginning now to
accumulate in the work of a small number of sociologists, psychologists, and linguists (e.g., Bernstein, Ervin-Tripp, Ferguson, Fishman, Goffman, Gumperz, Halliday, Labov, Lambert, Sacks, Stew-
art). Without elaborating upon the details of this work, let me
indicate something of the necessary nature of the sociological
contribution. I want to stress that there must develop a partially
independent body of method and theory—what might be termed
(adapting the title of a recent contribution to linguistics proper),
an integrated theory of sociolinguistic description. Let me try to
indicate why something less will not suffice.

First, the addition of language as one more sociological variable would not be enough. A linguistic variable may indeed prove
a useful indicator, say, of social class; but on this approach,
nothing has changed from the standpoint of the interests and
definitions of problems of sociology. Should other variables prove
better indicators in a given case, linguistic variables, reasonably
enough, fall by the wayside. A truly sociolinguistic approach, however, is interested in the relation of linguistic variables to group
membership for its own sake. If linguistic variables are not significant markers of group membership in a given case, sociolinguistic theory will be interested precisely because such a case
may help disclose the circumstances under which features of
language do and do not so function. Negative cases count.

There is a complementary point to be made on the linguistic
side. Social variables have played a sporadic role in descriptive
linguistics, inasmuch as they have sometimes obtruded themselves
in the core of grammar, e.g., respect forms (honorifics) in Korean
and Japanese. When not obtrusive, such variables and functions
have not been sought out. Presumably, however, respect relationships are universal to human society; perhaps they are always
expressed at least partially in speech. A sociolinguistic approach
will need to know how and when verbal means enter into respect
relationships in all types of society, so as to gain comparative
control over the dependence between the two. Obtrusive cases
such as the Japanese should come to be treated within a general
theory. (For exploratory work in this direction, see Tyler [1965].)

Second, a grossly correlational approach will leave much of
the heart of the subject obscure. To be sure, much can be learned
from the facts of the distribution of languages and subcodes with
respect to other variables, and at all levels, from world and nation-
state to village and family. Ultimately covariation of related fea-

tures will be a principal test of theories. It remains that language, as Malinowski put it, is a mode of action, even if linguists and sociologists have seldom described it as such; and in the study of language as a mode of action, variation is a clue and a key, but it is not just variation that is in question. To think so would be to concede the assumption that structure is to be found only in linguistic form. Two kinds of structure are in fact in question; the traditional structural linguistic view sees structure in the speech community as what Wallace (1961:26–27 and passim) has termed "replication of uniformity"; sociolinguistics sees structure in the speech community as what Wallace has termed "organization of diversity." The most novel and difficult contribution of sociolinguistic description must be to identify the rules, patterns, purposes, and consequences of language use, and to account for their interrelations. In doing so it will not only discover structural relations among sociolinguistic components, but disclose new relationships among features of the linguistic code itself.

The heart of what one is after in descriptive sociolinguistics is perhaps clearest from the standpoint of the socialization of the child. Linguistic theory treats of competence in terms of the child's acquisition of the ability to produce, understand, and discriminate any and all of the grammatical sentences of a language. A child from whom any and all of the grammatical sentences of a language might come with equal likelihood would be of course a social monster. Within the social matrix in which it acquires a system of grammar a child acquires also a system of its use, regarding persons, places, purposes, other modes of communication, etc.—all the components of communicative events, together with attitudes and beliefs regarding them. There also develop patterns of the sequential use of language in conversation, address, standard routines, and the like. In such acquisition resides the child's *socio*linguistic competence (or, more broadly, communicative competence), its ability to participate in its society as not only a speaking, but also a communicating member. What children so acquire, an integrated theory of sociolinguistic description must be able to describe.

Third, it will not do to begin with language, or a standard linguistic description, and look outward to social context. A crucial characteristic of the sociolinguistic approach is that it looks in toward language, as it were, from its social matrix. To begin with language, or an individual code, is to invite the limitations of the purely correlational approach, and to miss much of the organization of linguistic phenomena. Functions and contexts of use join together what structural description by itself may leave asunder, as has been suggested. The working assumptions of a thoroughgoing sociolinguistic approach must in fact be three:

1. A social relationship entails the selection and/or devising of communicative means considered appropriate and perhaps specific to it.

2. The communicative means will thus be organized in ways not perhaps disclosed apart from the social relationship.

3. The communicative means available in the relationship condition its nature and outcome.

It should be clear that a mechanical amalgamation of standard linguistics and standard sociology is not likely to suffice. Studies of groups usually treat speech as a medium through which to get at other things; as we have seen, grammars usually abstract from social variables. Neither normally attends to the patterning of speaking as an activity in its own right. Adding a speechless sociology to a sociology-free linguistics can yield little better than post-hoc attempts at correlation between accounts from which the heart of the relevant data will be missing. Useful inferences and insights may sometimes be obtained, but descriptive studies, couched in terms that integrate linguistic into social variables from the start, are the only basis on which it will be possible to progress. Some such studies are already available, as in the work of Blom and Gumperz (1972), Bernstein (1972), Labov (1973b), and others. Labov (1965, 1973a, b), for example, has shown how such an integrated approach is possible and necessary with regard to sound change and social dialect in New York City; the paper is of special importance for a sociolinguistic approach to linguistic evolution.

IV

The need for sociolinguistic descriptions may appear obvious and important to a social science audience. Such is not yet widely the case in linguistics. A decade ago American linguists, satisfied generally with the available theory for description of language, began to turn attention freshly to the use of linguistics in the study of society. A thoroughgoing critique of that theoretical basis has resulted in a new and ambiguous situation. While some linguists are at work on sociological problems, the issues that dominate linguistic discussion are almost wholly those of descriptive theory. And the tendency to separate linguistic form from social context has received renewed impetus from the insistence by the leading theorist of the present day (Chomsky 1965: 3) that:

> Linguistic theory is concerned primarily with an ideal speaker-listener in a completely homogeneous speech-community, who knows its language perfectly, and is unaffected by such grammati-

TABLE 3.1

	Descriptive	Comparative
Structure	Invariance	Variation
Use (Function)	Variation	Invariance

TABLE 3.2

	Descriptive	Comparative
Structure	Variation	Invariance
Use (Function)	Invariance	Variation

cally irrelevant conditions as memory limitations, distractions, shifts of attention and interest, and errors (random or characteristic) in applying his knowledge of the language in actual performance.

The goal of explanation in linguistics is set as universal properties of the human mind; the present interest and relevance of a sociolinguistic perspective is rejected.

There is underway, however, a long-term shift of emphasis in American linguistics, such that the appearance of withdrawal from sociological involvement may prove partial and temporary. The shift can be loosely phrased as one from focus on structure to focus on function—from focus on linguistic form in isolation to linguistic form in human context.

The pattern of the shift can be shown in terms of two fourfold tables. One dimension distinguishes description of a single case from comparative, or crosscultural, perspective. The other dimension distinguishes the structure of language from its functions, or use. Much of what has been discussed can be seen as summarized here, and comment can be brief. (See Tables 3.1, 3.2.)

Table 3.1 shows a distribution of emphases characteristic of structural linguistics as it developed during the 1930s and emerged into greater prominence after World War II. With regard to description of a single language, the point was to find the invariance, the homogeneous structure. As between languages, the expectation was to find diversity, or variation of structure—in some eyes, the greater the better. The use of language (speech) was not much attended and commonly seen as a realm of variation, a sort of ground to the figure of invariant form. Viewed comparatively, languages were regarded as functionally equivalent, and the functions of language mentioned in universal (invariant) terms.

A shift of emphasis, or a new pattern of emphasis, has shown itself first with regard to linguistic structure. As between languages, a renewed interest in typology and in universals has made the emphasis there one of finding invariance. The context is primarily a psychological one. With regard to description of a single case, focus on invariance continues, but attention to complex communities has established interest in social dialect, speech levels, and the like sufficiently to speak of a growing emphasis upon specifying varieties within a community and accounting for their interrelationships.

For the use and function of language, the context is primarily sociological. The implication of the two tables is that with regard to description of a single case there should be concern to find invariance (a sociolinguistic system); and, as between cases, a concern to find variation, or diversity, of use and function. Such emphasis is indeed emerging.

The general character of the differences between the two patterns of emphasis, and again, of much of the present discussion, can be summed up in another, more visible way, as shown in Table 3.3 (which restates with contrasts points made in ch. 1). The labels "structural" linguistics and "functional" linguistics are appropriate in the sense that linguists commonly speak of linguistic form as structure, and of function of language as a question of use; but structural analysis of course involves questions of functional relevance within the linguistic system, and functional analysis discloses structures of use, so that there are both structural and functional aspects in fact to both. Thus the necessity of the quotation marks.

V

The components of "functional" linguistics, like the components of sociolinguistic description (e.g., such as mentioned for the Menomini—community, values, role-models, types and occasions of interaction, social change) are patently sociological in nature. Yet they might be taken as anthropological, or social psychological as well. With regard to the former, indeed, one might rely upon ethnographers and the long tradition of linguistic work in anthropology for the success of the new pattern of emphasis. Why sociology? The answer is in part that sociolinguistics needs all the participation it can get; but in part the answer is that the nature of the world in which sociolinguistic description will be done points increasingly toward a major role for sociologists, if they wish to take it. The specification of the social relationships that provide the matrix for sociolinguistic description is increasingly a matter, not only of roles, but of role conflict; of stratification; ethnicity; sampling: covariation; in sum, of a kind of descriptive

TABLE 3.3

COMPARISON OF FOCI IN "STRUCTURAL" AND "FUNCTIONAL" LINGUISTICS

"Structural"	"Functional"
1. Structure of language (code), as grammar	Structure of speech (act, event), as ways of speaking
2. Use merely implements, perhaps limits, may correlate with, what is analyzed as code; analysis of code prior to analysis of use	Analysis of use prior to analysis of code; organization of use discloses additional features and relations; shows code and use in integral (dialectical) relation
3. Referential function—fully semanticized uses as norm	Gamut of stylistic or social functions
4. Elements and structures as analytically arbitrary (in crosscultural or historical perspective), or universal (in theoretical perspective)	Elements and structures as ethnographically appropriate ("psychiatrically" in Sapir's sense—cf. ch. 1, n. 6)
5. Functional (adaptive) equivalence of languages; all languages essentially (potentially) equal	Functional (adaptive) differentiation of languages, varieties, styles; these being existentially (actually) not necessarily equivalent
6. Single homogeneous code and community ("replication of uniformity")	Speech community as matrix of code-repertoires, or speech styles ("organization of diversity")
7. Fundamental concepts, such as speech community, speech act, fluent speaker, functions of speech and of languages, taken for granted or arbitrarily postulated	Fundamental concepts taken as problematic and to be investigated

On (1), cf. chs. 1, 2, 4; on (2), chs. 4, 7, 8, 9; on (3), chs. 6, 7, 8; on (4), chs. 3, 7, 8, 9, and Hymes 1964a; on (5), chs. 2, 4, 5, 8, 10, and Hymes 1961, 1971d; on (6), chs. 1, 2, 4; on (7), chs. 2, 4, 10, and Hymes 1964a.

work, which, if ethnographic, allows no clear distinction between social anthropology and sociology as its context. The work is increasingly a matter of ethnography of settings, situations, events, roles, groups, in complex societies of the sort typically studied by sociologists. And not only does one find American sociologists turning to work in other societies that is likely to involve them in linguistic experience of the sort that may lead to sociolinguistics; one also finds that the concepts necessary to a comparative and evolutionary perspective in sociolinguistics are developed as much, if not more, in the sociological tradition.

Descriptive sociolinguistics in the modern world is inseparable from encounter with social change. Indeed, for a systematic theory to emerge, many phenomena now treated as diverse types —acculturation, bilingualism, creolization, linguistic nationalism, pidginization, standardization, construction of artificial languages, vernacular education—must be seen as interrelated within the history of European expansion and the emergence of a world history. The linguistic acculturation of the Menomini and the decline of the English dialects are twin facets of the same process, which has as other facets the growth of new dialects of English in India and the Caribbean, no matter how separate the study of each of these has been hitherto. And it is in the sociological tradition that one finds the major precedent for the scientific study of European social history, and for the comparative study of the relevant insitutions.

It may be said to sociology, as to each of the social science disciplines, that various of its assumptions and claims are challenged by the phenomena of sociolinguistics, and that its own mandate requires it to take them up. As a problem area, sociolinguistics is not likely to become the possession of any one discipline, and it may indeed be the case that it will emerge as a generically social-science mode of linguistic description and explanation, without respect to individual disciplines. If sociology is not an exclusive partner with linguistics in the enterprise, however, it is still an indispensable one—in semantic analysis, for example (cf. Mair 1935, chs. 4 and 9 of this volume, and the lines of work reviewed in Kjolseth 1972 and Mehan 1972; as exemplars, note Garfinkel 1972, Sacks, 1972, and Schegloff 1968).

In general, the two major trends in the study of language concern semantic structures and structures of language use (cf. Hymes 1964d), and the two converge in kinds of problems faced in social research, especially in analysis of interaction. This is not to say that serious partnership in dealing with such problems does not make novel demands upon sociology. The social researcher, whether using survey instruments (cf. Hymes 1970a) or analyzing face-to-face interaction, confronts questions of referential and social meaning, in choices of words and of language, variety, or style, that may go beyond his or her usual practice. In this respect, the sociologist Duncan has rightly put as his first methodological proposition that statements about the structure and function of symbolic acts must be demonstrated within the symbolic event itself (Duncan 1968), and has compared sociology unfavorably with literature and art, where analyses are constantly referred to data, publicly accessible, that support them. The tradition of symbolic interaction has remained mostly a theoretical gadfly within sociology just because it has not taken the step from insistence on the central role of language and symbolic acts to analysis of the implicit form and textural detail through which that role is accessible.

Some sociologists are taking this step, one which requires linguistic knowledge and skills. The pitfalls are evident. One can get linguistics wrong, conceptually, ending up with a linguistic "model" that is not grammar, nor text analysis, nor good lexicography. One can fail to connect sociology with linguistic reality after all. Thus, Turner (1969) provides a sympathetic but sound critique of the late J. L. Austin's work on certain types of verbs called "performatives," which has stimulated so much of current interest in speech acts. Turner shows that "performative" (speech act) analysis applies generally to discourse, beyond performative verbs as such, and that it has autonomy, as a level separate from linguistic form; but his argument is entirely concerned with the autonomy, not at all with the complex interdependence, of speech acts in relation to the linguistic forms necessary to their realization and real analysis. One is left with a sociology that can talk about speech acts but not examine them. Strangely enough, one can also fail to connect language with social reality. Some sociologists become so absorbed in words as to fail to renew their relation to actual contexts. Admittedly, it is fascinating to discover the richness of speech, coming from a disciplinary background that has neglected it; but it is a bit absurd to treat transcribed tapes of interaction as if they were the Dead Sea Scrolls. When a society is gone, we must glean all we can from texts that remain, and contrary to some opinion, such work is arduous, disciplined, and often revealing. But again, it is a bit absurd to invent an amateur philology to deal with the life outside one's door. I have read elaborate analysis of verbal interaction that failed to consider the other aspects of the parties' presence to each other, attributing to complexities of words what may have depended on eye-contact; and imputations of intention and construal that neglected intonation (like many grammarians, to be sure) and that failed to consult or consider the interpretations of the participants themselves.

Let us hope that sociologists can extend their orientation and training to include linguistic skills, while not forgetting how to interview and observe. If they can, their discipline can play a major part in the general transition, now emerging, from philosophies to ethnographies of symbolic forms.

Chapter 4

Social Anthropology, Sociolinguistics and the Ethnography of Speaking

"Sociolinguistics" is the most recent and most common term for an area of research that links linguistics with anthropology.[1] "Ethnography of speaking" designates a particular approach. I shall sketch the context in which the two terms have emerged, then try to indicate the importance of the ethnography of speaking, not only to the area of research, but also to linguistics and social anthropology as disciplines.

To argue the study of speech is likely to seem only a plea for linguistics. To avoid that impression, I shall treat linguistics first, and at greater length, arguing the need for ethnography there,

1. This chapter is adapted from "Sociolinguistics and the Ethnography of Speaking," in *Social Anthropology and Linguistics*, ed. Edwin Ardener (ASA Monographs, 10), pp. 47–93 (London: Tavistock Publications, 1971). I want to thank Dr. Ardener for inviting me to participate in the 1969 meeting of the Association of Social Anthropologists, held at the University of Sussex, for which this paper was first prepared, and to express my admiration for his contribution to revitalization of linguistic work in anthropology. I should like to thank Clare Hall, Cambridge, for the fellowship that made possible a year of acquaintance with linguistics and social anthropology in Great Britain in 1968–69, and the National Institute of Mental Health (US), and the Guggenheim Foundation, for support of pertinent work. I benefited from opportunities to discuss some of the matters raised here at the Universities of Birmingham, Edinburgh, Leeds, London, Oxford, and York, and am particularly grateful to Roy Abrahams, Meyer Fortes, Esther Goody, Jack Goody, Edmund Leach, Stanley Tambiah, and John Trim for their interest and kindnesses at Cambridge.

before broaching the complementary need for linguistics in social anthropology. Behind both arguments stands a common conception of the study of speech.

I

Mixed terms linking linguistics with the social sciences, especially anthropology, are an old story. One can trace the use of "ethnographic philology," "philological ethnology," "linguistic anthropology," and the like from at least the middle of the nineteenth century. Until the second world war such terms were usually phrases—coordinate ("linguistics and ethnology"), genitive ("sociology of language"), adjectival ("sociological linguistics"). Only since World War II have one-word terms come to prominence. Their form, their relative chronology, and their prevalence, are revealing.

The form of these terms—ethnolinguistics, psycholinguistics, sociolinguistics—shows that it is linguistics, its concepts, methods, and prestige, that has become central. (Hence "ethnolinguistics," not "anthropology of language," for a field of research; and "anthropological linguistics," not "linguistic anthropology," as the prevalent term, even among anthropologists, for a subdiscipline.) To be sure, Malinowski had, much earlier, spoken (1920:69) of urgent need for an "ethnolinguistic theory" to help to elucidate native meanings and texts, but neither the term nor the theory received sustained attention. "Ethnolinguistics" first emerged into prominence in the late 1940s, followed shortly by "psycholinguistics" in the early 1950s, and by "sociolinguistics" in the early 1960s.[2] The sequence reflects the successive impact of recent linguistics, first on anthropologists, who had helped to nuture it, then on psychologists, and, most recently, on sociologists.

The currency of the term reflects, I think, a growing sense of the importance, not only of linguistics, but also of problems of language, and a hope for a combination of rigor and relevance in their study. Interest in sociolinguistics, indeed, is far from being a matter internal to academic disciplines. There are two main sources of practical interest and support: the language problems of developing nations (cf. Fishman, Ferguson, and Das Gupta, 1968), and problems of education and social relations in highly urbanized societies such as England and the United States. With respect to both one is pretty much in the position of wanting to apply a

2. This term also occurred at least a decade before it came into common use (Currio 1952); cf. Wallis (1956).

basic science that does not yet exist.[3] The creation of this basic science (whatever its ultimate label and affiliations) I take to be the defining task of sociolinguistics, and the chief warrant for the term.[4]

A more general sort of social relevance is that of seeking to transcend a long-standing "alienation" of language, and knowledge about language. On this view, language and linguistics often stand to human life in a relation parallel to that of goods and economics, as analysed in the first book of *Das Kapital*. Marx's comments on "fetishism of commodities," analysis of a human power and creation made to stand over against man, and understood in categories divorcing it from its roots in social life, could be applied, *mutatis mutandi,* to language. From this standpoint, the historical origin of standard languages and linguistic study as instruments of cultural hegemony (Hellenistic study of Greek, Indian of the Sanskritic Vedas, Chinese of the Confucian classics) is unwittingly reinforced by the contemporary methodological canon of defining

---

3. The need for such a scientific basis has provoked critical comment (e.g., the inaugural address of Alisjahbana 1965).
4. The practical relevance of sociolinguistics is a mixed blessing. It adds the justification of social relevance to a development that has a logic and importance within science itself; and work that is practically motivated can bring to light and help to solve issues of theory (cf. Hymes 1971 with regard to "disadvantaged" children). Research funds being scarce, and their sources sometimes shortsighted, however, energies are too often diverted into providing materials for which there has not been the chance to develop a scientifically adequate basis.

Practical concerns are sometimes associated with "macro," as distinct from "micro," sociolinguistics. The distinction sometimes reflects different priorities, and differences in professional origin. Some are attracted to work on large populations, and national institutions and policies, as being of more social relevance and theoretical importance. Others are attracted to work with small communities and social interaction, as offering a greater prospect of developing secure methodology and theory. Again, sociolinguistics is for some a new application of known social science; for others, an extension (and revision) of linguistics. The former may devise new questions and scales, the latter expand the scope of linguistic rules. Each may wonder about the validity and rigor of the other.

Obviously none of these differences need be one of principle. There are advances in method and theory to be made in the comparative study of larger social systems; rules of verbal interaction in a small community may be of immediate relevance for its teachers and schools. Policies and nationwide generalizations should be based on close knowledge of actual situations, just as local situations cannot be adequately understood in isolation. Use of quantitative and interview techniques presupposes close-grained qualitative analysis, and formal analysis of the sort congenial to linguists must come to terms with quantitative variables and social features. It remains that few have been able to balance practical relevance and scientific advance, and that perspectives that articulate the relations between "micro" and "macro" sociolinguistics are rare. (Several approaches are represented in papers by Albert, Bernstein, Fischer, Fishman, Garfinkel, Labov, and Roberts, in Gumperz and Hymes 1972).

linguistic theory as concerned only with an ideal speaker-hearer
in a perfectly homogeneous community, free from all limitations
of actual use. The effect is the same, closing off study of the social
realities of language by those most able to analyze their linguistic
dimension. From this standpoint, sociolinguistics has a contribution to make to what Wright Mills called the task of sociological
imagination, that of enabling men to understand their lives adequately in terms of the true determinants of them; here the perspective provided by ethnographic and comparative studies,
although of little engineering pertinence, may be of great intellectual importance. We have yet to gain the crosscultural perspective
on speech that we have on child-rearing, sex, religion. Both in linguistics and in social science, the roles of language in human life
usually are assumed or asserted. Research that seeks the actual
ranges and kinds of meaning that speaking and languages have,
and the conditions that support or frustrate each, has hardly
begun.[5]

Whatever one's conception of the relevance of sociolinguistics, two things should be made clear about it and the terms on
which it is modelled. First, these terms do not designate three
disciplines, but rather problem areas that draw members of different disciplines together. The problems and the participants overlap. Not only may scholars from different disciplines contribute
under the same one label, but also one and the same scholar may
in different contexts contribute under each of the three. The same
topic may appear under all three. (The issues raised by Whorf
have been discussed as "ethnolinguistics," "psycholinguistics,"
and "sociolinguistics" in turn.) In effect, the three terms mediate
between particular social sciences and linguistics, and, increasingly, between linguistics and the social sciences as a whole.
Sociolinguistics, the last to emerge, and the one more suggestive
of social science as a whole, benefits from this trend, and tends to
displace the others, where their putative content is shared. It
remains true that there is more willingness to identify one's work
as "sociolinguistic" than to define oneself as a "sociolinguist."

Second, the domain of such terms is subject to shifting definition of the disciplines between which they mediate. For something
like a generation, say, from *Coral Gardens* (1935) to Katz and
Fodor (1963), a technical study of a folk taxonomy might readily

5. See, now, the development of this theme by Lefebvre 1966 (ch. 8, "La
Forme merchandise et le discours," esp. pp. 348 ff.). Thoughts of my own are
found in papers of 1961, 1966c, and 1967a: 646. The analogy with Marx's
critique of economics was part of our prepared discussion of "Marxism and
Sociology" by I. M. Zeitlin, at a symposium of the Socialist Scholars Conference, New York, September 1967. Cf. Barthes's notion of *l'ecriture* (1953),
Bernstein (1964), Sherzer and Darnell (1972), and Hymes (1961, 1966b).

have been labelled "ethnolinguistic." Today, given the renewed legitimacy of semantics among linguists, such a study can be taken as part of linguistics (cf. the excellent textbook by Lyons 1968). Given the renewed attention to cognitive structures among anthropologists, such a study can equally well be taken as part of social anthropology. A similar fate may await sociolinguistics. Having arisen to fill a gap, it may find itself absorbed from both sides. A generation from now, one still may speak only of linguistics and anthropology (and of sociology and psychology) when disciplines are in question. Sociolinguistic, ethnolinguistic, and psycholinguistic will remain useful adjectives for kinds of research but their corresponding plural nouns will be seen as having marked a transition.[6]

If this should happen, it will be in the context of a linguistics and a social anthropology in some respects radically recast, such that adjacent sectors merge.[7] I shall return to this prospect in the conclusion. Let me emphasize what I mean by saying here that the prediction would not be verified by increased cooperation between linguists and anthropologists, in the field and after, although there is of course much need for that. It would not be made true by some ethnographers coming to do what some linguists now do, and conversely, although that is essential; or by investigations that are jointly linguistic and ethnographic on just those occasions when the special importance of a feature (linguistic or social) dic-

6. It will, of course, remain possible to speak of ethnolinguistics as a field in which progress can be gauged (Whiteley 1966: 154n.9), in so far as one is speaking of a relation between linguistics and anthropology, exclusive of other disciplines. This relation is most likely to remain specific for historical problems. Among social scientists, only anthropologists are likely to be found proposing genetic relationships, reconstructing vocabularies, tracing population movements and diffusion through loan-words, etc. It remains to be be seen to what extent the extension of other social sciences to work in areas conventionally anthropological (Africa, Asia) will lead to a sharing of synchronic interests in language. When one wants to designate a branch of anthropology parallel to "physical" and "social," "linguistic anthropology" will continue to recommend itself.

This discussion of terminology draws on Hymes (1966a), which goes into greater detail from the standpoint of anthropology. Such reflexive use of our means for understanding other cultures—here, analysis of terminology— seems to me essential. It tests our methods and our self-knowledge against each other.

7. This is not to define linguistics as part of anthropology (though some linguists have done so), parallel to, but opposing, Chomsky's definition of linguistics as a branch of cognitive psychology. Many branches of linguistics are hardly confined to being parts of either anthropology or psychology. Such statements are possible only if one ignores or denies part of linguistics itself, or moves to a level of abstraction remote from actual practice. For a view of the place of linguistics within a more general field, see Hymes (1968 h, and cf. ch. 8, n.2).

tates intensive study, although of course one wants such work. These things are needed, most obviously with regard to semantics.[8] No amount of combination of disciplines as presently constituted, however, asking just the questions each now normally asks, will serve. The essence of the prediction is in the hope for disciplines radically recast. It will become true only if linguistics and social anthropology revise their conventional scope and methodology, so that matters now let fall between them are seen as indispensable to each.

The multiplicity of terms, over the past century and more, for the common interests of linguists and anthropologists suggests a recurrent need, and a recurrent tension—a need met often by ad hoc coinage, a tension persisting owing to failure to resolve the relationship of the two fields in a form capable of sustained growth. Just as practical problems require an as yet inchoate scientific field, so do some of the tasks of linguists and anthropologists.

8. As long realized, of course, and pointed out by Mair (1935) in criticizing "linguistics without sociology," and by J. R. Firth (1935), advocating "sociological linguistics," in the same year as *Coral Gardens* also. A decade later Nida [1945: 208, and in Hymes (ed.), 1964: 97] advocated a "combination of analytical social anthropology and descriptive linguistics [as] . . . the key to the study of semantics. "Two decades later, Whiteley advocated the combination afresh in a valuable paper (1966). The reiteration suggests that a commonsense principle has yet to become a commonplace of practice. This interpretation would seem to be borne out by a sentence in a recent Malinowski memorial lecture: 'Would not then an analysis of the words used directly in the ritual advance this kind of interpretation further?' (Tambiah 1968: 200, n.2.) That a social anthropologist should find it necessary to propose this to his colleagues in the year 33 CG (after *Coral Gardens*)! Especially since the very point is consciously important within the established church of their own society. The Scottish church insists on an order in the service the opposite of the English, because a fundamental point of doctrine is involved (Buchanan, 1968: 143–44). The precise choice of words, or even use of words at all, poses unresolved problems (Buchanan, 1968: 13, 21). Regarding a desire for a "definite association of the people" with the preparation of the Table for the eucharist, one finds:

"The fact that the laymen bring the elements to the Table . . . whether during a hymn or during silence, does not of itself convey any representative symbolism or include the congregation as a whole. The introduction of a formula can change that, but immediately words are introduced they seem to say too much. . . . Texts appropriate to gifts of money cannot of themselves say anything very helpful about the elements. Recourse is then had to symbolism; but . . . This is not to say that the Lambeth statement has had no effect on texts. The big effect, already noted, is in the "Accept us in him" terminology. This clearly has many years to run, as it comes not only in the LFA [Liturgy for Africans], but also in its derivatives EAUL [East African United Liturgy] and NZ [New Zealand Episcopal Liturgy]. It is a far less controversial form than open self-oblation, for it emphasizes both God's grace, and the mediation of it by Jesus Christ. But another decade may well show that this pharseology is a liturgical by-product of a late doctrinal formulation, and it may thus go back into the melting-pot, as Christians strive to find exactly what they do want to say at this point of the eucharistic prayer."

Such a resolution requires changes in present ways of thinking about and working with language in the two disciplines. By "ethnography of speaking" is meant work to bring about the change.

II

The issues are implicit in the term "ethnography of speaking" itself. "Ethnography" has sometimes been considered "mere" description, not itself a theoretical task, but only fodder for one. Often it has been taken as a part of the scientific division of labour concerned with societies other than one's own. "Speaking" has been regarded as merely implementation and variation, outside the domain of language and linguistics proper. Linguistic theory has mostly developed in abstraction from contexts of use and sources of diversity. But by an ethnography of speaking I shall understand a description that is a theory—a theory of speech as a system of cultural behavior; a system not necessarily exotic, but necessarily concerned with the organization of diversity.

Let me now sketch what is entailed with regard to linguistics, considering first the scope and goals of linguistic theory, then issues of methodology.

The Scope of Linguistic Description

As a term for the activity of linguists that corresponds to ethnography, I shall use simply "linguistic description." What portion of language linguists describe, or attend to most carefully, depends of course upon their theoretical outlook. The development of linguistic description in this century must be seen in relation to the introduction of, and changes of foci for, the notion of structure. The concern first was to secure recognition of the synchronic state of a language as a legitimate object of scientific study, as one indeed of theoretical importance and of precedence, independently of practical, historical, cultural, or other considerations. This goal is the culminating theme of Saussure's *Cours de linguistique générale* (1916), the posthumous book regarded as the starting-point of modern linguistics; it is assumed by Boas (1911) (except that cultural considerations are important), and it is the theme of Sapir's first theoretical essay (1912), developing into the leitmotiv of his book *Language* (1921).

To a great extent it was the conquest of speech sounds as an area of pattern belonging to linguistics that gave structural linguistics its impetus. (Sound had been the domain of phonetics as a *Naturwissenschaft,* only grammar the domain of linguistics, a *Geisteswissenschaft.*) Internationally the area of concentration, where battles of method and theory were first fought, thus was phonology. In American linguistics Boas, Sapir, and Kroeber had already criticized traditional conceptions of word structure; Bloomfield (1933) generalized the notion of morpheme, and morphology came to be intensively cultivated in the late 1930s and the 1940s. Syntax came more to attention in the 1950s, and Chomsky (1957), building on work of Harris, made it the centre in a way that radically challenged earlier work in phonology and morphology as well. Semantics has become a major concern in the 1960s, and in some hands in a way that would radically recast previous work in syntax (including that of Chomsky). Very recently the notion of sociolinguistic description has been advanced (Hymes 1967b), essentially as a synonym for "ethnography of speaking." Here in one sense is the theme of this paper—that the next change of focus for linguistic descriptions entails social description (ethnography), and that with this change the process that began with phonology and morphology will have come full circle—linguistic description will find its own development to require, on a new plane, considerations from which at first it sought to be free (cf. ch. 8).[9]

Structure and Freedom

A principal issue is the relation seen between structure and freedom, or, from another point of view, between structure and human nature. To put it in grossly simplified form: in seeking structure, Saussure is concerned with the word, Chomsky with the sentence, the ethnography of speaking with the act of speech. That is, for Saussure, the object of linguistic theory was language as a structured social fact, and its sphere was the word. Combinations of words in sentences (conventional phrases apart) were aspects of speech, a matter of individual free creation in particular acts outside the sphere of structure. Later linguists extended structural analysis to the sentence, but structure was conceived as segmentation and classification of occurrent forms. With Chomsky, both (a) the scope of syntactic structure and (b) its relation to human nature were reformulated.

As to (a): beyond occurrent forms and distributional patterns was a network of relationships, distinct from, yet basic to, them. In part, Chomsky revitalized traditional conceptions, making them explicit in a formal theory. In so doing Chomsky was carrying further a logic in the recognition of linguistic levels that can be

---

9. There were always some linguists who insisted on the social character of linguistics, but without much effect on the character of linguistic description or the foci of attention.

traced from Sapir's "Sound Patterns in Language" (1925). Briefly, the logic is this: a level (or component) of linguistic structure is to be recognized when there appear systematically two one–many relations (on 'pragmemic' level cf. ch. 1). Thus a sentence such as "Visiting anthropologists can be amusing" may be ambiguous. A single structure, so far as occurrent forms and relations are concerned, it may yet express two different sets of underlying relationships. In one "anthropologist" is subject, in one object, of the verb from which the gerund "visiting" derives. (Loosely, it is as if the sentence derived in the one case from "Someone visits anthropologist," and "It is amusing." This is the relationship Sydney Lamb calls "neutralization." Conversely, the same set of relationships may underlie a number of different sentences, e.g., "Visiting anthropologists can be amusing," "To visit anthropologists can be amusing," "It is amusing to visit anthropologists"; or "It is amusing to be visited by anthropologists," "Anthropologists who visit can be amusing," etc. This is the relationship Lamb calls "diversification." Notice that in the last pair "anthropologists" is object of a preposition ("by" in one case, subject of "be" in the other, yet, fundamentally, subject of "visit" in both. The level of underlying relationships in syntax is "deep structure." It is actually more abstract, more remote from the manifest forms (surface structure), than these examples show.[10]

As to (b): Chomsky also interpreted the relation of structure to individual freedom and human nature. The deeper structures discovered are not opposed to freedom, but its condition. The child is conceived, not as passively learning linguistic patterns, but as actively constructing a theory to make intelligible the scattered and limited sample of speech that comes his way. Within a remarkably short period, from remarkably limited data, the child is seen to acquire essential mastery of a finite device capable of producing an infinity of sentences. These conditions of acquisition are argued by Chomsky to necessitate postulation of a quite specific innate basis (faculté de langage). Herein lies the "creative aspect of language," the "rule-governed creativity," acquired and used largely

10. If "deep structure" and "surface structure" are to be used as terms in anthropology, any analogue to linguistic structure should be explicitly disavowed, if some such formal, transformative relationship between levels is not intended. In particular, it would wholly miss the point of Chomsky's linguistic theory to regard deep structure as simply a more abstract set of patterns of the same sort as the patterns of surface structure. The point is that the levels of structure are related in a finite system of generative principles. I should add that it is not necessary that the relation be expressed in terms of a concept of "rule." (Some linguists, notably Lamb, maintain that "rule" is inappropriate.) The points made here, as to linguistics and ethnography, would still hold, whatever the manner of formulating the systematic relations underlying sentences and acts of speech.

free of stimulus control, which permits a speaker to respond appropriately to novel situations. For Chomsky, the ultimate purpose of linguistic theory is to characterize this underlying ability.

The goal of the ethnography of speaking can be said to be to complete the discovery of the sphere of "rule-governed creativity" with respect to language, and to characterize the abilities of persons in this regard (without prejudice to the specific biological basis of the abilities). In extending the scope of linguistic rules beyond sentences to speech acts, and in seeking to relate language meaningfully to situations, this approach, although compatible with Chomsky's goals, does critically recast certain of his concepts, as well as reject his ignorance (blissful or willful) of the relevance to questions of freedom and dignity of social science research.[11] To see how this is so, let me consider two concepts that Chomsky has made central to discussion, then discuss particular lines of linguistic research.

Competence and Performance

Chomsky's work is a decisive step, not only in extending the scope of linguistic theory, but also in redefining the nature of its object. For "language" Chomsky substitutes "competence" defined as a fluent native speaker's knowledge (largely tacit) of grammaticality—of whether or not putative sentences are part of his language, and according to what structural relationships. The goal of linguistic description is thus changed, from an object independent of men, to a human capacity. Both changes (deep structure, human capacity) are felt to be so great as to lead transformational grammarians to reject "structural linguistics" as a name for their work, and to use it solely to describe other schools as predecessors. From a social standpoint, transformational grammar might equally well be seen as the culmination of the leading theme of structural linguistics. To center analysis in a deep structure, one grounded in human nature, is to fulfill an impulse of structural linguistics to treat language as a sphere of wholly autonomous form. Such a theory perfects and gives the ultimate justification to a study of language at once of human significance and abstracted from actual human beings.

Chomsky's redefinition of linguistic goals appears, then, a halfway house. The term "competence" promises more than it in fact

11. It is indeed difficult to understand how the relevance of Lee 1959, for example, or of contributions to the sort of outlook found in Hymes (ed.) (1973), could have escaped attention. Social science is not all Skinnerian behaviorism and counterinsurgency, as writings such as the chapter on "Psychology and Ideology" (Chomsky 1973: 318–69) would seem to imply.

contains. It is restricted to knowledge, and, within knowledge, to knowledge of grammar. Thus, it leaves other aspects of speakers' tacit knowledge and ability in confusion, thrown together under a largely unexamined concept of "performance" (cf. Chomsky and Halle 1968: 373). In effect, "performance" confuses two separate aims. The first is to stress that competence is something underlying behavior ("mere performance," "actual performance"). The second is to allow for aspects of linguistic ability which are not grammatical: psychological constraints on memory, choice of alternative rules, stylistic choices and devices in word order, etc. The intended negative connotation of the first sense of "performance" tends to attach to the second sense; factors of performance —and the theory must place all social factors here—are generally seen as things that limit the realization of grammatical possibilities, rather than as constitutive or enabling. In fact, of course, choice among the alternatives that can be generated from a single base structure depends as much upon a tacit knowledge as does grammar, and can be studied as much in terms of underlying rules as can grammar. Such things equally underlie actual behavior are facets of knowledge, and would be aspects of competence in the normal sense of the term. On its own terms, linguistic theory must extend the notion of competence to include more than the grammatical.

The need of some such revision is being recognized within the dominant trend in grammatical theory.[12] What may not be accepted at present is a need to complement its reductionist theoretical thrust, and to revise its intuitive mode of practice. Chomsky's interest is in moving from what is said to what is most abstract and elementary in grammar, and from what is social to what is innate in human nature. That, so to speak, is but half a dialectic. A thoroughgoing linguistics must move in the other direction as well, from what is potential in human nature, and elementary in a grammar, to what is realizable and realized; and conceive of the social factors entering into realization as constitutive and rule-governed too. The present tendency is to ignore factors external to grammar, or to treat them in the same way as formal grammar, reducing most of their interesting features to the status of deviations from a few hypothetically intuitive postulates. Need for observant attention to people speaking, and in general, for the services of ethnography and ethnology, is ignored.

An ethnography of speaking approach shares Chomsky's concern for creativity and freedom, but recognizes that a child, or

12. In a conversation (July 1968), Chomsky remarked that the original competence/performance dichotomy was inadequate, in reference to my critique of it (Hymes, 1967 MS).

person, master only of grammar, is not yet free. Chomsky's attempt to discuss the "creative" aspect of language use (Chomsky 1966) suffers from the same difficulty as his treatment of competence. The main thrust is independence of situation. Chomsky specifies freedom from stimulus contol, infinity of possible sentences, yet appropriateness of novel sentences to novel situations; but the first two properties, and the grammatical mechanisms he considers, can never account for appropriateness. A novel sentence might be wildly inappropriate. Appropriateness involves a *positive* relation to situations, not a negative one, and, indeed, a knowledge of a kind of competence regarding situations and relations of sentences to them. As with competence, so with creativity: I share Chomsky's goals for linguistics, and admire him for setting them, but they cannot be reached on his terms or by linguistics alone. Rules of appropriateness beyond grammar govern speech, and are acquired as part of conceptions of self, and of meanings associated both with particular forms of speech and with the act of speaking itself. (For a statement of the social import of human linguistic capacity, revitalizing a long-standing thesis of Boasian anthropology, see "Language and Freedom," ch. 9 in Chomsky 1973).

The issue is especially clear with regard to education and schooling. Chomsky's insistence on the universal capacity for linguistic fluency is essential against the pervasive tendency to blame the failures of a social system on its victims, but in itself provides only a partial remedy.

To say that children could be fluent and are not is poignant, perhaps to invite drastic intervention techniques (some American "authorities" advise taking black children from their mothers at the age of six months). What is needed as well is a realization that the standard of the schools is not the only standard, that more than one system of speaking, each with rules, values, and satisfactions and accomplishments of its own, is involved. Lower-class black children in the United States, for example, are probably much more sensitive to the aesthetic and interactional uses of language than are many middle-class white children.

In such respects a conception of linguistic theory concerned exclusively with an ideally fluent speaker-listener in a perfectly homogeneous community in theory, and in practice only with one's own intuitions and formal logics, may unwittingly play into the hands of those whose views about people the theory's exponents would wish to reject. Not only are motivations and rules and values for use neglected, but also the competence of which they speak is unlocated, merely glossed with a conventional language name, e.g., English. The entire theoretical potential of the formal system is imputed willy-nilly to all individual speakers. Such reliance on one's own sense of communicative conduct can result in unintended intellectual and social "imperialism," attributing parochialisms to the rest of the society in the name of the frontiers of theory. The difficulty is analogous to the circularity with which Whorf moves between an imputed world-view and the linguistic data (from one informant in New York City) from which the world-view had been inferred. In fact, of course, similar bodies of data are compatible with different underlying organization, and degree of knowledge, in individual speakers. One serious difficulty for some children in fact is that their speech is referred by teachers to the same grammatical system as standard English. In the case of West Indian and many American black children, it may have a distinct history involving past creolization, so that a grammar superficially similar may be importantly distinct (cf. Dillard 1968). In the case of many native American children, a distinctive cultural tradition may inform their English discourse.

An adequate approach must distinguish and investigate four aspects of competence: (a) *systemic potential*—whether and to what extent something is not yet realized, and, in a sense, not yet known; it is to this Chomsky in effect reduces competence; (b) *appropriateness*—whether and to what extent something is in some context suitable, effective, or the like; (c) *occurrence*— whether and to what extent something is done; (d) *feasibility*— whether and to what extent something is possible, given the means of implementation available.

The last three dimensions would have to be "performance" in the system of Chomsky's *Aspects* (1965), but knowledge with regard to each is part of the competence of a speaker-hearer in any full sense of the term, and "performance" should be reserved for a more normal, consistent meaning (see below). There is no notice of occurrence in *Aspects,* or in most current linguistic theory, but it is an essential dimension. Most linguists today scorn quantitative data, for example, but Labov (1973a, b) has shown that systematic study of quantitative variation discloses new kinds of structure and makes possible explanation of change. In general, this theoretical dimension provides for the fact that members of a speech community are aware of the commonness, rarity, previous occurrence or novelty, of many features of speech, and that this knowledge enters into their definitions and evaluations of ways of speaking.[13]

13. Conversation interaction may proceed in terms of awareness of frequencies of features, as when Prague speakers are reported to move from the phonology of standard Czech to that of conversational Czech by degrees.

In terms of these dimensions, one can say of speech that it is, for example, grammatical, awkward, overly formal, and rare, as in the conversation of the American ambassador to the Court of St. James in the TV film, "The Royal Family"; ungrammatical, difficult, expressively appropriate, and individual, as in the speech of Leontes in Act II of *The Winter's Tale* (Thorne, 1969); ungrammatical, awkward, appropriate, and common, as in the bumbling speech required of Burundi peasants before aristocrats (Albert, 1972); grammatical, easy, correct, and avoided, as indicated in these remarks under "Dukes and Duchesses . . . Style of Addressing in Speech": though the necessity for using the full title would generally be avoided . . . in conversation it is best to make as sparing a use as possible of titles" (*Titles and Forms of Address*, 1967: 46).

One must recognize not only knowledge, but also ability to implement it, with respect to each of these dimensions, as a component of competence in speaking. Especially, one must provide for motivation and value.[14] And, as indicated, the competence to be attributed to particular persons and communities is in each case an empirical matter. Transformational theory recognizes that what seems the same sentence may enter into two quite different

---

Japanese are said to be able to identify foreigners who have learnt the language formally because their speech is too correct (on quantitative aspects generally, see now G. Sankoff 1974). Here belongs "the disitinction between the merely and marginally possible and the actually normal: between what one will accept as a hearer and what one will produce as a speaker" (Quirk 1968: 195). The category also allows the feature of social life summed up in the medieval rubric, *factum valet* (Harold Garfinkel, pers. comm.): something contrary to rule may be accepted, in fact done, e.g.:

> The prefix "The" is now by general custom used in addressing the daughters of dukes, marquesses and earls, e.g., "The Lady Jean Smith". Although it should therefore be used, the practice exists only by courtesy, and is not recognized as correct by, for example, the College of Arms (*Titles and Forms of Address*, 1967 edn: 45).

14. The simplistic view of transformational generative grammar is that competence is essentially a maturational unfolding. Many hold the equally simplistic view that quantity of exposure should shape children's speech (a view once put forward to explain linguistic change by Bloomfield, 1933). In fact, of course, maturation and exposure both play some role, but identification and motivation are equally fundamental (cf. Labov 1966, LePage 1969). Many black boys use substandard speech, not through interference with unfolding or lack of exposure, but as a sign of masculinity. Is it surprising that black lower-class boys do not take white middle-class women teachers as models? Non-standard-speaking children hear as much TV and radio as other children, and their teachers all day. At Columbia Point School (Boston) last summer, in a discussion in which teachers had raised just these points, the one black mother present observed: "I've noticed that when the children play school outside, they talk like they're supposed to in school; and when they stop playing school, they don't."

sets of relations, syntactically; it must recognize the same thing to be true, socially.

Finally, the negative connotation of performance, as the realization of knowledge and ability, must be replaced with recognition of its positive aspect as well. There are properties of performance, essential to the social role of speaking, that go beyond the knowledge and ability referable to particular persons. In part these properties are functions of the social organization of speech (complementary of roles, etc.), in part they emerge in the actual events of speech themselves (as when one speaks to a responsive or a "cold" audience).[15]

Such a perspective calls for a descriptive method, a methodological approach, different from that common in present linguistics. Ch. 2 has outlined it from an ethnographic standpoint. To indicate further what it would be like, let me consider some ways in which linguistics itself is moving in the required direction.

Directions of Linguistic Description: Dimensions of Discourse

In the present situation in linguistics the main frontiers of relevant work have to do with extension of analysis of the organization of coherence of texts; beyond the force of speech acts to the formation of conversations; beyond a chosen language to choices among forms of speech; and beyond the referential function to functions that may be grouped together as stylistic. Each of these extensions can be seen as involving kinds of knowledge and ability, i.e., competence, on the part of members of a community, and as entailing ethnographic analysis of speaking. These extensions enrich the adequacy of linguistics, on both the syntagmatic and paradigmatic planes, in terms both of sequences and of the sets of features from which sequences are selected; but together their effect is more than two-dimensional. Language can no longer be taken as horizontal, as Bloomfieldian "discovery" procedures might have had it, nor as derivationally vertical as Chomskyan "recovery" procedures might have it, but only as the composite of many intersecting planes or sectors. A language is, so to speak, multifaceted, and different aspects of its history and character are illuminated with some of its faces, obscured with others.

15. E.g. in a review of records by Joan Chissell (*The Times Saturday Review*, 5 April 1969):
"Stephen Bishop . . . in Beethoven's Diabelli Variations, a work which did much to make his name on the concert platform. Here, the daemonic, visionary Beethoven takes a bit longer to break out than when aided and abetted by audience reaction, but progressively Bishop's superb strength and discipline take fire."

Discourse: Texts

Chomsky has alluded to coherence (1968: 11), perhaps in response to the attention given to it by Halliday, Gleason, and others (coherence was not discussed in Chomsky 1965, despite the attribution of it here to a Cartesian view). Just as one has the ability to recognize a series of sentences as discourse, rather than an arbitrary list (Hasan 1968: 1). The ability depends in important part on properly linguistic features and is increasingly recognized as a necessary facet of investigation (cf. Daneš 1964; Halliday 1967). Three brief examples must suffice.

Kiparsky (1968), for example, in a brilliant article explaining diverse Indoeuropean phenomena in terms of a single type of rule, conjunct reduction (by virtue of which the second occurrence of a feature may be omitted or expressed by an unmarked form), notes that the scope of such rules applies across sentences (p. 34, n.4) and even across change of speakers in dialogue (p. 43). Gunter (1966) explicitly attacks the restriction of *la langue* to the sentence, and notes that the placement of accent cannot be explained without the assumption that a given variety of a sentence signals its own particular kind of relevance to its context. (By variety of sentence is meant that a given sentence is in effect chosen from among what another linguist, Henry Hiz, has called a battery. There are paradigms not only of morphemes, but of sentences as well.) The format of the usual transformational grammar is criticized for obscuring the relation among the members of a paradigm of sentence varieties. With particular reference to accent, Gunter goes on to show that some placements in dialogue make nonsense of it, others provide intelligibility; that in general one has a knowledge of "context grammar" that enables one to tell whether a sentence is relevant to what has just been said, or whether relevance to an implicit (nonverbal) context must be sought; if the former, what the connection is, and if the latter, what limits the form and content of the nonovert must satisfy. (See Gunter's article for detailed interpretation of English examples.) As a third example, let me cite (Wheeler 1967), who found that his Siona informants would allow variation in the enclitic chosen to mark subject and object relations, where single sentences were involved, but would stubbornly refuse to vary the presence or choice of enclitic in texts. There was decidedly a fixed order for use or nonuse of the markers, if a narration or dialogue was to be acceptable, yet no clue within the sentence as to the rationale. Wheeler discovered (partly with the aid of kinesic behavior on the part of informants) that not one but two dimensions underlay the grammatical markers in question. The markers signalled both subject, object, or goal within the sentence, and degree of focus—emphatic, normal, or none—within the discourse. This last, purely discourse, function is indeed their primary function.

The study of texts is of course familiar to linguists and ethnographers both; and transformational grammar itself began in work of Zellig Harris in the early 1950s on certain recurrent properties of texts. The work cited above makes clear the development of text analysis in terms of an extended understanding of the competence of speakers. There is much to be learnt just from such study of syntactic relations. At the same time, analysis must go beyond purely linguistic markers. Much of the coherence of texts depends upon abstract rules independent of specific linguistic form, indeed, of speech. Such are the kinds of knowledge that the sociologist Harvey Sacks analyzes as hearers' and viewers' maxims. One such maxim in brief form is: if the first of two sentences can be heard (interpreted) as the cause of the second, hear it that way. Sacks (1972) uses the start of a children's story as illustration: "The baby cried. The mommy picked it up." He notes that we spontaneously take the mommy to be *its* mommy, and to have picked the baby up *because* it cried, although neither relationship is stated (or implied by the underlying syntax).[16]

A familiar example of structural analysis of texts is of course the work of Lévi-Strauss, Greimas, and others. From the standpoint of an ethnography of speaking, such work has a complementary limitation: it has little or nothing to do with specific linguistic form at all. This is not to deny the existence of narrative structures independent of linguistic form, but to question that their function can be validly inferred apart from a knowledge of such form. In a Chinookan myth, for example, any translation,

16. An entry from *Pears Cyclopaedia* (Barker, 1968–69) illustrates this point, and a further one of some importance:
    "1901. Queen Victoria dies, Jan. 22. Trans-Siberian railway opened for single-track traffic."
For many people, as for myself, this entry is momentarily humorous. One can read it in terms of Sacks's maxim: *post hoc, ergo propter hoc*. The railway opened for single-track traffic *once* (because) Queen Victoria had died. This response reflects the fact that discourse, like syntax, has ambiguities, entailing relation of a surface structure to more than one underlying structure. Were only Sack's maxim applicable, there would be only a puzzling causal relationship. Were only conventions of chronicle applicable, no relationship except occurrence in the same year would be considered. The humour is in entertaining the causal connection of narrative where one knows it is not intended (conjuring up perhaps an image of Queen Victoria bodily blocking the single track). Notice that the discourse rules are seen to be sensitive to genre (narrative, chronicle). An important part of humor, and creative use of language generally, is to be understood in terms of such *conjunctive* (simultaneous derivation, not selection of a single derivation, as in disambiguation). Use of this resource of language seems to vary a great deal crossculturally, and competence for it probably depends very much upon cultural context.

even an abstract, would make clear the presence of a structure, "Interdiction: Interdiction violated," and imply that the outcome (a murder) follows from the violation, as so often is found to be the case. Analysis of the myth in terms of its specific development, in Clackamas Chinook, discloses structures that place almost an opposite significance on the myth. The myth is to be understood in terms of a specifically Chinookan theory of myth (one requiring constant moving back and forth between linguistic form and cultural meaning for its discovery, as in the classic structural linguistic principle of form—meaning covariation) such that it is here not the violator, but the one who issues the interdiction, who, in Clackamas terms, is culpable. Only through control of the original linguistic form, moreover, is one able to discover that an inherited plot has been shaped to express through imagery and style a personal meaning, as well as to see that the terse myth has a unity (see Hymes 1968b).

The particular contribution of linguistics presumably will be to explore to its limits the formally linguistic coherence of texts, and, as in the work of Gunter, Labov, and some others, to explore conversational interaction as well. The contribution of social anthropology may be to explore the structure of conversational interaction more directly and thoroughly, as part of ethnography, and to insist on understanding discourse structures as *situated*, that is, as pertaining to cultural and personal occasions which invest discourse with part of their meaning and structure.[17] There

17. My understanding of these issues owes much to Kenneth Burke, who has long insisted on analysis of language as the enacting of strategies to encompass situations (see the title essay in his *Philosophy of Literary Form*, 1941). Burke has also pointed out the value of theology, as well as of poetics and rhetoric, for the understanding of verbal action. In general, anthropology has much to gain from the disciplines of rhetoric, literary criticism, and textual interpretation. Both points are nicely exemplified in the parables of Jesus. The early Church interpreted the parable allegorically; critical scholarship freed them from that in the late nineteenth century, but form-criticism, despite some insights, failed when it tried to treat them in terms of formal distinctions not present in the original Aramaic folk-category (*mashal*). Recent work has established the primacy of two considerations: reconstruction of the original linguistic form (Aramaic), wherever possible, by triangulation from the variant Greek, Syriac, and Hebrew renderings, and reconstruction of the place of a parable in Jesus' career, as "uttered in an actual situation . . . at a particular and often unforseen point . . . they were preponderantly concerned with a situation of conflict" (Jeremias 1963: 21). A major cause of misinterpretation was the tendency of Gospel writers and the Church to take the parables as addressed to their own subsequent situation rather than as addressed (as was the case) to an immediate situation, often to an opponent or doubting outsider. The parables are *par excellence* instances of what Chomsky (1966) terms the "creative" aspect of language use, an essential criterion of which he gives as appropriateness of new sentences to novel situations; and they bring to the fore what Chomsky omits, the dialectic relation. Chomsky analyses the grammatical conditions

is as yet relatively little work that integrates both aspects. These points bring us to a central concept, that of speech act.

Discourse: Speech Acts

Some linguists, recognizing the significance of speech acts, now wish to incorporate them into syntax, so that a sentence carries with it in deep structure a performative verb, something like "I ask you," "I tell you," and the like (normally deleted in overt form). There is indeed evidence to support this approach in some cases (McCawley 1968: 157), but as a general solution to the problem it is cumbersome and counterintuitive, and appears a last-ditch effort to keep within the conventional boundaries of linguistics. An approach that insists on the complex, abstract knowledge of speakers with regard to other relationships quite distinct from manifest form need not cling to a literal verbal embodiment of acts of speech (as I argued in a letter to John Ross as early as the summer of 1968). Some assertions, requests, commands, threats, and the like are known to be such on the basis of a knowledge, *jointly*, of the message-form and the relationship in which it occurs. For example, the same sentence commonly serves as a serious insult in some relationships and as a badge of intimacy in others.

A related point—obvious, yet needing to be repeatedly mentioned—is that the rules that govern speech acts govern more than single speakers and more than speech. As to single speakers, the Sanskrit rule for conjunct reduction across interlocutors has been mentioned. The constraining power of the second part of the Summons-Response sequence in American English interaction has been noted by Schegloff (1968), and many many analogues are to be found in other societies. An example of expected "conjunct replication" is reported by Jacobs (1940: 130):

---

for sentences to be independent of control by a situation; the ethnography of speaking investigates the conditions for sentences to define and change situations.

On the crux in Mark 4: 10–13, as to Jesus' own intention, Moule (1966: 149–51) defends the authenticity of the saying, but fails to deal with the linguistic and contextual evidence for its being an interpolation here (Jeremias, 1963: 13–18). Hunter (1964: 110–22) reviews the problem, adopting Jeremias's solution. (All authors agree that the apparent meaning that the parables are intended to prevent outsiders from understanding is wrong.) The issue hinges on two conjunctions, the original Aramaic *de*, which can mean 'who', whereas the NT Greek *hina* can mean only 'that', and the original Aramaic *dilema*, to be taken (as rabbinical exegesis shows) as 'unless', not as 'lest'. The necessity of original text—*pace* Lévi-Strauss, and some of his followers—for accurate understanding of fundamental relationships, the inadequacy of translations, could not be more clearly demonstrated.

when the Coos were still living in their native area and villages, myths and possibly also narratives were told only in the winter-time, according to Mrs. Peterson; it was expected that the child auditors, if not older people, repeat in unison each phrase or sentence verbatim after the raconteur. "They kept right on telling it until the children got it right. They wanted them to have it right. They did not want them to get it mixed up and 'lie' when they told it." When folktales were told to an audience composed only of adults, that is, of persons passed puberty, just one of the auditors repeated each sentence verbatim following the raconteur. But this repeating of what the other person said is only an aspect of conversational etiquette in general: the person spoken to usually if not always repeated verbatim what was said to him.

An especially nice example of both more than single speakers and more than speech is found among the Haya of northern Tanzania (Sheila Seitel, pers. comm.). When mentioning a quantity, a speaker will say something such as "We saw this many of them, "holding up a certain number of fingers. It is the listener who then says the number. Again, rules for summoning in English in American society subsume both verbal and nonverbal acts: "George!," a telephone ring, a knock on a door (Schegloff 1968). By the same principle that rejects compartments in syntax and phonology, when unitary treatment of unitary phenomena is presented (Mc-Cawley 1968: 166ff.), the boundary between verbal and nonverbal features must be rejected, once sentences are studied as addressed acts of speech.

Within speech itself there is more to performances than performatives, and more than logical presuppositions and postulates too, interesting as these cynosures of attention in formal linguistics are. As noted in ch. 2 with regard to speech acts, they comprise sets of features, in relation to functional foci or components of speech events; and these sets require to be validated in relation to the actual rules underlying communicative conduct in a community, and the verbal styles and strategies available to its participants. Formalisms can foreclose too soon. The first commandment in the study of discourse must be: Let people surprise you, as to what they can do, and what they can use to do it.

Still, to consider discourse as situated is not to refer it to an infinity of possible contextual factors. (cf. Friedrich 1972: 299, the failure to develop a method beyond the handling of discrete instances vitiated the influence of Malinowski's work.) Linguists and perhaps others do tend to imagine that when a door is opened on a level beyond the familiar, everything in the universe outside will rush in. From the standpoint of the ethnography of speaking, there is in a community a system of speech acts, a structured knowledge accessible to the members of the community, and so, to a great extent, to science.

Discourse: "Code-switching"

"Code-switching" has become a common term for alternate use of two or more languages, varieties of a language, or even speech styles. Studies of code-switching are important, because bilingualism and bidialectalism are important, and because such work necessarily breaks with an image of the notions of language and speech community as identical.[18] In such studies one finds that the very question of what counts as unit or object of description in a community is dependent on ethnography. (See discussion of *speech community* and forms of speech in ch. 2.)

Just to locate the referent of its analysis, then, linguistics must locate some particular body of judgments of acceptability and kinds of knowledge with regard to the plurality of forms of speech found in a community. For formal linguistics, the task may be only a way of excluding some phenomena and of ensuring the validity of those selected. For sociolinguistics and ethnography of speaking, such an account of the repertoire of a community is an essential framework. In this regard Denison (1968) provides a valuable account of a trilingual community (cf. also Denison 1970). He delineates thirteen factors involved in the selection of one or the other of the three languages in the north Italian community of Sauris (German, Italian, Friulian). These factors can be seen to be ingredients of four or five general components of speech events: situation (here, formality of the scene, home setting); genre (here, sayings, written genre depends on relationship to what I would term key—the attitude or spirit in which the act occurs, here, spontaneity versus non-spontaneity); participants (here, capacities and preferences of sender, receiver, auditor for a variety, plus age and sex); and the act-sequence itself (here, shifts in topic, and the variety of the preceding discourse).

Selection and switching of forms of speech point beyond themselves in two important respects. First, their description requires, and helps to create, an adequate general framework for the discovery and analysis of rules of speaking. In addition to the components of speech events found pertinent in Sauris, choice of

18. Compare the following remarkable statement (Chomsky 1973: 326–27): "Consider, for example, the notion 'likelihood of producing a sentence of English rather than Chinese'. Given a characterization of 'English' and 'Chinese' by an abstract theory of postulated internal states (mental states, if you like), it is possible to give some meaning to this notion—*though the probabilities being negligible under any known characterization of determining factors,* will be of no interest for the prediction of behavior." Chomsky's ignorance of linguistics, outside a narrow sector, become downright embarrassing at moments like this. He presumably intended the argument to apply to any arbitrary pair of possible languages known by a person. In sweepingly denying predictability to social science, he also denies it to millions of multilingual people in whose lives and communities code-choice has a high and valued degree of regularity (cf. e.g., Blom and Gumperz 1972).

form of speech may depend upon ends in view (e.g., Kaska Indians in northwestern Canada switch to English to curse, Malagasy-speaking peasants use French to drive their cows); the instrumentalities available in terms of *channels* and their use (oral, written, singing, etc.); the norms of interaction holding between persons (e.g., as to whether choice of the variety best known to an interlocutor is obligatory, ingratiating, or insulting, as implying that he or she does not know some more prestigious variety); and norms of interpretation (e.g., belief that the cries or calls of a certain creature are in a certain code, requiring to be answered in the same). Commonly rules for use of a form of speech will involve a relationship among two or more components. Just these two steps—identifying what can count as an instance of such a component relevant to communication, and discovering the relations obtaining among components—are the initial steps of ethnography of speaking (and communication).

Second, the dimensions and meanings found to underlie selection and switching of forms of speech are general. Social distance is a dimension that underlies choice of Haitian French or Creole in Haiti, of one among a hierarchy of languages in Nigeria (Hymes 1972d); choice of word in "pronouns of power and solidarity" (Brown and Gilman 1960) and "pronominal breakthrough" (Friedrich 1972); use of phonological variables (Labov 1966); use and construal of a verb affix (Swadesh 1933); choice of intonational features and contours; and so on. This is not to say that means different in character and scale do not condition different outcomes and rules, but it is to say that they do not uniquely determine, do not control, them. The creative aspect of language use involves a measure of freedom and diversity, cutting across compartments habitual to linguistics, in the selection and grouping together of means. Early in the development of modern linguistics, syntactic relations ("inflection," "incorporation," etc.) has to be generalized beyond association with particular grammatical types (cf. Boas 1911, Kroeber, 1911, 1916: 91–93, Sapir 1911, 1922: 52–54) to universal features and dimensions. A similar need has been recurrently recognized in semantic description (e.g., Jespersen 1924: 39–40, 45ff., Jakobson 1957, Fillmore, 1968). Sociolinguistic description broaches such a need at the most inclusive level of all; relations and dimensions, the organization and meaning of linguistic features, have to be generalized beyond any one sector of language, and indeed, beyond language itself.

If pursued in a thoroughgoing way, then, the study of choice among the forms of speech brings one to a novel starting-point, which is to recognize that the fundamental organization of linguistic features is into community-relative forms of speech, or, even more generally perhaps, speech styles. "Languages," "dialects," "codes" are not equivalent to, but components of, these. Whole-language choice is important and salient, but not in practice or in principle fundamental. The true structure of choice of linguistic means, of a theory of the creative aspect of their use, lies deeper. Thus, shift in the provenance of linguistic means (e.g., from German to Italian), while striking, goes together with shift in any component of speaking, as prospective evidence of underlying organization: shift between normal voice and whispering, between direct and indirect address, between deliberate and hurried tempo, between one topic and another, between one proportion of stylistic features and another, etc. Here is the kind of form-meaning covariation that is basic to sociolinguistics, the sociolinguistic commutation test, as it were, corresponding to the principle of contrast and nonrepetition basic to the relevance of features in linguistics proper. Such work of course requires intimate command of a community's linguistic resources and also raises the question of stylistic perspective.

Discourse: Stylistic Perspective

The concern of most work called stylistic is with literary or other written texts, and the scope of the analysis is defined by some principle of selection among elements given by linguistic analysis. (Three selections of relevant work are Chatman and Levin 1966, Steinman 1967, and Chatman 1970.) Such stylistics is relevant insofar as selection entails a relation between linguistic elements and contextual factors. It then points beyond itself in the same two ways as "code-switching": the principles of selection point to a general framework, and the kinds of dimensions and meanings are general. Broadly conceived, indeed, stylistics can be almost indistinguishable from ethnography of speaking (of. Guiraud 1961, "Conclusion"), although the ethnographic approach must concern itself with speech styles generally in a community.

Much of the work involving the notion of style, of course, is not concerned with the general foundations implied by it. The notion (or speech level) may be invoked only when some contextual factor inescapably intrudes into ordinary linguistic analysis (as with men's and women's speech in some languages, age, status, formality of context, or the like in others). Or "style" may be the ready label for a dimension of variation in what is conceived as a strictly linguistic problem, e.g., the "contextual styles" in Labov 1966, as a dimension specifically of socially motivated sound change. Finally, style may be regarded as departures or deviations from a standard or norm. In contrast to such work, stylistic perspective is taken here to apply to all of speech, that is, all of speech is referrable to the set of styles in the repertoire of a person or community; it is taken as bringing into view verbal elements not necessarily given by the usual linguistic analysis (so-called "expressive," "emotive," "attitudinal," etc., elements—cf. ch. 8); and it is taken as concerned with departures or deviations from a norm only in those cases in which departure or deviation is indeed the intention of the source (as it is with some writers and speakers). In the vast majority of communities and cases, style is understood rather as the arousal and accomplishment of expectations, following the lead of Kenneth Burke (1931) in his essay on "Psychology and Literary Form." It is such a perspective that is taken to be implied as general foundation by the various particular uses of the notion of style.

From this standpoint, the identification of speech styles is a vital descriptive task at the frontier of current linguistics. (For statement of the basic descriptive concept, rules of co-occurrence, see Ervin-Tripp 1972). Obviously speech styles do not exhaust functional investigation of speech, which involves not only the organization of linguistic means, but also the consequences of their use. Nevertheless, knowledge of speech styles is essential to complete discovery of the sphere of rule-governed creativity with regard to language. It is often complex use of styles that underlies individual acts that are creative in the sense of involving unique meanings and mediations, and innovation with regard to rules, or styles, themselves. (On unique mediation, cf. Tillich 1964: 56–57; on such innovation as a general human experience, cf. Williams 1961, part 1, ch. 1). By disclosing the conventional means available and organized, one makes possible a clearer understanding of the personal and transcendent (cf. Sapir 1927, Tillich 1964: 53–67).

Methodological Summing-Up

Clearly, much of what has been discussed from the starting-point of linguistics could be approached from an ethnographic starting-point as well. That is in keeping with the prediction that an ethnography of speaking would represent a merging of the two disciplines at certain points; and it is inescapable. The logic of the discussion of linguistics has been to provide linguistic description with a necessary ethnographic base: to extend the scope of linguistic description from an isolated sentence-generating single norm to the structure of speaking as a whole, and to see description of speaking as situated and purposive. In short, to see larger structure, and to see structure as dependent on explicit broader conceptions of function. But to have presented these matters from an ethnographic starting-point would have involved a critique of social anthropology, just as much as the presentation above has been a critique of linguistics. If linguistics needs to look to the foundations of its work, social anthropology needs to look to the linguistic content. It perhaps has a special responsibility and opportunity to do so, and to this I now turn.

III

There are neglected kinds of knowledge to be made explicit as goals of analysis in social anthropology as well. I shall be able to mention only two examples, one having to do with members of other cultures, one with those who study them.

A few years ago Max Gluckman wrote on the importance of gossip and scandal (1963). Among the groups taken as illustrations (Elizabeth Colson's Makah, English fox-hunting aristocracy), knowing how to gossip was found to be essential. This case may be taken to represent many ethnographic accounts, wherein some such ability is noted.

Consider what is entailed. Presumably it is not the case that gossiping and speaking are the same, that all speech is gossip. There must then be criteria for recognizing some speech as gossip, as being better or worse at it, as making mistakes, and as learning how. In short, members of the group presumably share a knowledge, and have ways of acquiring it, that an ethnographer might be expected to describe. Typically, ethnographers do not do so. Ethnographic accounts are rife with terms that in fact denote ways of speaking, though they are not always recognized to be such. (For reconstruction of a contrast drawn by Lowie in this respect between Crow and Hidatsa, see Hymes 1964b.) One may be told that it is important, for men, say, to be good at a certain way of speaking. Commonly it is impossible to tell what would consist of an instance of the activity in question, or what being good at it would be like. Members of the world's cultures pray, curse, reproach, taunt, invoke, gossip, answer, instruct, report, joke, insult, greet, take leave, announce, interpret, advise, preach, command, inquire, duel verbally, etc., etc. At least they do so in the language of ethnography. What they would be found to be doing in terms of their own languages and cultures—or in terms of a general theory and terminology of speech, one that was systematic, not an ad hoc adaptation from the ethnographer's culture —it is seldom possible to tell. Sometimes who may or should speak, how, when, and where, to whom, can be glimpsed, but seldom in sufficient detail to permit explicit formulation.

(Here is a respect in which linguistics has a lesson for ethnography. If it does not direct its attention sufficiently to ethnographic matters, in its own domain it is explicit and vulnerable. Linguists write rules, or formalize relationships in data in other ways, and study the conditions in which one or another formalization is to be preferred, not to ape mathematics, but in order to do a decent job of work. Rule-writing commits one in explicit terms, as to what is being claimed and comprised. A good deal of the extension of ethnography into knowledge of speech is probably best handled by amplification of linguistic rules to comprise the ethnographic factors. The attitude to take toward the formalisms involved is to regard them simply as necessary book-keeping.)

Straight lexicography would sometimes serve, as when there is a specific verb stem for an act such as "to tell A in the presence of B of the bad thing B has said of A" (Wasco Chinook). Translation itself, of course, would not suffice: "to pronounce" is the best English gloss for Chinookan -pgna, but the specific constitutive force of the latter comes out only in its use in ceremonies and myths (cf. Hymes 1966b). To define the act concealed in the Chinookan stem that can be politely rendered "to sing of someone with whom one has slept" requires some knowledge of its place among possible types of song. Investigation of the stem "to curse" would lead one into intonation and social relationships; with a minor exception (qalaq baya, something like "darn you") there are no words in the language that are curse-words or obscene in themselves: cursing and obscenity depend on what is said, in what way, to whom. Lexicography might stop with recording the only Chinookan expression analogous to a European greeting (dan miuxhúlal, "what are you doing"); it would not itself lead one to explore the absence (as in many Amerindian societies) of the complex greeting patterns found in Africa, or to notice that common Wasco practice is not to greet someone who joins a group: courtesy requires that one does not call attention to the newcomer until he or she no longer is such—a practice in keeping with another, that one can pay a visit simply by coming and need not speak, if there is nothing more to convey. To pursue the analysis of speech acts, then, involves one in ethnography with speaking as its focus.

It would be easy to respond that such ethnography might be interesting but a luxury. In fact, I think it will prove both valuable and in some respects indispensable. First of all, inquiry into speaking—just into occasions in which speech is required, optional, or prescribed—discloses patterns of importance in a culture. Among Chinookans, for example, investigation of patterns of expected speech and required silence discloses that certain scenes are defined as formal by the fact that an audience is addressed by one whose words are repeated from another source, and that both grammar and conduct reflect a belief that matters dependent on the future, especially where relations with nature are concerned, should not be spoken while still uncertain. The pattern unites a number of practices, including the major ceremony in individual life (conferring of a name), the central public ideological activity (myth narration), and the major personal one (the guardian-spirit quest). For each there is a period in which something said (pronouncement of name, myth, guardian spirit's instructions) can be quoted but not disclosed in full, and a point at which, having been validated, the words are repeated in full. In terms of the pattern, a number of isolated and puzzling items fall into place (see Hymes 1966b). Again, attention to the interpretation put upon infant speech may reveal much of the adult culture. Both Chinookans and Ashanti believe that infants share a first language not the adult one (on native theory, the "native language" is always a second language). For Chinookans, the baby's talk is shared with certain spirits, and shamans having those spirits interpret it lest by "dying" it return to the spirit world from which it came; the attempt is to incorporate the infant communicatively within the community. Ashanti traditionally exclude infants from a room in which a woman is giving birth, on the ground that an infant would talk to the baby in the womb in the special language they share, and, by warning it of the hardness of life, make it reluctant to emerge and so cause a hard delivery. The evaluation of spontaneous speech as intrinsically dangerous (and a pairing of men: women: culture: nature, in this regard) is brought out in this. Interpretations of the intent of first utterances—e.g., as an attempt to name kin (Wogeo), to ask for food (Alorese), to manipulate (Chaga)—may indeed be something of a projective test for a culture, as regards adult practices and the valuation placed on speech itself.

At the very least, then, analysis of speaking would enhance ethnographies. Beliefs and practices with regard to children may be an especially revealing area—one important for general theory, since the usual commonplaces concerning the role of language in the transmission of culture are patently inadequate to the great empirical diversity as to what is and what is not, and how much is, transmitted verbally. Some attention to speaking is in fact essential to ethnography itself, if seldom consciously thought of as part of one's analysis. In learning to get along with informants and other members of a community, to obtain information and the like, an ethnographer willy-nilly acquires some working sense of the very things with which we are here concerned. He or she does not normally make that working sense an object of conscious attention or reflection. (A number of times such patterns seem to have come first to awareness in conversation about fieldwork.) With respect, then, to what may be called the domain of *interrogative behavior,* investigation of the sort proposed here would entail no more than making one's own process of investigation part of the object of study.

In just this respect social anthropologists can make a vital contribution to sociolinguistics and the ethnography of speaking, while perhaps contributing to their own work, whatever its main concern. A social anthropologist once posed the following problem: in a Mayan-speaking community in Mexico her questions were typically responded to by a Mayan expression translatable as "Nothing." She also noted that children's questions to parents would receive the same answer. I am not sure how the ethnography got done, or what solution was supposed to be drawn out of a sociolinguistic hat, but clearly, it cannot be the case that members of that Mayan community have no way of obtaining information from one another. Presumably there are appropriate ways of ascertaining things one does not already know from others who know them, and circumstances in which those who know things think it appropriate to tell them. I would suspect that a direct question was interpreted as rudeness. (Speakers seem generally to have and evaluate alternative ways of asking information and giving commands.) In any case, facts such as these—that among Araucanians it is an insult to be asked to repeat an answer, that a prompt answer from a Toba means he has no time to answer questions, that a Wasco prefers not to answer a question on the day of its asking, that Aritama prefer intermediaries for request— point to a sector of behavior that successful ethnographers presumably master, just as they master some command of the local language. To make such matters the object of explicit attention would serve the interests of social anthropology and sociolinguistics both.

There is a second area in which these two interests appear to coincide, the study of kinship terms. Formal analysis of kinship ("componential analysis") has sometimes forgotten in practice what it honors in theory, the need of an ethnographic approach that treats verbal behavior as situated, as answers to explicit or implicit questions, whose local status must be determined. Schneider (1969) has brought this point forcibly home. He shows that analyses of American English kinship terms have conflated two separate questions: when asked as to relatives, American informants may understand either biological relationship (relationship at all) or social relationship (relationship that counts). And he shows that the priority of terms of reference over terms of address is a dogma at best, and empirically wrong in known cases. In these respects Schneider's critique of componential analysis is at one with the critique of linguistics made earlier in this paper. To his points may be added the question of the setting of questions: Tulisano and Cole (1965) observe that informants may use different terms in introducing kin from those they use in responding to ethnographers, and Murphy (1967) reports that the Tuareg use a Sudanese system for explaining kin relations to nonkin, but an Iroquois system in address and reference among kin themselves. Conant (1961) has shown that systems of address may be more revealing than systems of reference, and at the same time contain other than kinship terms in the narrow sense, and Fischer (1964) has taken a specific setting, the family, to show the significance of patterns of address drawing upon several different domains (kinship, pronouns, personal names).

Social anthropologists are thus familiar in the area of kinship with exactly the problems that the ethnography of speaking raises about verbal form in general. The starting-point must be the purposes and strategies of persons in situations: what terms, what language indeed, what type of system even, are found in the data, will depend on that. At the same time there is, perhaps, an extension of focus. The fundamental problem may be seen to be, how do persons address each other? How are formally and comparatively distinct domains (personal names, kin terms, pronouns, titles, nicknames) integrated in the service of address?

One value of terms, or modes, of address as a focus is that it makes so clear that the relation of linguistic form to social setting is not merely a matter of correlation. Persons choose among alternative modes of address, and have a knowledge of what the meaning of doing so may be that can be formally explicated. An approach that has seemed successful with choice of speech level in Korean address would be, briefly, as follows: a mode of address (term, style, speech variety, whatever) has associated with it a usual, or "unmarked," value—say, formality. Social relationships and settings have associated with them usual, or "unmarked," values. When the values of the mode of address and the social context match—when both, say, are formal—then that meaning is of course accomplished, together with the meeting of expectations. When the values do not match—when, say, an informal mode of address is used in a formal relationship or conversely— then a special, or "marked," meaning is conveyed. The unmarked and marked meanings are each defined by a particular rule or relation, mapping the set of linguistic alternatives onto the set of social relationships and settings. What the particular marked meaning—deference, courtesy, insult, change of status—will be is of course an empirical question, as are the options available to the recipient (to overlook, acknowledge, take as irrevocable). Some generalizations seem likely to emerge, e.g., that mappings of terms onto categories higher and lower than normal matching have positive and negative import, respectively.

I stress this point because there is a strong tendency to consider the relation of linguistic form to setting only in terms of one-to-one matching. The "rule-governed creativity" of speakers is not so restricted. "Registers," for example, are not chosen only because a situation demands them; they may be chosen to define a situation, or to discover its definition by others (as when the choice can be taken in two different ways, depending on the relationship).

In the study of interrogative behavior and modes of address, then, social anthropologists would serve their own interests while dealing with problems essential to an ethnography of speaking. There are other respects in which the contribution of social anthropology is essential, if it can be secured. I shall indicate four of these.

First, as noted above, analysis of the meaning of modes of address requires knowledge of the "semantics" of social relationships as well as of the semantics of verbal forms. Attempts to deal with these problems from the standpoint of linguistic meanings alone cannot succeed; nor can treatments in terms of contexts alone. Each has structure of its own that is essential, but not sufficient. There are ten features of use of second-person pronouns in Russian, for example, according to Friedrich (1966), not two, because ten are needed to account for switching and other aspects of use. Yet this goes against the obvious fact (stressed by Einar Haugen in discussion in the same volume) that the Russian pronouns do essentially contrast on just the dimensions of authority and intimacy. If the additional features are packed into the pronouns, one obscures their semantic structure and leaves unexplained their varied efficacy in different situations. Nor would it serve to displace the meaning onto the contexts alone (as Malinowski's approach seemed in danger of doing); that way would lie sheer confusion. The pronouns, like features of address and style generally, have "an identificational-contrastive" value, to use the term of Kenneth Pike (1967), essentially that of authority and distance versus absence of authority and closeness. The personal relationships in which the terms are used have also their values on these dimensions. The additional features seen as needed by Friedrich contribute to defining the values of these situations. The actual implications of pronoun use so nicely explicated by Fried-

rich arise from the interaction of the two sets of values, or meanings (taking into account preceding discourse as part of situation).[19]
In short, semantics and ethnography of speaking simply are not
possible without social anthropology.

Second, it is essential for sociolinguistics, and ethnography
of speaking as its part, to explain the absence as well as the
presence of phenomena, and their differential elaboration. To take
up again the example of men's and women's ways of speaking:
one needs accounts of cases where there is little differentiation as
well as of cases where there is much; of cases where grammar is
affected and where it is not, in order to explain, if possible, why
the cases where sex is marked in grammar occur. It is not, then,
that intrusion of a social feature into grammar is unimportant;
rather, it represents a particular linguistic means of implementing
a universal function of speaking. An adequate sociolinguistic theory must have something to say about such relationships (cf. Tyler
1965, for a suggestion with regard to one such relationship). In
consequence, one cannot ask for the study of such phenomena
only when they are salient and central to a language or society—
one needs the full range of cases. (And it would be just the other
side of the same error to do as some have suggested, to study such
phenomena under the heading of "marginal linguistics" in just the
cases where they are not central.)

The point applies to linguistic marking of social status, of
knowledge and responsibility, and any other feature of anthropological interest.[20] Anthropologists have tended to point to obliga-

19. Cf. Gluckman (1959), where two or three Barotse terms for property
concepts serve complex judicial proceedings, through interaction with a
complex vocabulary for relationships among persons.

20. Missionary linguists may be specially interested in the conditions in
which a language gives grammatical status to a major theological category,
such as kerygma. The development of an approach to language as situated
action, as against a purely semantic and formal approach, parallels, if much
less successfully, the development of a view of theological interpretation as
directed to kerygma, the proclamation of the Church as an act (and of
Christ, indeed, in some writing, as a word-event) for which one takes
responsibility, as against mere acceptance of institutional authority and
credal propositions. The distinction is grammatical in Siona (Wheeler 1967).
One mode-aspect indicates awareness of the circumstances of the action of
a verb, as opposed to non-awareness (definite:indefinite), and association
with them, as opposed to no responsibility for them (involvement:non-
involvement). Wheeler (1967: 71–73) translated Bible narrative in the
"definite involvement" mode; informants then, and most Siona still, retold
it as they would a myth, or another person's experience, in the "indefinite
non-involvement" mode, "but a few have accepted the Scripture as God's
personal communication to them and narrate it to others in the definite
involvement mode" (p. 73). Cf. Ebeling (1966, ch. I, III (2), VI (3)); Kasper
(1969: 29–32, 42n.1., 47–51); Richardson (1961, ch. 5, ch. 6: 126 ff.), from
Lutheran, Catholic, and Episcopalian standpoints, respectively.

tory grammatical categories and terminological elaboration as direct expressions of a society. Here, as elsewhere, there are always two possibilities, and no general rule to decide between them in advance: the particular trait may be directly expressive, or it may be compensatory. Thus, Trukese personal names emphasize individuality, Nakanai names social relationships—both are compensatory, on Truk to secure some measure of individuality amidst pressing social obligation, on Nakanai to remind ambitious individuals of social obligations (Goodenough 1965). One might refer to this as the "Chinese music principle," agitated music accompanying quiet action, quiet music agitated action, in classical Chinese drama (I owe the example to Kenneth Burke's account of an experience with the musician Henry Cowell). Moreover, a language is never a direct inventory of a culture, but always a selective metalanguage. The circumstances, and a theory, of linguistic explicitness ought to be a major problem uniting linguistics and social anthropology.

Third, a matter related to the preceding two, it is essential to sociolinguistics and the ethnography of speaking to develop an adequate theory of the kinds of speech acts and the dimensions of speech forms, both as a basis for analyses and as a result of them. The familiar task of anthropology—of providing comparative perspective—is especially needed here. In a sense this task could be described as that of providing a truly comparative rhetoric, drawing on, but transcending and establishing on a different basis, the insights of rhetoric and poetics in his own civilization.[21] In this respect the problem parallels that which confronted linguistics in reconstructing the basis of grammatical and phonological concepts in the light of the languages of mankind as a whole, and that which confronted social anthropology in reconstructing adequate dimensions for the understanding of kinship, the family, marriage, and the like. To cite two examples of kinds of problem:

1. Among the Iatmul, a speaker cites a myth in terms of exoteric clichés, fragmenting its plot, in manifesting the correct knowledge that proves a kin claim to land while keeping outsiders in the dark. In contrast, among the Cashinaua of Brazil (Ken Kensinger, pers. comm.) the citation of a myth in dispute calls for verbal exactitude (whereas the ordinary narration may be interrupted, adapted to circumstances, etc.). What are the varieties of speech acts found with regard to the social function of myths? Where are they found? And how can their occurrence be explained?

21. Cf. ch. 7 and Burke (1950: 43): "We are not so much proposing to import anthropology into rhetoric, as proposing that anthropologists recognize the factor of rhetoric in their own field."

2. Basil Bernstein has pioneered in the recognition of diverse varieties of speech within a single community, and with regard to England he has distinguished elaborated and restricted codes. Ethnographic data indicate that the three dimensions linked to these types sort separately: "now-coding" versus "then-coding," personal versus positional social control, elaboration versus limitation of verbal form. Thus two Quakers, both remarkable men, are described as follows:

> G's style has some sparkle at particular points, but, for the most part, it is unexciting. B, on the other hand, rose to great heights which enabled him to produce memorable and quotable prose. If G was asked why individual worship was insufficient, and therefore social worship required, his natural tendency was to quote the Bible, leaving the matter there, but B could invent an appropriate figure of speech. . . . G, to our ears, sounds pious, using largely predictable phrases, but B's expressions often have a startling freshness. [Trueblood, 1960: 146–47]

G was in fact a preacher of great influence through the eastern and southern United States. Trueblood ascribes the difference in part to B's being more nearly original in his thought. Neither social control nor limited verbal form seems involved. Again, among the Chaga, a proverb, an instance of then-coding *par excellence*, is used just because the personal feelings and motives of a child are taken into account: rather than speak directly to the child, a proverb is used to call attention indirectly to the matter for which he is at fault. Again, in a Newfoundland village, the genre of "cuffing" is precisely an elaboration of verbal form, where, in the absence of actual news and controversy, argument over a past occurrence is carried on, but with the rule that personal involvement and feeling disqualify a participant. Faris (1966: 247) reports that there was marked reaction to his own attempts to gossip or attempt the technique of the "cuffer," and anxiety that, as a "stranger," "my information was personal and not the formalized and routinized communication of local people." (Faris notes that he did not persist in "cuffing" attempts, but more from lack of sufficient skill than from community reaction.) Further, whole communities may seem to contrast on the personal:positional control dimension (Arapesh and Manus, according to Mead 1937) in the handling of speech and communication, but a third independent type may also occur (Bali, according to Mead). The occurrence and interrelations of these features and dimensions, and possible related others, badly need crosscultural investigation.

Fourth, social anthropologists have been concerned to explain the role and meaning of religion, kinship, myth, etc. As have linguists, they have tended to take the role and meaning of speech for granted, to note only that it is everywhere important. But it is not everywhere important in the same way, to the same extent or purpose. Communities vary grossly in the sheer amount of talk, in the place assigned to talk in relation to touch or sight, in trust or distrust of talk, in the proportion and kinds of roles dependent on verbal skills (cf. ch. 2). While any one instance of these phenomena is likely to seem familiar, when two or more are seen to contrast—e.g. that the Bella Coola chatter incessantly whereas Paliyan men after the age of forty talk almost not at all (Gardner 1966)—one begins to see a problem for comparative analysis. The place of speaking in human lives has hardly begun to be understood in the ways in which anthropologists would seek to understand the place of other aspects of life. With religion, kinship, and the like, one at least can argue in the light of data from many ethnographic accounts. For speaking, the ethnographic accounts are still mostly to come.

IV

Ethnography of speaking, as sketched above, would be a linguistics that had discovered ethnographic foundations, and an ethnography that had discovered linguistic content, in relation to the knowledge and abilities for use of knowledge (competence) of the persons whose communities were studied. "Sociolinguistics," it was said, is a term of a type that mediates between disciplines. Its currency reflects general recognition that inherited disciplinary boundaries do not suffice, their unity being as much social as intellectual. In the study of man, as in Christian churches and radical movements, once-vital distinctions seem about as pertinent to present needs as disputes between medieval baronies. We can no longer believe wholeheartedly in disciplines with exclusive claims on levels of reality or regions of the world. The institutionalizations that confront us appear as obstacles as often as they do as aids. Pursuing a problem, or a student's training, one continually finds the unity of both fragmented among disciplines and faculties.

Still, I do not think that the answer is to create new disciplines, even though sociolinguistics may have in it the makings of one. What is needed is opportunity to combine the kinds of training and knowledge required to pursue sociolinguistic problems, in short, flexibility in institutional structures. Whether the center be a faculty of linguistics or anthropology or sociology, a school of English, or some of these jointly, is secondary, and depends on local conditions and initiatives. What is primary, given recognition of the field, is the means to pursue it.

Anthropology has here a special opportunity and, one might say, even responsibility. Of the sciences concerned with men, it has the closest and fullest ties with linguistics. In principle it already recognizes linguistic research as part of its concern, and already includes some acquaintance with language and linguistics in its training. The required combination of training in linguistics and in social analysis can perhaps be effected under the aegis of anthropology more readily than under any other. (Important here also is the humanistic aspect of anthropology, its ties with attention to texts and verbal art.) There being a social need for such training, anthropology would enhance its recognized relevance in sponsoring it. And insofar as the internal unit and direction of anthropology are in question, it may be fair to say that problems of the sort described in this paper could be one center of unity, a new one that would be yet in some respects but a renewal of some of anthropology's oldest concerns at the center of contemporary social and scientific problems.

Chapter 5

Bilingual Education: Linguistic vs. Sociolinguistic Bases

Bilingual education is a sociolinguistic subject par excellence.[1] The skills of linguists are both necessary and insufficient. The role of linguistics in research on bilingual education may seem to be a matter only of application of a linguistics already given. The contrary is the case. Research on bilingual education requires a kind of linguistics not yet fully constituted. The use of linguistics in such research challenges linguistics to develop conceptual and methodological tools able to deal adequately with the place of speech in human life—with the place of actual speech competencies in actual lives.

A goal of education, bilingual or other, presumably is to enable children to develop their capacity for creative use of language as part of successful adaptation of themselves and their communities in the continuously changing circumstances characteristic of contemporary life. And linguistics indeed has already addressed itself to this goal, as witnessed by the concern within descriptive theory for the "creative aspect of language use"

1. This chapter was first published in the *Bilingualism and Language Contact: Anthropological, Linguistic, Psychological Aspects, and Sociological Aspects*, Report of the 21st annual Round Table, ed. by James E. Alatis (Monograph Series on Languages and Linguistics, 23) (Washington, D.C.: Georgetown University Press, 1970), pp. 69–76. An abstract and remarks directed to the context of the occasion have been omitted; the concluding three paragraphs and last footnote have been added to round out the argument.

(Chomsky 1965, 1966) and the recognition of the role of the child's first language long advocated by many linguists and anthropologists. In both respects, however, linguistics falls short until it is able to deal with ways of speaking in relation to social meanings and situations, until, in short, the starting point of description is not a sentence or text, but a speech event; not a language, but a repertoire of ways of speaking; not a speech community defined in equivalence to a language, but a speech community defined through the concurrence of rules of grammar and rules of use.

The leading view of the nature of linguistic competence and creativity has been dubbed "Cartesian linguistics" (Chomsky 1966), not as a historically exact label, but in recognition of a direction given to theory of language in the period following Descartes by an emphasis on the nature of mind as prior to experience, and an analytic, universalizing, reconstituting methodology (cf. Cassirer 1955, ch. 1, "The Philosophy of the Enlightenment"). In similar vein, one may dub a subsequent tradition of thought 'Herderian linguistics' (Hymes 1970a), not as a historically exact label, but in recognition of a direction given to theory of language in the period following Herder (1744–1801) by an emphasis on language as constituting cultural identity (cf. Barnard 1965: 117, 118, 142), and on a methodology of sympathetic interpretation of cultural diversity sui generis—Herder coined the German verb einfühlen—if within a larger universal framework. (The two traditions might be labeled "Enlightenment" and "Romantic," but the individual names perhaps are better, in that they less imply two mutually exclusive periods, or simple uniformity within each.)

"Cartesian" and "Herderian" approaches have contributed much to our knowledge of language. In the past the differences between the two approaches have been salient, but here what matters most is what they have fundamentally in common: isolation of a language as the object of linguistic description; equation of a language with a speech community (or culture); taking of the social functions of language as external, given, and universally equivalent; restriction of study of the structure of language to units and relations based on reference.

The emergence of sociolinguistics is in important part a response to social needs; but as an intellectual stage in the history of linguistics, the recent history of sociolinguistics can be seen as a response to the hegemony of Cartesian and Herderian assumptions, first, by critical analysis of the assumptions themselves, and, secondly, by effort to replace them. Just as Boas, Sapir, Bloomfield, Pike, and others can be seen as concerned to develop concepts and methods adequate to the description of all languages, so the current work of Ervin-Tripp, Fishman, Gumperz, Labov, and others can be seen as concerned to develop concepts and methods adequate to the description of speech communities. And where Boas, Sapir, Bloomfield, Pike, and others had to empty some concepts of normative or ethnocentric content (e.g. "inflection," "incorporation" vis-à-vis compounding), extend some (e.g. *morphème*), and invent others (e.g. phoneme), with regard to grammars, so have contributors to sociolinguistics today the task of emptying, extending, and inventing with regard to the identification and organization of ways of speaking.

The concern with competence and creativity in Chomsky's Cartesian linguistics is an advance toward sociolingistics, but, on analysis, an advance more nominal than real. To make competence central, rather than *la langue,* to reconcile the sphere of creativity with that of structure, does focus discussion on actual human beings and their abilities, and regard them as acquirers and shapers of culture, rather than merely as "culture-bearers." Just such a transformation was projected for anthropology and linguistics by Sapir in his last writings (see discussion in Hymes 1970b and ch. 7). But whereas Sapir turned attention to "living speech," understood as requiring that received categories be reconsidered within the matrix of social interaction, Chomsky's "Cartesian" linguistics seems a cogent, thoroughly thought out perfection of the impulse to the autonomy of language that spurred so much of structural linguistics and in an earlier stage, Sapir himself. From origin as possibly a physico-chemical accident to the assumptions of wholly fluent use free of situation in a homogenous community, any dependence of language on social interaction and adaptation is excluded.

In effect, Cartesian linguistics reduces "competence" to knowledge of grammar, "performance" to behavior, and "creativity" to novelty. Those concerned with linguistic aspects of education and with sociolinguistic theory must thank Chomsky for making competence and creativity central to linguistic theory, but must reconstruct the concepts for themselves.[2]

Indeed a sociolinguistic critique of the conception of language made explicit in Cartesian linguistics is markedly parallel to the critique by Marx of Feuerbach, from whom he learned, but whose limitations he had to transcend. By substituting "he" (or "Cartesian linguistics") for "Feuerbach," and "linguistic" for "religious," one has a remarkably applicable statement:

> He resolves the linguistic essence into the *human* essence.
> But the essence of man is no abstraction inhering in each single

2. Chomsky's treatment of "competence," "performance," and "creative aspect of language use" is discussed in more detail in ch. 4.

individual. In its actuality it is the ensemble of social relationships.
    He, who does not go into the criticism of this actual essence,
is hence compelled:
    (1) to abstract from the historical process and to establish
        linguistic intuition as something self-contained, and to
        presuppose an abstract—*isolated*—human individual;
    (2) to view the essence of man merely as "species," as the
        inner dumb generality which unites the many individuals
        naturally (i.e. not socially).
                                    [Easton and Guddat 1967: 402]

I do not think one can abandon some conception of a generic
human nature (human essence), as the thesis might be taken as
saying; but the man for whom Chomsky's competence and theory
is a model is indeed an isolated man in the abstract. There is
nothing to be said about men (or women).

    Cartesian and Herderian linguistics differ most obviously with
regard to the place of differences among languages. There is not,
to be sure, a complete opposition. The most celebrated early figure
in the Herderian tradition, W. von Humboldt, was concerned with
universals as well as specific difference, as were Boas, Sapir, and
Whorf later. Indeed, what Herder, von Humboldt, and Goethe are
linked by is a conception of form that links the individual and
universal. The notion of form is linked to that of creativity and
individuality both, so that in contrast to the Cartesian sense of
particularity and uniqueness of personality (language, culture) as
negative limitation, such limitation is seen as positive. It is not
the absence of universality, but realization of a universal power.
The universal finds realization only in the actuality of the particular; form is truly acquired only through the power of self-formation
(Cassirer 1961: 20–25). (On this development, see Cassirer 1950:
224–25, 252; 1955: 32–36; 1961: 20–26. On von Humboldt as having
found his way into the study of language through his concern with
the characterization of individuals and individual peoples, see
Lammers 1936 and Leroux 1958: 69, n. 2).

    Chomsky treats von Humboldt in terms of his continuity with
the general approach of the Enlightenment; he acknowledges but
omits much of that aspect of von Humboldt which, according to
Cassirer, is his distinctive achievement. He follows von Humboldt
in concern with the universal power, but neglects von Humboldt's
understanding of form as something not given, but historically
emergent and acquired.[3] The treatment of von Humboldt is in
keeping with the treatment of competence and creativity.

    3. One might argue that transformational generative grammar ought by
rights to be especially concerned, as was von Humboldt, with individual
form. By establishing that marked departures from universal, or natural,
features and relations entail costs, it is able to recognize the great extent to
which languages, or rather their speakers, pay such costs, and to appreciate
the power of the sociohistorical forces that motivate such payment.

The Herderian approach, as developed by von Humboldt, is indeed the approach needed in sociolinguistics. The focus, however, must be changed from a language as correlate of a people, to persons and their ways of speaking. The inadequacy of a monolingual approach has long been recognized and, indeed, no one has ever denied the obvious facts of multilingualism, the prevalence of linguistic diversity in the world. The difficulty remains that in informal thought one tends to fall back on the Herderian model of one language, one people, one culture, one community— the Hopi and their language, etc., (on the persistence of "savage anthropology" of this sort, see Fontana 1968), because we are only beginning to have sociolinguistic models and taxonomies adequate to thinking in terms of multilingual situations. But, as the work of Gumperz, Labov, and others has shown, more than plurarity of languages is involved.

First of all, what counts as a language boundary cannot be defined by any purely linguistic measure. Attitudes and social meanings enter in as well. Any enduring social relationship or group may come to define itself by selection and/or creation of linguistic features, and a difference of accent may be as important at one boundary as a difference of grammar at another. Part of the creativity of users of languages lies in the freedom to determine what and how much linguistic difference matters. The alternative view, indeed a view often taken, conceals an unsuspected linguistic determinism. (For a recent issue of this sort, involving the notion of ethnic unit and mutual intelligibility, cf. Hymes 1968.)

Secondly, speech communities cannot be defined in terms of languages alone in another respect. A person who is a member of a speech community knows not only a language but also what to say. A person who can produce all and any of the sentences of a language, and unpredictably does, is institutionalized. For some range of situations, itself to be empirically determined and perhaps varying significantly across communities, a competent member of the speech community knows what to say next. And speech rules may be shared across language boundaries, not only in space but also through time. The Ngoni of Africa, for example, mostly no longer speak Ngoni, but use the language of the people in Malawi whom they conquered. However, they use it in Ngoni ways, ways whose maintenance is considered essential to their identity. Analagous situations obtain in some American Indian communities in the use of English.

In general, both theory and relevance to education require that one break with the equation between a named language and a functional role. Beyond cognitive differences possibly attributable to differences of language, there are cognitive differences due to differences in speaking. There is interference not only between phonologies and grammars, but also between norms of interaction and interpretation of speech. One must take the vantage point of the person acquiring competence in speech in a community, and discover the number and organization of ways of speaking that result.

In sum, there is no quarrel with the Cartesian concern for universals and the human mind. There is much concern with the Herderian stress upon individuation and emergent form. Only the focus of theory and description changes, from rules of language to rules of speaking. It is the latter that are fundamental, embracing the former as one constituent. And an understanding of rules of speaking is indispensable to understanding failures and to increasing success in bicultural education.[4]

I should not end with the implication that the contribution is all in one direction, from sociolinguistics to education. Work in bicultural education, and in education generally, is important to the development of sociolinguistics. Scientific and practical interests in understanding of ways of speaking coincide, and indeed, the practical interests may not only contribute to, but shape the future of the subject. For one thing, linguists are indispensable to the work that is needed, but what some of us argue on linguistic grounds may be advanced on practical grounds with greater effect. Concern with education, more than concern with theory, may cause linguists to recognize how far brave talk about the nature of language and of mind is from being of use to the minds and languages of children; how far intuitions of relationships and contexts are from being adequate to the relationships and settings of discourse in classrooms and communities.

Again, those who are "native" to the contexts of communication in communities and classrooms are indispensable sources of insight into the features, and organizations of features, of speech, that matter there. And change can be accomplished only if the participants in classrooms become participants in the ethnography of the speaking in classrooms. No sociolinguistic finding, however valid, can be effective if merely published, announced, or even imposed, if on persons who misunderstand and resist it.

In sum, theoretical considerations call linguistics to become a social science; social considerations call linguistics to become a community science. Concern with education may be the key to the realization of this vocation.

4. Philips 1972 is an outstanding demonstration of this point. The present paper was in origin an introduction to the first version of her paper (Philips 1970); see now the revised conclusion in Philips (1972). The volume containing her revised paper has an introduction (Hymes 1972b) in which I develop the theme of this and the remaining paragraphs in detail; the entire volume is relevant.

Chapter 6

The Contribution of Folklore to Sociolinguistic Research

The folklorist is accustomed (inured might be the word) to having some other discipline, such as linguistics, pointed out to him as important to folklore.[1] I should like to point out the importance of folklore for work in linguistics. Certain lines of folkloristic research, I maintain, are essential to the progress of the trend in linguistic research called "sociolinguistic."

What is the task of sociolinguistic research? It is, in my view, to lay the foundations for an adequate understanding of the place of language in social life. But have not a good many scholars been about that task for a considerable period of time? Very partially, and very inadequately. The plain fact is that speech, the true nexus between language and social life, has been largely neglected. It has not been studied in its own right.

Linguists have observed speech but have systematically

1. This chapter is adapted from the paper of the same title published in the *Journal of American Folklore*, 84 (331): 42–50 (1971) as part of an issue on "Toward new perspectives in folklore" with Richard Bauman as special editor. The issue has also been published as a book, *Toward New Perspectives in Folklore*, ed. by Américo Paredes and Richard Bauman (Austin: University of Texas Press, 1971). The paper was read at the annual meeting of the American Folklore Society, Atlanta, November 7, 1969, and I should like to thank the program chairman, Dan Ben-Amos, for inviting me to participate. I should like to dedicate this chapter to my teacher, Stith Thompson, with whom I first studied the ethnography of folklore.

analyzed just those aspects of it that have answered to problems
of formal grammar. They have abstracted from speech as a structured activity. Social and expressive aspects of speech have been
attended to only when they have intruded inescapably into grammar. One can hardly characterize personal pronouns, for example,
without noting that certain pronouns identify the role of speaker,
others that of hearer, or even that the same pronoun may be plural
or singular in reference, depending on social relationships. But a
more exact or general study of the rules governing the interaction
between participants in speech events has been left aside.

Anthropologists and other social scientists have used the data
of speech, but typically they have abstracted from its linguistic
characteristics. They have usually gone straight through the form
of speech to get at its content, what speaking is presumed to be
about. They may discuss the importance of a verbal genre, such
as myth or gossip. Almost never do they specify what one would
need to know to recognize an instance of a verbal genre or to
perform it. They do not characterize the ways in which what is
said is a function of how it is said.

Exaggerating the situation perhaps to an unfair extreme, we
may say that from linguists we have grammars, in terms of which
(in principle) everything grammatical that a language permits can
be said; but in terms of which any particular thing is as likely as
any other, whether it be nonsense, a greeting, a chemical formula,
a quotation from the Gettysburg Address, a proposition, or an
answer to a question that has not been asked, and in any style or
none. From anthropologists we have ethnographies, in terms of
which (in principle) what the members of a community do can be
understood; but only if one subscribes to the implicit convention
that they do it in silence, or that when they greet, command,
request, promise, gossip, insult, pray, narrate, announce, invoke,
curse, wheedle, orate, glaver, or dispute, the fact that they are
doing one or the other has nothing to do with the way it is said.
In short, linguists have abstracted from the content of speech,
social scientists from its form, and both from the patterning of
its use.

It might seem that little of importance is at stake; a certain
kind of information slips away between the two approaches—that
of grammar and that of ethnography—but nothing consequential.
In my view, quite the opposite is the case. We shall not be able
to have a theory that accounts for the meaning of language in
different lives and cultures, that can deal with the many linguistic
problems of the contemporary world, until we examine this "slip-
page" and reconstruct the study of language from its vantage point
—that of the actual functioning of language.

The situation has not been seen for what it is partly because we are accustomed to generalize statements as to the functions of language, commonplaces as to the great importance of language in general. These commonplaces do us a disservice. Praising language in general, they obscure the need to study just what functions it does have in particular cases. They lead us to act as though language has the same functions in every community (indeed, that all languages have the same functions and that each community has just one language having these functions). The facts are otherwise. Hockett (1958: 535), for example, generalizes, "The story-teller must be a fluent and effective speaker. . . ." But among the Gbeya of Central Africa no one is regarded as skilled in narration (Samarin 1969: 323). Malinowski (1923) has stressed "phatic communion," talking for the sake of talking. The Wishram Chinook of the Columbia River take just the opposite view; one does not talk when one has nothing that needs to be said (personal fieldwork). Sapir (1933) has written of the tendency to fill up one's world with language; but among the Paliyans of south India, by the age of forty men are reported to speak almost not at all, and a communicative person is regarded with suspicion (Gardner 1966). Often one reads of the role of language in the transmission of culture, the social heritage, but among many peoples the great bulk of adult roles and skills are transmitted nonverbally.

It has often been said that language is an index to or reflection of culture. But language is not simply passive or automatic in its relation to culture, even where there is only one language to consider (much of the world of course being multilingual). Speaking is itself a form of cultural behavior, and language, like any other part of culture, partly shapes the whole; and its expression of the rest of culture is partial, selective. That selective relation, indeed, is what should be interesting to us. Why do some features of a community's life come to be named—overtly expressible in discourse—while others are not? Why do communities differ in the extent to which language, or a language, serves this function of a "metalanguage" to the rest?

To speak of the functional importance of language, or of folklore, has sometimes been a way of saying something nice about the subject without getting down to cases. Such statements seem to recommend study of the subject; but after all, if the most important general conclusion is already known, why go to the trouble? When one speaks of language or folklore as an index or reflection of culture, it may be that one is trying to persuade the student of culture in general that our special study is relevant—it fits. But this sort of argument presupposes that culture is not to be found in the special subject, and when analyzed it defeats its own intent.

If language or folklore is a simple reflex of culture, there is no reason other than personal predilection for the serious student of culture to consider it further. "Oh yes," he would be able to say (having studied a culture apart from its language or folklore), "if you examine the language (or folklore) you will find that it fits."

From the standpoint of a serious interest in language and folklore as aspects of culture, the ways in which each is partly autonomous and partly a self-governing factor in the life of a community are precisely what make their study necessary. The ways in which language and folklore differ in function from one community to another are the most revealing. Indeed, a case in which a language or a body of folklore is not important, or not important in a particular way, is important to scientific theory. Such a case contributes to explanation of the conditions that govern importance.

A considerable list could be given of the ways in which communities differ with regard to the functions of language—the amount, frequency, and kinds of speech that are typical; the valuation of speech with respect to other modes of communication; and the valuation of different languages and ways of speaking. Just as it is not possible to speak glibly of *the* function of myth (or of any other folkloristic genre), since it is necessary to investigate its functioning in the particular community, so with genres of speech generally and language itself.

To build a systematic theory we require what I have called "ethnographies of speaking." How does folklore contribute to this goal? Ultimately in many ways, but most immediately, I think, with respect to the concepts of performance and of genre.

The term "performance" has come into prominence in recent folkloristic research. In the most ambitious and challenging effort so far to integrate linguistic and social aspects of a folkloristic genre with a descriptive model and explanatory theory, Lomax (1968: 155–61) refers to "the performance orientation of the research." He treats performance situation, rules of performance, and particularly five levels of performance style in song. Abrahams (1968) states that "what is needed is a method which would emphasize all aspects of the esthetic performance," and has developed (1970) a pioneering analysis of "gossip as performance." Ben-Amos (1967, 1971: 5) writes that "the performance situation, in the final analysis, is the crucial context for the available text."

It would not be correct to say that there is an agreed definition of "performance" among these or other authors; but there is, I think, a common thrust. Lomax focuses his use of "performance" upon the norms governing relations among performers, singling out the following as the primary conditions of any performance:

1. The size of the vocal group, one or many
2. The interplay, if any, between the leader and the chorus
3. The degree of dominance of the leader, if any
4. The level of organization within the group

The five levels discovered in his research are designated as "interlocked," "simple social unison," "overlap," "simple alteration," and "solo and explicit." The relation of performer to audience is implicitly defined, ranging from no distinction—all present in the group participating in performance—to solo—necessarily defined by the presence of others who are not performing (Lomax 1968: 155–61).

Abrahams (1968: 144–45; see also Abrahams 1970, 1971) has a somewhat different focus, one linking the notion of performance as a structured event to performance as stylized behavior. When he specifies the components of the esthetic performance as "performance, item, and audience" he seems to have in mind a structured event, entailing reciprocity (mutual participation between performer and audience as the general focus), with the stylized behavior of the performer also designated "performance" in a more specific sense. Such usage of a term on two levels of generality is common in science as well as in daily life; compare the use of "grammar" both for the general object of linguistic description and for a component of it distinct from phonology.

Ben-Amos argues for a redefinition of folklore, as concerned not with things, but with a communicative process. In delineating his conception, he stresses, as do Lomax and Abrahams, a relation between performer, esthetically marked (stylized) material, and audience. Dundes (1964), on the other hand, has shown the difference between knowing folklore materials and knowing how to use them, and has shown ways to study folklore as communication in terms of rules of use (see also Ben-Amos 1969).

The essential element common to all these approaches is the movement from a focus on the text to a focus on the communicative event. The term "context" takes on a new meaning, or new force in this regard. To place a text, an item of folklore, in its context is not only to correlate it with one or more aspects of the community from which it came. Or if that is what "context" means, then the new direction goes beyond a merely "contextual" approach. It is not content to take folkloristic results on the one hand and results of other studies on the other, each independently arrived at, and then to try to relate the two after the fact. It wishes to study the relation between folkloristic materials and other aspects of social life *in situ*, as it were, where that relation actually obtains, the communicative events in which folklore is used.

This concern is precisely parallel to the motivation of sociolinguistic research into the ethnography of speaking. The theoretical failure of past attempts to relate language and culture has resulted from just such a lack. In discussing language and culture, one was discussing grammars and ethnographies from which the essential ingredient in which the relation exists—speaking—was missing. Adequate theories of the place of folklore, as of language, in social life must be based on studies of use.

So far only a convergence of approach has been sketched, one to which, indeed, some of the early writing on the ethnography of speaking has already contributed (see the review by Hendricks 1967). It can be maintained, indeed, that folklore is a special case of the ethnography-of-speaking approach. Whatever one's view on that, my concern here is that folklore has a special contribution to make. The study of stylized genres in communicative events has a critical role to play because it can direct attention to essential features of language that are now neglected or misconceived in linguistic theory. Let me briefly indicate how this is so.

From its beginnings early in this century, modern linguistics has slighted the study of the use of language. Ferdinand de Saussure's twin conceptions of *la langue* and *la parole* have commonly been interpreted to mean that linguistics had for its object only *la langue,* and that that was the exclusive domain of structure. There have been notable exceptions (men like Sapir and Jakobson), who have thought through a broader, dynamic approach to language; but the main trend in linguistic theory has been as described. Recently Noam Chomsky has substituted the terms "competence" and "performance" for de Saussure's *la langue* and *la parole.* Nominally the substitution is an important advance. "Competence" and "performance" imply abilities and actions, rather than as "language" does an object of study abstracted from human beings and their behavior. The improvement, however, has remained merely nominal.

Here is the rub. In studying verbal performance, both in sociolinguistics and folklore, we need to be able to specify the verbal means employed. Linguists must contribute their skills, yet the dominant trend in linguistics today is in quite the opposite direction. The skills that are mostly taught and cultivated in linguistics are those for unravelling the logical properties of syntax and semantic relations internal to language conceived as an idealized norm, used only for referential utterances. Judgments as to the acceptability of utterances are sought intuitively, not from use in the community. The model of explanation is to relate diverse utterances to a common underlying source in the basic structure of a language, and perhaps to a deeper source in the human brain.

There is little attention to the skills that would disclose the social properties of syntax, semantics, and phonology as used in situations. There is little or no awareness of a direction of explanation that would relate an underlying structure to the conditions for selection of the alternative ways of saying it. Most of all, there is no adequate conception of language as having organization beyond the sentence—and even the text—in terms of speech acts and speech events.

There is indeed a good deal of work on discourse and style, but when all is said and done, it will only have arrived at a point already recognized in folklore as a limit to overcome, the text isolated from context. Moreover, the main thrust of such work is to seek relations beyond or larger than the sentence, through the distribution of elements already identified within the sentence. There is little or no attention to aspects of language that are obvious and essential to folkloristic research—features of emphasis and expressivity not part of the referential organization of the language, organization of features into coherent styles, or ways of speaking, that cut across the compartments of the ordinary grammatical description; organization of speech into acts in ways that are independent of the sentence as a unit, now comprising more than one sentence, now occurring within a sentence. For example, the same insult (serious or jocular) conveyed by the first of two sentences: "You're a bastard. Do you know what you've done?" Or a sentence part: "You bastard, do you know what you've done?" And by an intonation, alone with the words: "Do you know what you've done?"

Such are the strengths of trained incapacity that it is difficult to get many linguists even to see the existence of such phenomena, let alone to admit their relevance. Elsewhere I have tried to show the necessity of attending to such matters within linguistics itself and developed a critique of the notions of "competence" and "performance" that stand in the way of such attention (see chs. 4, 7). There is no opportunity to go into these arguments in detail here or to present evidence indicating what consideration of language from the new standpoint would be like. I should like simply to summarize some of the ways in which folkloristic research both challenges and is challenged by the linguistic outlook described above.

1. Chomsky's attitude is rather neoplatonic. Competence is an ideal grammatical knowledge: performance, the use of language, is largely an imperfect falling away. Folklore recognizes the use of language as a positive accomplishment, and not only in literature with a capital L but in the verbal art of ordinary people and com-

munities. Folklore, par excellence, understands the normal use of language as drawing on kinds of knowledge and organization that are parts of "competence" beyond the purely grammatical.

2. Chomsky's idealization of the "fluent speaker-user" in a homogeneous community makes the object of linguistics implicitly an abstract individual. There is nothing for linguistics to study that is not part of, or product of, the knowledge of such an individual. In its analysis of performance, folklore recognizes the differentiation of knowledge and competence within a community with regard to speaking; it recognizes the structure that obtains beyond the individual in the norms of interaction of communicative events; and it recognizes the emergent properties of such interactions, both normally and as specific to particular performances (as when an audience is "warm" or "cold").

3. Chomsky's conception of the "creative aspect of language use" reduces "creativity" to novelty. This indeed is the focal point of his theoretical impact on linguistics—a conception of linguistics as concerned with explaining the use of language as an indefinitely large number of new sentences. As alluded to in the preceding section, this approach cannot accomplish its own goal, that of explaining the occurrence of novel sentences that are accepted as appropriate, since its linguistics accounts only for the novelty of the sentences, not for their appropriateness. Appropriateness is a relation between sentences and settings, and the settings must be analyzed as well. Moreover, creativity may consist in the use of an old sentence in a new setting just as much as in the use of a new sentence in an old setting. More than any other discipline, folklore is in a position to develop the implications of this fact in a general theory of the "creative aspect of language use." Only with the aid of folklore can we hope to understand the meaning of language in social life and in comprehensive terms. For the role of language is not only to enable persons to adapt to new situations with novel utterances but also to do so with familiar utterances. We have to explain familiarity as well as novelty of utterance. We have to account for what people wish to or must say again. I apologize for emphasizing something that is well known to folklorists; my excuse is that it is ignored in linguistics.

4. Linguists who concern themselves with such matters tend to work from grammar, from what is familiar to what is unfamiliar. Experience shows, I think, that such an approach is not sufficient. It consists in seeking additional organization and function for familiar elements and structures. In fact, some of the organization of linguistic means can only be discovered by starting with higher level functions and contents, such as acts and genres. There is no internal linguistic makeup that would lead one

to group together "See you later, alligator," "Ta Ta," "Au revoir,"
"Don't take any wooden nickels," "Glad you could come," and
"I'm going, I'm going," as leave-takings or "Hi" and "Well, I'll be
a son of a gun, if it isn't Sid Mintz" as greetings. Moreover, any
social relationship or event tends to develop an organization of
verbal means (perhaps some innovation of means) specific to
itself. By working from the usual grammatical description of a
language, one would never arrive at many of the features and
relationships detectable to a folklorist working toward language
from the analysis of a communicative event.

5. The perspective and sensitivity of the trained folklorist is
requisite to recognizing what goes on in speech in yet another,
quite general way. There is, of course, the matter of recognizing
well-known traditional materials and genres. It must strike a folklorist as odd indeed that a major work on the English language
(Chomsky and Halle 1968) can discuss the internal organization of
"This is the cat that caught the rat that stole the cheese" without
mentioning the internal rhyme (cat, rat), let alone noting the existence of a traditional way of chanting it. More vital is the fact that
even if the performance is identified with stylization, rather than
with behavior, there is a continuum, not a dichotomy. In many
communities, as Abrahams points out, almost all public verbal
behavior will be stylized. Here I must go beyond one possible
implication of Ben-Amos' statement that "Folklore . . . is a social
interaction via the art media and differs from other modes of
speaking and gesturing" (1967; 1972: 10). I think the folklorist has
a contribution to make, not just to one mode of speaking, but to all.

What is folklore? Forgive me for raising this fundamental
question just towards the end of a paper, but let me consider it in
respect to two kinds of criteria that seem of great interest today.
One approach is to define folklore in terms of the study of genres,
the other to define folklore in terms of the study of communicative
behavior with an esthetic, expressive, or stylistic dimension. In
my opinion all of speaking is to be approached as having an
organization in terms of ways of speaking, and thus as manifestations of a community's repertory of acts and genres of speech.
There is no speech that is not an instance of some such act and
genre. Again, I think that all speech is to be approached as having
an esthetic, expressive, or stylistic dimension. The stylistic and
referential are interwoven and interdependent in all of communication. Obviously there are degrees here, both of organization and
of esthetic or expressive quality, and folklorists will be most concerned with the more highly organized, more expressive end of the
two continua. But because the ethnography of speaking can be
said to have as its goal a view of the speech of a community as

ways of speaking, and as always conventionally expressive, it is of the greatest importance to have the contribution of those who are best trained to attain this goal in any discipline. If linguistics has certain necessary skills to contribute to folklore, there are certain necessary skills that folklore has to contribute to linguistics.

The contribution of folklore to sociolinguistic research may provide a special opportunity for the development of folklore itself. A linguist cannot help reflecting that the two fields were in much the same situation earlier in this century in the United States. Both linguistics and folklore were interdisciplinary activities, contributed to by students of English, modern languages, and anthropology. Although it attained a separate professional association and its own journal much later than folklore, linguistics burgeoned rapidly following World War II, while folklore did not. The rapid development of linguistics was due, I think, to the development of an autonomous methodology, that of structural linguistics. The new methodology provided for the discovery of new kinds of units and organization in language. The analysis of verbal performance in terms of genres and expressivity may now offer folklore a similar opportunity.

Chapter 7

The Contribution of Poetics to Sociolinguistic Research

Language as symbolic action[1] is for those for whom linguistics is linked to poetics and rhetoric, and to insights that can be gained from study of the workings of words and motives in significant texts.

The author is not concerned with recent trends in linguistics. The present book (15), does cite Sapir, and an essay exploring the ways in which the notion of words as the signs of things can be reversed (359–79) is reprinted from *Anthropological Linguistics*; Boas is cited in an ethnographic connection; and I am mentioned for a suggestion as to the interpretation of the novel *Nightwood*, and for an ethnographic anecdote that led to publication of the paper just cited (243, 360); but the gap is patent in Burke's statement that his essays are intended to exemplify "a theory of language (as symbolic action), a philosophy of language based on that theory, and methods of analysis developed in accordance with the theory and the philosophy" (vii). Burke's insights and style of exposition and evidence, moreover, are rooted in literature—in assimilation of major works of Western tradition, on the one

1. This chapter was first published as a review of *Language as Symbolic Action: Essays on Life, Literature, and Method*, by Kenneth Burke (Berkeley and Los Angeles: University of California Press, 1966), in *Language* 44: 664–69. Page references for the Burke volume are given in parentheses in the text. I want to thank the editor, William Bright, for giving me the opportunity to write about Burke in this Journal.

hand, and intimate acquaintance with the rise of modern American literature, on the other. The range and originality are impressive, but to many linguists the enterprise will seem wholly foreign. Thus the essay on the origin of language (419–79) is concerned, not with formal universals, but with the principle of the negative as a distinctively human trait embodied in language (recalling Whitehead's reported challenge to Skinner to explain language by explaining the statement, "There is no black spider on this table").

Nevertheless, underlying parallels can be found between Burke's work and recent trends in linguistics, and there are possibilities of convergence of the two. Indeed, it would seem that Burke has been first in the field, commonly enough by a generation, with regard to standpoints toward language that recent linguists take to be recent on the American scene. He is still ahead of us in some respects. It is worthwhile to place the man, and see what he is up to.

As user of language, Burke is a recognized poet; author of an early collection of short stories and an admired novel (1932) just reprinted (the preface and text adumbrate the motives of his turn to generic concern with language); and, since the beginning of the thirties, writer of essays, reviews, and books that have found audience among political scientists, sociologists, social psychologists, and anthropologists, as well as students of literature (cf. his dissection of the verbal techniques used for scapegoating, 1957: 164–88), and "Freud and the analysis of poetry," 1957:221–50). A great autodidact and trenchant nonconformist, with but one year of college, he has become a major and honored figure in American literary life, yet has maintained autonomy of life style and thought, never closed off from the sources of his own experience.

By principal profession, Burke is a literary critic, but of a special sort. His concern with symbolic motivation and linguistic action in general has led him beyond literary criticism. That fact has opened him to attack from other critics (for such attacks, and Burke's response, see 480–506); but it is also the measure of his seriousness and of the interest of his goals to those concerned with, to quote Chomsky (1957:102), "some more general theory of language that will include a theory of linguistic form and theory of the use of language as subparts." Let me single out certain features:

1. Since the thirties, Burke (e.g., 1941) has waged war against the inadequacy of mechanistic, empiricist, anti-"mentalist" approaches in the human sciences. The point is drawn in terms of a distinction between motion and action, the latter comprising the symbolic dimension of human motives and behavior.

2. Rather than reject earlier insights in the name of modernity

or science, Burke has sought to assimilate and build on traditional rhetoric, poetics, and dialectic (cf. 306).

3. Burke asserts that, to establish the forms of symbolic action, one needs cases sufficiently stable to be methodically observable, and sufficiently complex and mature to be representative. The primary object of study thus is taken to be an idealized, normative one—the definitive literary text, abstracted from performances and posited as unified (homogeneous). Results obtained from such study can be applied to the more fluctuant and obscured world of daily action (1955:264–65, 274–75).

4. Analysis must first of all be formal, that is, within the realm of what Burke terms "poetics," the analysis of a work or genre in and of itself, in terms of the working out of principles and interrelationships internal to it as a structure (486–87, 496–97; 1958:61), as apart from concern with expression of character ("ethics"); persuading or moving of an audience ("rhetoric"); and provision of information, or universal resources of verbal placement, symbolic action ("grammar," or dramatistic grammar—1945; here, 59–60). "Poetics," "rhetoric," "ethics," and "grammar" are the four categories into which Burke divides his project here (28). It is revealing to trace (in Burkean fashion) the recurrence of "pure(ly)" and "sheer(ly)" as modifiers in contexts where the formal is in question, either to the intrinsic characteristics of a given work (poetics) or the characteristics intrinsic to some set of verbal resources generally—in either case, apart from contextual considerations. I have traced them with forms of *formal* (19, 221, 296, 494), *grammar* (329, 388), *linguistic* (221, 408, 419, 461), *terministic* (18, 250), *technical* (92); cf. also 25, 29, 91, 92. In terms of Burke's own motives, these modifiers are an almost perfect marking of his concern to delimit and insist upon such a domain of study.

5. Analysis must be explicit in two respects: (a) it must make explicit the principles (underlying structure, rules) that are only implicit for the originators of texts studied (33; cf. discussion of "derive," 85–87, 117, and of "prophecy after the event," 36–37, 75, 81, 85); (b) it must explicitly define the structural type ("literary species") of the work, i.e. give an adequate formal definition with corresponding rules (42–43, 223–25). Burke's finest instances, perhaps, are those (1951a) of the lyric, the Platonic dialogue, and Joyce's *Portrait of the Artist as a Young Man*; see also his paradigm (1951b) for *Othello*.

6. Analysis of particular works and forms must both make use of and seek further to disclose universal characteristics of symbolic action (formal, substantive). Such universals are seen as intrinsic to human nature (cf. 20–23, 53, 73–74, 149, 152, 158, 182,

189, 253, 296, 409, 494–96; in Aristotelian fashion, man's nature is seen as including participation in a social order). Indeed, it is Burke's concern for a sort of explanatory adequacy that has opened him to one kind of attack from narrower critics, namely, that of devising modes of analysis applicable to all texts, not just to those considered good.

7. The tactics of the method can be described as a kind of discourse analysis built upon a concordance of key terms. Key terms are not mechanically found. Three articles—1941 (the title essay), 1954, and 1958 (60–61)—give practical guidance. An essential part is played by the analytic concepts and suggested recurrent or universal elements of the general theory; these, together with examples of analysis, are found developed throughout his critical works (1931, 1935, 1937, 1941, 1945, 1950, 1961). Key terms are traced for features of placement, substitutability, and co-occurrence ("subcategorization," selection) proper to them in the given work (establishing underlying symbolic interrelationships and the motivational structure on which they rest). The formal logic of the work is sought: its sequential development (why the parts are in precisely that order and no other), and the transformations that govern the motivational development (Burke uses the term, 1950:10–13; here 134–35, 180, etc.). For Burke, underlying motivational structures are to a completed work rather like underlying semantic structure to a complex sentence.

These features show parallels, but something also of the clear differences between Burke's work and current linguistic theory. Burke calls his perspective "dramatism" (53ff., 366–69; an article appears in the new *International Encyclopedia of the Social Sciences*, 1968). The title, and the terminology in which it is implemented, express his belief that the necessary foundation and unity of the human sciences lies in study of language and thought as situated modes of action, that is, as motivated in origin and dramatic (dialectic) in form (1957:87–100). It follows that understanding of structure requires understanding of function, or purpose (1957:62–63, 245–47); every text must be treated as a strategy for encompassing a situation (1957:3, 93). Thus, if Burke is for "action" as against "motion" (mechanistic and behavioristic reductions), he is also for the complex scope of a "dramatic" model of human action as against models that reduce it to any single or unbalanced set of motives, such as restriction of concern to the informational and referential functions, as is the case with much linguistic theory at the present time (1957:121–44; cf. Hymes 1964a).

Two implications are of particular relevance here. Both can be approached through the notion of language expressed in Burke's definition of his book's purpose (cited above) and in its title. In brief, the notion of language and the linguistic is taken to include reference to (1) the general symbolic resources involved in use of language, and (2) the plurality of modes of action (motives, functions) that use of language may constitute. A tracing of Burke's use of the words "language," "linguistic," and "grammar" shows this. On the one hand, while the terms include and sometimes specify sounds, words, and syntax (e.g., 467), much more commonly they are a way of insisting upon goal-directed symbolic activity as intrinsic to human nature (language being the case par excellence), and of referring to such activity as underlain by universal symbolic operations that in part might be, and occasionally are, called dialectic (299, 372). On the other hand, the "intrinsic" satisfactions, or functions, of languages (of "symbol-using," 1958:57, 61) are at least four; and designation (naming, reference) plays a small part beside unfolding of form (poetics), inducement to action (communication, persuasion), and expression. More particularized analysis of components of speech acts, functions, and their interrelations is given in Burke 1945, and throughout his other books. One significant list of speech acts is that in the preface to his novel (1966:xii–xiv), wherein he describes discovery of his motives for writing it as "to want to lament, rejoice, beseech, admonish, aphorize, and inveigh."

Thus, for Burke the organization and selection of linguistic resources in verbal performance (action) is underlain by kinds of *symbolic competence* that transcend linguistic competence in its present technical sense. An extension of the notion of kinds of competence underlying linguistic performance is necessary in any case, if the convergence in outlook between much of modern ethnography and transformational grammar is to be recognized and made fruitful. Linguists would seem to have no good reason to want to deny ethnographers the right to be "mentalists," or to try to insist that ethnographers must henceforth approach patterns of language use on only, say, Skinnerian terms, rather than continue to see them as reflecting underlying sociocultural (symbolic) competence.

Furthermore, if linguistic performance is equated to all use of language, then it is not seen by Burke as adulteration of ideal competence (cf. Katz 1967:144), but often as *accomplishment*, a creative coping with situations that may entail emergence of new levels of structure, to which terms such as "underlying," "completing," "transcending" can be applied. If "linguistic performance" is restricted to particular behavioral manifestations; or if it is articulated so as to provide for use of linguistic competence in the accomplishment of verbal art; or if verbal accomplishment is taken as based on additional kinds of competence beyond the linguistic—or, finally, if linguistic competence itself is extended beyond the grammatical and semantic—then the apparent conflict would dissolve. In the interim Burke would undoubtedly observe (45–57) that a restricted terminology restricts the adequacy of possible observations and understanding.

The revival of interest in the ethnography of symbolic forms (myth, ritual, song, chant, dance, and the like, and the subtler forms of daily life), and the analysis of patterns of language use, linked with a desire to emulate linguistic methodology, promises development of work from which a truly comparative "rhetoric" and "poetics" may yet emerge. I should not misrepresent Burke's place with regard to such work. Especially when working in another culture, the linguistically trained student of symbolic forms will face problems, and set goals, for which Burke provides no specific guide. Yet such linguistic ethnography will impoverish itself if it does not build on the insights accumulated in the tradition that Burke extends and enriches. Differences of terminology and style aside, there is in it, to use words of a well-known linguist, *much that is substantially correct and essential to any adequate account of language.*

Some final remarks on the book. It is organized in terms of (I) five summarizing essays, (II) particular works and authors, and (III) further essays on symbolism in general. Particular studies deal with *Coriolanus* (in I), *Antony and Cleopatra, Timon of Athens,* the *Oresteia, Faust* (both parts), Emerson's *Nature, Kubla Khan, A Passage to India, Nightwood,* Theodore Roethke, and William Carlos Williams. Kant's ethics comes in for analysis in III, the terministic screen of psychoanalysis in I. Some essays seem classics of their kind—I would single out the essays on the strategies of Shakespeare's plays, especially *Coriolanus,* and that on Emerson's *Nature.* This last essay contrasts the two kinds of transformation: dramatic catharsis in the plays (through symbolic sacrifice, victimage), and dialectical transcendance in Emerson's essay. The development of the contrast would seem to relate to two motives that emerge strongly in the book (cf. 97). In the Shakespearean essays, Burke's well-known sensitivity to implications of works for social tension and social order is still brilliantly present, but is complemented by heightened emphasis on biological components of symbolic expression, especially "the thinking of the body" (he is marvelous on Mallarmé, 308–43), on the one hand, and on formal thoroughness, transcendence, and the pure play of symbolic prowess for its own sake. (Several essays end with mention of thoroughness—carrying out the full implications of a form or set of terms.) Indeed, the book can be said to be pervaded by interrelations of the term *poetic(s)* as pure or sheer act: (a) as department of study, i.e. as analysis of a work in and of itself (496–97), and in terms of internal consistency and inter-relationships required by its own nature (486–89, 221); (b) as an office (purpose) of speech, either in the narrowly Ciceronian sense of entertaining, or the wider sense, introduced by Burke, of the self-consistent and self-developing (see 1958:60–61, and this book, 139, 146, for the links); (c) as fundamental motive of man ("the sheer exercise of 'symbolicity' (or 'symbolic action') for its own sake, purely for the love of the art" (29)), so that in one recent essay, not included here (1958), all functions of language become derivative of the poetic motive as intrinsic pleasure in language use. One suspects a personal dialectic of transcendence here.

Part Three

Linguistics as Sociolinguistics

But General Forms have their vitality in Particulars, & every
Particular is a Man, . . .

'For Empire is no more, and now the Lion & Wolf shall cease'

William Blake, *Jerusalem,* ch. Four, section 91;
America: A Prophecy

Chapter 8

Linguistic Theory and Functions in Speech

The late Uriel Weinreich (1966: 399) observed:

> Whether there is any point to semantic theories which are account-
> able only for special cases of speech—namely humorless, prosaic,
> banal prose—is highly doubtful.

The purpose of this chapter is to generalize Weinreich's statement, and to remove the qualification: linguistic theories accountable only for such cases of speech cannot be consistently justified.[1]
I shall try to bring out the plurality, priority, and problematic
(empirical) status of functions in speech.

1. This chapter is based in "Linguistic Theory and the Functions of
Speech," in *International Days of Sociolinguistics/ Giornate internazionali
di Sociolinguistica*, 111–44 (Rome [: Istituto Luigi Sturzo, 1970]). The original
paper appears in Italian in the same volume (145–71) with the title "Teoria
linguistica e le funzioni della lingua," and in Czech in *Slovo a Slovesnost :
Časopis pro otázky teorie a kultury jazyka* 31(1): 7–32 (1970), with the title
"Lingvistická teorie a promluvové funkce" (translated by František Daneš)
(Praha: Československá Akademie Věd). I am indebted to the Istituto Luigi
Sturzo for inviting me to take part in its Second International Congress of
Social Sciences, September 15–17, 1969, in Rome; to its secretary, Dr. Ughi,
for his kindnesses; to František Daneš, Norman Denison, Paolo Fabbri, John
Gumperz and Gillian Sankoff for their comments at the conference, and
Virginia Hymes, William Labov, and Joel Sherzer for their comments later;
and to David Sapir in whose home in Philadelphia the paper for the Congress
was completed with the aid of some of his and his father's books.

In speaking of "functions," I do not intend to raise here the many issues that attach to the notion of "functionalism" in the social sciences, and, more generally, in the philosophy of the sciences and humanistic disciplines. I use the term first of all because its use by the Prague School has associated it with the perspective developed here, and because it does seem the appropriate general term for a necessary idea. In their methodological reflections on worlds of human knowledge, scholars such as Ernst Cassirer and Kenneth Burke have found the question of function, and, in human action, the question of the function known as purpose, indispensable. That the burden of proof lies with the advocate of the relevance of concern with such questions in linguistics today, does not reflect the nature of language, but the limitations of current linguistics. The burden of proof ought to be, and I believe will come to be, on those who think that linguistics can proceed successfully without explicit attention to its functional foundations.

I do not try to say here what functions speech has overall or in particular communities. I try only to show that, whereas linguists usually treat language in terms of just one broad type of elementary function, called here "referential,"[2] language is in fact constituted in terms of a second broad type of elementary function as well, called here "stylistic." Languages have conventional features, elements, and relations serving referential ("propositional," "ideational," etc.) meaning, and they have conventional features, elements and relations that are stylistic, serving social meaning. Substantive functions, in the sense of human purposes in the use of speech, employ, require, and indeed give rise to characteristics of both kinds. A general study of language comprises both, and even a study seeking to limit itself to what is referentially based cannot escape involvement with what is not. Involvement with stylistic function, and social meaning, reveals that the foundations of language, if partly in the human mind, are equally in social life, and that the foundations of linguistics, if partly in logic and psychology, are equally in ethnography (cf. Hymes 1964a: 6, 41).

The term "function" is so readily misunderstood in linguistics today that I should explain something I do *not* intend. In many minds, the term "function" in the study of language has become

2. "Referential" seems to be the most convenient term. It is of course distinct from denotation, and understood as entailing an intensional conception of meaning. I reserve "meaning" for the import of a form or utterance generally (cf. Firth 1935). To equate "meaning" with grammatical and lexical meaning, as ordinarily analyzed, is a reduction, indeed, one might say, a category mistake. (Cf. Jakobson 1957, 1965 on indexical and iconic meanings in language).

associated with behaviorism as espoused by B. F. Skinner. It should be clear that the appeals to knowledge, creativity, and even freedom and liberation (chs. 4, 10) in this book bring my approach under Skinner's obloquy. A commitment to an ethnographic "mentalism," however, does not require one to avert one's eyes from functions, just because Skinner has written about them (cf. Hymes 1964e). The trouble with Skinner is not that he writes of such things as "mands," but that, lacking linguistics, he has no way to specify and analyze the features and relationships to which such terms point. Thus, a "mand" is an utterance that elicits goods, services, information—one might want to recognize a category of this type, but one would want to warrant it too, as part of a valid system of speech acts, and determine its identifying and contrastive features in speech. (For a sociolinguistic use of the notion of "mand," see Ervin-Tripp 1972: 245). Skinner may make a convenient target, for discrediting interest in functions generally; perhaps that is his latest function in current controversy (cf. Chomsky 1973, ch. 7). Most linguists should be sophisticated enough not to be misled by such tactics. One does not have to choose between "mands" and "minds."

It is indeed something of a contradiction, an irony at least, that we have today a general linguistics that justifies itself in terms of understanding the distinctiveness of man, but has nothing to say, as linguistics, of human life. The voice is the voice of humanism, of a rationalist idealism; the hand, one fears, is the hand of mechanism. I want to insist that willingness to take functions for granted, as given, as unproblematic for linguistic practice and theory, is ideological and self-serving. Such a posture enables linguists to credit themselves with studying "language," when they only make models of logic and grammar. Linguistics cannot claim to be a science of *language* without constituting itself on an adequate functional foundation, as the present chapter seeks to show.

GETTING AT GRAMMAR

Accepting Sentences

For many linguists, a description is intended to account for all, and only, the grammatical sentences of a language. Such an account abstracts from hesitations, interruptions, incompleteness, errors. The point, of course, is not only to exclude such sentences, but also to explain their excluded status. It is success in only a weak sense just not to provide for such sentences. It is success in a strong sense to show why the grammar provides for other kinds of sentence and for the kinds excluded. Now, a grammar can readily illuminate the fact that syntactic jumbles (The a which hurry horse magnificently two) are not grammatical. It cannot illuminate the status of hesitations, interruptions, unfinished sentences, and certain kinds of errors, but only say that they are not its business. It is embarrassing at the very outset for a grammar, conceived as illuminating speakers' abilities, to be able to explain nicely mistakes that speakers almost never make (one really has to concentrate to invent a nice syntactic jumble), and to have nothing to say about "mistakes" that speakers make all the time—"mistakes," indeed, that are often the proper "mistake," so to speak, to make.

A description that takes as its criterion *acceptable* sentences must account for hesitations, interruptions, stops in mid-sentence, and errors, that are appropriate to a situation or a style. A grammarian really has to do so also; he or she has to get at his or her intuitive judgments of grammaticality *through* the surrounding, more immediately intuitive, network of judgments of acceptability.

Acceptability, of course, has a social dimension, as just indicated, and has to do with genres, norms of interaction, and social meanings and stylistic features, quite in addition to the considerations of feasibility in mental processing in terms of which it has been discussed (Chomsky 1965). Consider, for example, a Burundi peasant, who, when speaking to an aristocrat, must bumble verbally in a culturally prescribed manner (Albert 1972), or a Surinam black, whose fellows will admire him if he speaks Dutch with grammatical and lexical correctness, but resent his airs if his pronunciation is correctly Dutch as well (Eersel 1971). Quite generally, to complete a certain sentence, to speak without hesitation, to speak with perfect grammaticality, can, under certain conditions, be offensive.

Description cannot be restricted to fully "semanticized" sentences, if the semantic import and structure of some parts of sentences is to be understood, and if all the conventionalized units and relations in sentences are to be analyzed. In American society "Would you like to bring me the paper?" commonly asks the addressee's wishes—"like" has referential force. For some Americans, and commonly in England, "like" does not, and "Would you like" is a politeness formula. Americans and Britons experience a fair amount of mutual interference in this regard, Britons finding many American requests (e.g., "Cup of coffee") tersely rude, and even refusing to honor them, while Americans may find British requests annoyingly indirect or elegant. Americans who adapt to British habits while abroad may have some difficulty on return, as when my daughter Alison asked in Philadelphia, "May I have one of those candies, please?" and the clerk replied, "Sure, honey, I'll sell you anything you want."

Surface structure of sentences, in other words, is not to be taken at face value—not only because of underlying syntactic relationships, as grammarians now fully recognize, because of Chomsky's work, but also because the surface structure itself is not just a matter of grammatical formatives. It is a matter of formatives of two types, both grammatical, but one "referential," the other "stylistic." To use an example from Sydney Lamb: if a secretary, answering the phone, asks "May I say who's calling?," an appropriate answer is not just "Yes." As an act of speech, the immediate constituents of the sentence are something like [Politeness formula] + [Operational element]; the question asked is "Who's calling?" The status of "May I say," and the dependence between an appropriate answer and "Who's calling," are part of a speaker's linguistic competence, even if one restricts the "competence" to grammatical knowledge (as I do not, of course—ch. 4). The principled investigation of such phenomena makes social factors inescapable in grammatical analysis.

Further as to the status of elements such as "May I say." It is a familiar fact that lexical elements and phrases, if they acquire grammatical function, may lose their earlier lexical force in their new paradigmatic relationships; thus, in English "keep" and "get" now mark continuate and inceptive aspect in sentences such as "Keep going" and "Get going," not "retain/obtain possession of" something called "going." Just so, lexical elements and phrases, if they acquire grammatical function in a social or stylistic sense, may lose their earlier lexical force in their new paradigmatic relationships. The two processes are quite parallel, if not identical: it is the difference in the function that has drawn the linguist's attention to the referential cases and not the others.

One may find a particular process only partly accomplished—one of the sources of diversity in judgments of sentences. I myself find "May I say" "semi-grammaticalized," as it were, so that I often reply to the sentence in both interpretations, with "Yes" and my name. In the United States "Thank you" has commonly the force of expressing thanks for something received. In England "Thank you" may be said by a cab driver as he opens the door to let a passenger out, and even by a host handing a guest a plate at the dinner table. The expression seems to be more of a polite acknowledgment, an abstract marker of junctures of interaction with a guest (or customer), and to have gone part of the way toward the pole of repetitive acknowledgement represented by Japanese "hai" and "dozo." (Though it may be that the English cases cited are analogous to French "merci," differing from the American expression in features of context toward which thanks is directed; here, not the immediate transaction, but the relationship of longer duration now being acknowledged at its salient point of transaction. The need for ethnographic study of interaction is clear in either interpretation.)

Every language has a great many such elements, internally (morphologically) uninteresting perhaps, and uninteresting too, perhaps, syntactically, through lack of apparent interdependence with referential grammatical categories. Indeed, such elements are seldom presented in descriptions (but compare the long interesting list of 50 or more in Sapir's Takelma grammar, 1922). An ordinary grammar can only list and gloss them, even so, if it does not take into account the contexts and function in terms of which they have contrastive relevance. Analysis in terms of speech acts, such as summons, may however show such elements to have syntagmatic and paradigmatic properties (cf. Schegloff 1968), and so may analysis in terms of interconnection with intonation in expressive function (cf. Seiler 1962, Van Holk 1962). It may be that a more comprehensive approach to familiar grammatical categories within ordinary syntax would have to deal with such particles and expressions as well. In many sentences in languages such as Wasco Chinook and Warm Springs Sahaptin, for example, an initial particle, such as Wasco *ani'* or *adé*, has not only its own local force, but a scope which comprises and colors the rest of the sentence to follow, as to mood. It in effect defines the interpretation of what follows, disambiguating in advance. Initial position for elements defining mood over the scope of what follows may be widespread, even universal.

Consider also proper names in vocative sentences. They are more than arbitrary in reference, as Lévi-Strauss (1958) has brought to attention, and as the inspired rightness of the names invented for *The Lord of the Rings* by Tolkien abundantly demonstrates; they have internal structure, have social meaning (cf. Hymes 1966b), have semantic invariants (Franklin 1967), and phonological or other markers (cf. Smith 1969). When viewed from the standpoint of address, in relation to social groups and settings, they enter into contrastive sets, among themselves, and with forms from other domains (pronouns, kin terms, titles, zero —cf. Fischer 1964), demonstrating again that recognition of social function brings recognition of new structure, transcending conventional compartments.

These are elements of neglected structure within sentences, which social meaning and stylistic function bring into view. It is being increasingly recognized that the single sentence is itself an arbitrary boundary (cf. ch. 4 on discourse), generalizations being lost if the sentence is the limiting unit. Let us add that if it is essential to consider how a grammatical feature may be expressed now in a single sentence, now across sentences, it would be artificial to consider only the larger scope, and not the differences in social and stylistic meaning between both realizations. Conjoining of structures, as distinct from their disjunction, is not just a larger sphere of syntactic operation; it opens up an additional sphere of significant choice.

If grammatical rules are pursued to the full extent of their application, moreover, more than grammar must be analyzed. As has been pointed out in earlier chapters, the very formal dependencies of a sentence in relation to a preceding sentence may also be found in relation to a nonverbal context (cf. ch. 4, citing Waterhouse 1963, Gunter 1966, Schegloff 1968). Further, the status of a sentence, its features as a request, a command, etc., of course differ according to the social relationship and situation. Thus the film "The Royal Family" shows Queen Elizabeth II beginning a morning's work at her desk in Buckingham Palace by saying over the intercom, "Do you think you could bring up those papers I was looking at yesterday?" In all these respects, an analysis of sentences, of the scope of their formal relationships, requires a coordinated analysis of social meaning. Each aspect of structure and meaning disclosed enters into judgments of acceptability, and perforce, grammaticality.

Many linguists may wish to ignore, or relegate to another day, such relationships and meanings. As the above examples indicate, and as work of Labov (1966) in New York City demonstrates in detail, one will miss linguistic structure that way. Even more, one will not be able to establish the limited structure that one seeks. Postal (1964) and others, for example, have based analysis of the reflexive pronoun in English on the assumption that the occurrence of the same proper name as both subject and object of a sentence must refer to two distinct persons. "Paul admires Paul" must be concerned with two different Pauls. (I owe this example to Werner Winter's discussion of the problem at the Conference on Linguistic Method organized by Paul Garvin, Los Angeles 1966). Many American speakers agree, however, that the two "Pauls" may be the same person. I have heard in spontaneous conversation such a sentence as "But you have to remember, Ben looks after Ben." About 1951, the following could be seen painted on a wall at Harvard: "Pitirim loves Pitirim" (Philip Curtin, pers. comm). Such cases must be dealt with.

It is hardly satisfactory to invoke differences of "dialect" here, or ad hoc in other cases of apparent difference of opinion as to the acceptability of a sentence. There seem always to be different "dialects," and "dialects" that differ for different examples, in the audiences of linguistic papers in recent years. Notice that as soon as there are two such disputed examples, there are four possible "dialects": that of those who accept both proffered examples, that of those who reject both, and the two of those who accept one, reject one. (Thus, some of those who reject "Ben looks after Ben" might be among those who do not think that a noun marked (+ feminine) can also be marked (+ agent) with certain verbs of sexual activity in English (Dong ms.); others might be among those who think such a noun can be so marked; and so on). As the number of disputed examples increases, the number of theoretically possible "dialects" increases as the power of 2. The actual groupings are no doubt fewer than the number of disputed examples would lead one to calculate; 5 disputed cases probably do not evidence 32 dialects. No doubt there are interconnections and contextual factors. The point is that one must know what they are.

The failure to find consensus, to find generally convincing examples, for crucial points, brings present practice and theory to an impasse. One does not wish to retreat to analysis of a corpus, a supposed "idiolect," or to arbitrary methodological canons. One intends to analyze English, not some uncertainly located variant of English; more than that, one proposes to analyze something that is somewhere, by someone, known. The contradiction between intended theoretical scope and restrictive methodological practice becomes ever more glaring and frustrating.

The way out of the impasse would be to recognize, first, as Jakobson has long maintained, that a language is a "system of systems." That is to say, it is not enough to recognize a multiplicity of forms of speech and to abandon hope of uniting them, or diverse analytical topics, into a common theory, as some formal linguists appear to be doing. There is indeed a certain practical wisdom and significant precedent for abandoning a general theory that proves a Procrustean bed. J. R. Firth concluded in such a spirit [1935] 1957: 29): "Unity is the last concept that should be applied to language. . . . There is no such thing as *une langue une* and there never has been."

But this is to neglect the possibility of a unified theory from a social, rather than grammatical, standpoint. Noting that "the London group is in virtual accord with the group of Prague" (in taking a functional approach that recognizes both the diversity and conventionality of forms of speech), Vachek (1959) rejected Firth's conclusion as one to which only "stubborn nominalists could subscribe." He argued that "all the existing varieties of

English can be said to be mutually complementary with regard to the types of social situation in which a speaker of English may find himself placed" (1959: 109). Just so some linguists have defined "register" as a functional variety in one-to-one relation with a defining situation. Such "mutual functional complementariness" saves the unity of a language (see the discussion of the similar tactic taken by Pike later in this chapter); but it repeats on the level of variety and situation the same error so long made on the level of language and community (see ch. 2). The mapping between means and contexts is not in principle one-to-one; that is indeed a cardinal tenet of the sociolinguistic perspective of this book. It is precisely the contrastive relevance of varieties within the same situation, the possibility of alternation and choice within the same situation, that defines the relevance of the rules of co-occurrence obtaining within them, and provides for their social meaning. It is such a complex unity, having to do with repertoires in relation to situations, persons, and communities, that answers to a conception of language as a "system of systems." (This paragraph is elaborated from Hymes 1961d.)

Such a complex unity provides for the fact that the functions served in a language, and warranting its elements and relationships, are social, or stylistic, as well as referential, and that what appear as "deviations," "violations," "variations," or "dialects" from the standpoint of only the latter function may appear as choices within the more complex system of rules. "Ben looks after Ben," for example, may be taken to be marked for stylistic effect. If not dismissed, but analyzed together with "John looks after himself," the desired analysis of latter is empirically saved, and the equally valid force of the former explained. The cases with "-self" manifest a widespread regularity in English, and it is no part of the purpose of a sociolinguistic approach to discard such regularities; the purpose is rather to place such regularities within a more adequate analysis of the relation between sound and meaning in English (and languages generally).

In general, then, the sentences that trouble syntactic analysis are subject to interpretation and selection in the first instance on the dimensions of social context and speech style. The two dimensions have long been noted (e.g., Kenyon 1948), but in its initial advances into syntax, recent American grammatical theory seemed able to ignore them. It can do so no longer, if it is to have other than an ad hoc, arbitrary base. If it is possible to isolate judgment of grammaticality from the more general judgment of acceptability, this can be done only if the contextual and stylistic dimensions of judgment are known.

Being Sensitive to Context

Grammarians have often enough taken dimensions of context and style into account, but commonly in an ad hoc and unprincipled way. That is, discovery of the nature of grammatical elements and relations has often depended upon discovery of social conditions for their use. In analyzing Siona, for example, Wheeler (1967) was unable to account for speakers' indifference to choice among certain forms in individual sentences, yet their rigorous insistence on consistent selections in discourse (this being a good example of grammatical regularities missed if only the sentence is analyzed, as noted in ch. 4). Nonverbal and other contextual information brought out that the forms were selected on two simultaneous dimensions: voice, and relative focus. Another set of important categories, mood-like in character, required considerable ethnographic inquiry to establish their defining properties: definiteness vs. indefiniteness of the knowledge reported, and responsibility, involvement, commitment vs. their absence, in relation to it. Mothers, for example, discuss their own children with the one category, the children of others with the other.

In this admirably explicit account, rich in interesting detail, Wheeler makes clear a common practice of linguists: knowledge of the social contexts governing the selection of grammatical features is obtained in order to define the categories, but then abandoned, except for the residue of a relatively abstract category label. Two terms of a relationship are necessarily studied but only one is formally described.

Aaron Cicourel has related a particularly telling instance of this practice. In a linguistics class analyzing Indonesian, the informant was regularly relied upon to supply social meanings and cultural knowledge which would permit the linguistic analysis to proceed, but the meanings and knowledge were themselves excluded from the description. In other words, the description was to make explicit only part of the knowledge that the native speaker indicated he needed in order to speak grammatically. The linguist in charge of the class was determining the relevance of data, not by the goal of explicating the native speaker's knowledge of language, but by the goal of writing what would be considered a proper grammar by professional colleagues. Such instances clarify the ideological status of claims that grammatical analysis is concerned with something that can be properly called "competence."

Sometimes features of context, especially attributes of one or more participants in the speech event, force attention to themselves. Sometimes simply status as addressor or addressee is involved, as in the definition of pronouns and other "shifters" (Jakobson 1957) or in the statement of a rule (such as the conjunct reduction in Sanskrit that applies across change of interlocutor in question and response). Sometimes generic features of participants are involved, as when different indicative and imperative paradigms (the surface result of several intersecting phonological rules) are selected in Koasati (Haas 1944), according to whether the addressor of record is male or female. (Men use female forms when quoting the speech of women in tales, and conversely, so the features are part of common competence; indeed, children are corrected for them, according to their sex.) In Yana words have one phonological shape when the addressor and addressee are both adult males, another (shortened and altered) otherwise. (Both styles are thus part of the competence of men, and the entire lexicon marked accordingly.) Sometimes more limited status is involved, as when in Abipon all words add -*in* if any participant to a conversation is a member of the Hocheri (warrior society) (Sherzer 1970), or in Ainu, where several pronouns are plural, or singular, plus respectful, according to the relative age-grades of the addressor and addressee (Hattori 1964). Relationship between participants is also entailed when a Hindu sentence such as *ve dəsərəth ke lərke the* "He (they) Dasharath of son(s) was (were)" is ambiguously singular or plural, depending upon the respect relationship between addressor, addressee, and person spoken of (Jain 1969: 94).

Such features usually are treated as marginal. Once used in order to define grammatical meanings, or to save the referential unity of alternative shapes, they are ignored. The rest of the data is not examined for further elements and relationship governed by the features now unavoidably invoked. In sum, such features are treated in an ad hoc, rather than a principled way. Often enough a prose comment would suffice, or the implicit formalism of parenthetic glosses and annotations, such as "(man speaking)," "(woman speaking)," "(said to children)," "(respect form)." Some scholars have indeed begun to introduce the requisite social features formally into the contexts in which linguistic forms are generated.

Now, the methodology of context-sensitive grammar normally requires features used in contexts to have been previously introduced. (Chomsky and Halle 1968: 384 decide not to make this a formal condition, but observe that their own practice has followed it; others have in fact given it as a requirement). Insofar as this canon is followed, *any analysis that requires social features in the contexts of forms is evidence of the need for a prior analysis of the social features.*

Some scholars have already grasped this point with regard to the selection of features in terms of styles or genres of discourse (cf. Bloomfield and Newmark 1963: 70–71, 85–86, 245, and DeCamp 1970). Explicit analysis, let alone differentiation and interrelation of the features and dimensions, has hardly begun. The point, of course, is that designation of discourse features as governing contexts cannot be ad hoc, and requires analysis of what constitutes contrasting styles, genres, in the community in question.

Recently a need has been recognized to identify lexical elements as native or foreign, or of specific provenience, e.g., Romance or Greek in English, French or English in Mohawk (Chomsky and Halle 1968, Postal 1968). Standard dictionaries, of course, go farther, identifying forms according to several social dimensions. Webster's *Third International Dictionary,* for example, incorporates regional provenience, level (substandard, but not hypercorrect), technical genre (mostly by subject, such as music, cricket, mineralogy, Semitic grammar), style (slang, but not literary and such, so that *e'en, e'er* are unlabelled), and currency (obsolescent, archaic, as defined by date of most recent attestation). Leonard Bloomfield once observed that even in a small nonliterate community the dimension of level would require one "to annotate almost every item of the grammar, and many of the lexicon" (1927, cited from Hymes [ed.] 1964: 395, regarding Menomini). The point again is that annotations, and dictionary features, require an analysis of the terms that enter into them.

Using Appropriateness Creatively

To insist that analysis of social meaning has priority is not to impose an arbitrary requirement, or conduct a critique that linguistic practice can afford to ignore. Such analysis is required by what some regard as an essential goal, justifying much else, namely, to illuminate the "creative aspect of language use" (Chomsky 1966). A defining property of this aspect is response to novel situations with sentences that are both novel and appropriate. The crux of the matter is that ordinary grammatical analysis may explain the possibility of novel sentences (not all novel sentences, if stylistic features are neglected), but a novel sentence may be inappropriate, bizarre or uninterpretable. Appropriateness is a *relation* between sentences and contexts, requiring analysis of both. Indeed, creative language use is often not a matter of a novel sentence, or a novel context either, but of a novel relation. Sentence and context may be familiar; the use of one in the other may be what is new.

Contextual rules probably can account for a great deal of the appropriateness of discourse (more generally, relations, however modelled, since nothing depends on the relations being expressed in a certain rule-format), given analysis of contexts as well as of linguistic forms. For example, the dimension of social distance appears to be universal in languages, as in social life, connected with a series of related meanings, such as informality-formality, intimacy-respect, equality-authority, private-public. Let me take informality-formality for illustration. In the paradigm of greeting forms in American English, "Hi" could be specified as [−formal]. Its use in a context defined or interpreted as [−formal] would be unmarked. Such a matching of the values, or social meanings, of forms and contexts can be taken as one manifestation of appropriateness, in a narrow sense of the term. Often of course the values of form and context do not match, as when a [−formal] form, such as "Hi" is used in a context defined or intepreted as [+formal]; such a relation is marked. It may of course also be appropriate, in a somewhat broader sense of the term, a sense more adequate to the competence and creative ability of persons. Marked uses are often judged the appropriate uses to employ. They may define an attitude, signal a change in social relationship (as in what Friedrich 1966 calls "pronominal breakthrough"), be a way of accomplishing many things, by way of humor, irony, insult, praise. Much of appropriateness in this broader sense can be analyzed then in terms of (1) a set of alternative linguistic forms; (2) a set of contexts (specified in terms of participants, etc.); (3) unmarked values (social meanings) of forms and contexts; (4) a set of relations between forms and contexts.

To give briefly a few examples: a common, perhaps universal, phenomenon is for one and the same term to be "fighting words" in some contexts, a badge of intimacy in others (cf. Swadesh 1933). In all societies there are age-graded terms for persons. If unmarked usage is to refer to a person by the term for the category in which, by age, he or she belongs, then derogation can be expressed by referring to a person by a term for the category below that to which, by age, he or she belongs (calling a man "boy," a boy "big baby"). Praise can be expressed by referring to a person by a term for a category above that to which, by age, he or she belongs (short of decrepitude) (calling a boy "young man," an infant "little man"). (Such a pattern is found among the Klamath Indians of southern Oregon). The set of terms and the set of social categories remain constant. What contrast are the relations between them, that is, the rule, operation, or mapping relating one to the other.

In large part the kind of analysis adumbrated here only makes systematic and formally accountable familiar observations, of the sort dealt with by Metcalf in his study of German modes of address. Thus (Metcalf 1938: 43): "*Ihr* was not uncommonly employed for 'symptomatic' purposes where a different type of address would be expected under normal circumstances."

The essential thing is that the present analysis *locates* the kinds of import summed up as "symptomatic" in a different place, not in subcategorization of the form (e.g., "distancing" *Ihr*, "discourteous" *Ihr* (Metcalf 1938: 44—the quotation marks are his), but in alternative *relations* between form and context, and the social meanings involved. The present analysis avoids the tendency to invent pseudo-homonyms, investing individual forms with meanings that are really relational properties (e.g., "literary *Du*," "emotive *Du*"), when the form simply contrasts on a single dimension (here, with *Sie* on the dimension of social distance), but is made to bear the contrastive relevance of properties of genre, voice, social relationship, and the rules connecting it with them. The analysis also avoids the opposite tendency to obscure the structure of context by attributing all social meanings mechanically to it.

Such analysis of course does not exhaust the meaning, or import, of what is said. Contextual rules of the sort discussed are really context-*selective* rules, allocations of forms and contexts, and not in themselves fully sensitive to the ways in which collection and contextualization of forms may augment meanings, such that the whole is more than the sum of the parts. (J. Peter Maher calls this property of collocations *investiture*). And there are of course also emergent meanings, as when unexpected concurrence of two or more relations, intended or imputed, produces humor, irony and other effects. Further, the full meaning depends upon additional characteristics of what is present, done and said —intonation, tone of voice, gesture, and local norms of interaction and interpretation, such as whether an addressee has, or does not have, the option of ignoring a putative insult, or as when, by responding "You must be joking," one conveys that joking is not the apparent interpretation. Such creative aspects of language use seem to require even more clearly an analysis of social meanings and social contexts. One may not need to know all the contexts and categories of a community to discern the essentials of its patterns in these regards, but one must know the dimensions on which contexts and categories contrast. For linguists who take the creative aspect of language use seriously, the difference between linguistic and sociolinguistic description will tend to disappear.

FINDING AND USING UNIVERSALS

Finding Universals

The need for a functional approach can be seen from a some-what different vantage point, that of universals in a general theory of language. The principle to be applied is an extension of one stated by Ferdinand de Saussure. De Saussure argued the necessity of including lexicon in the description of language, as well as grammar, because a given category might be expressed in the one sector in one language, and in the other in another. For a general theory to deal with such categories, its descriptive base would have to include both sectors. The same logic applies to stylistic features and social meanings, alongside those that are referential, and in a way applies more completely. A certain category may be expressed within the effective scope of a referential description in one language, but be expressed outside that scope in another; moreover, conversely, a certain feature may express a category within the effective scope of description in one language, but also express it (or another category) outside that scope in another language. In both respects, true universal properties of language will be missed, if description is not extended to the scope of two types of function, rather than restricted to one. Let me consider first some instances having to do with sound patterns.

Sound Patterns

Despite its great interest in universals, recent transformational generative phonological theory remains explanatorily inadequate because of its restriction to "referential" function. The restriction appears most seriously in an argument such as the following with regard to labiovelar stops in some West African languages (Chomsky and Halle 1968: 298).

> Since clicklike suction is clearly an independently controllable aspect of the speech event, the data just cited establish suction as a separate phonetic feature, regardless of the fact that apparently in no language are there contrasting pairs of utterances that differ solely in this feature.

The data are taken from Ladefoged (1964: 9), and refer to Late (without the suction) and Yoruba (with it). Ladefoged in fact contrasts more generally many Guang languages (e.g. Late, Anuin) to Yoruba, Senadi, Ibibio, Idoma, Bini and some others on the articulatory features in question (1964: 9–11; in some of the languages a third factor enters).

160   FOUNDATIONS IN SOCIOLINGUISTICS

Chomsky and Halle, like most linguists, conceive of contrastive relevance solely as serving the function of reference
between forms within a language. On this basis, the additional
articulatory trait in Yoruba, Bini, and other languages is only an
unmotivated local habit. Matters need not be left there, if social
function is recognized.

There is first of all the possibility of contrast with forms not
in the language. Native speakers of Yoruba are in fact astonished
if a nonnative speaker produces these stops with the ingressive
suction. Native speakers of Bini (which shares this feature with
Yoruba, but with an additional difference at closure) also distinguish native: nonnative speakers in this way. Generative phonology now marks lexical items for language identity for other
purposes, and it also employs a convention of treating elements
as marked for the category to which they belong, e.g., a noun as
marked (+Noun). It would seem a simple extension to treat the
forms of language as normally marked (+Yoruba), (+ Bini), etc.
A pronunciation of labiovelar stops in Yoruba without the ingressive velaric movement or suction does not indicate a change in
the referential marking of forms; but a phonological marking as
(−Yoruba). Second, there is stylistic function within a language.
In Bini (the only language for which I have information) velaric
suction enters into the system of emphasis in the language. (For
information on the perception of native: nonnative pronunciation,
I am indebted to J. David Sapir and Miss Becky Aghéyisi; for the
information on stylistic use, to Miss Aghéyisi and Dan Ben-Amos.)

All independently controllable phonetic features should be
regarded as functional. The point is simply that there is more than
one kind of function for phonetic features to have.

The relation between the phonetic features of particular languages and linguistic universals is misconceived on another score,
if social, or stylistic, function is not taken into account. Chomsky
and Halle (1968: viii) explain their attention to English stress contours on the grounds of light shed on "linguistic theory" (universal
grammar). Neglect of aspiration in English is explained on the
same ground. English aspiration, in point of fact, is a perfect
example of a feature that does have relevance for general theory.
It has contrastive relevance, not in reference, but social meaning.
(Such features may be grouped together as "stylistic" as distinct
from "referential"). Strong vs. weak aspiration of an initial stop
is a conventionally recognized way of conveying emphasis,
whether for reasons of metalinguistic clarification, conveying of
attitude, self-expression, or whatever. The contrast strong: weak
aspiration of initial stop is available as a diacritic of social meaning, just as the contrast voiced: nonvoiced is available as a dia-

critic of referential meaning. (Cf. velaric suction in Bini, glottalization in Siuslaw (Hymes 1966c: 336), and many other cases.)

Furthermore, aspiration is probably contrastively relevant in
every language. Probably it is a universal, not only as a matter of
inventory, but as a matter of functional relevance. In some languages it distinguishes lexical forms (e.g., Hindi); in others, uses
of the same form (English). It is perhaps universally part of the
normal linguistic competence of speakers and hearers. From a
more adequate standpoint, then, descriptively one establishes *all*
the conventionally recognized contrastive phonetic features of a
language and community. One investigates membership in the
universal list of potentially relevant features, membership in the
list of features factually relevant in all languages, *and the function*
(referential, stylistic) *in which features are relevant.* (What is stylistic in a given context cannot at the same time be referential,
although the same feature may serve different functions in different contexts.) From the standpoint of general theory, in other
words, one has to do with four lists. The list of features potentially
relevant is not in fact changed so far: aspiration, vowel length,
labiovelar (see below) and the like are already present in it,
although of course functional investigation of this sort may
enlarge the list, by finding independently controlled features used
only stylistically (such as the Yoruba, Bini, et al. ingressive velaric
suction appears to be). (The possibility of such a feature having
once had referential function, or gaining it, is of course always
present.) There is next the list of features empirically found to be
relevant just in referential function; the list of features empirically
found relevant just in stylistic function; and the list of features
found relevant in either or both. It may be, of course, that the
second and third lists will prove to be small, almost empty. If so,
the importance and pervasiveness of stylistic function will be
inescapably demonstrated. In any case, such an approach will
make possible understanding of the hierarchy among sounds with
respect to degree of universality.

The explicit development of such an approach will bring out
the interest of features, and forms containing them, otherwise
perhaps overlooked or merely itemized in individual languages.
Typological and areal statements may be put into a new light.
Thus, one would think offhand of West Africa as a characteristic
area for labiovelar stop consonants (Kpelle, etc.); that is of course
because they are prominent in referential status in languages of
the area. It now becomes of interest to look for stylistic use of
labiovelar stop consonants in areas in which these sounds are not
reported referentially. What might seem an odd or unnoticed fact
of incidental distribution in the *kiksht* dialects of Chinookan be-

comes of general interest. (I am indebted to Michael Silverstein for discussion of the *kiksht* phenomenon). A labiovelar stop complex is attested in Clackamas Chinook only in an emphatic form of the stem for "large" (itself already augmentative—see below on symbolism in stem-initial position in these dialects); cf. *-quaitł* : *-qbaitł* (the latter form is from Jacobs 1959: 301, line 4), and in Wasco only in what Wascos consider the only intrinsically cursing word, *qalaqbaya*. (The latter form is not wholly analyzable, but elements of the shapes *qala-*, *qana-*, *gwala-*, etc. are found derivationally initially in stems with a general sense of augmentation. The word is said by Wascos to have no meaning (apart from its insulting force); it is in a sense pure phonesthematic poetry. The rarity of the sounds is fitting to the uniqueness of the word. (Wascos can curse in Wasco, but apart from this word they do so by saying what they mean; they have no other lexical items inherently imprecatory.)

Such functions of phonetic features have of course been taken into account, when they could not be ignored, and even seized upon as a special trait of certain languages, as is the case with aspects of social meaning. The Chinookan *kiksht* dialect Wasco (equivalent to the Wishram of the published literature) is fairly well known for augmentative-diminutive symbolism in consonants, especially in stem-initial position. The pertinent facts are briefly these. Voicing is not referentially contrastive in stops, except in stem-initial position. Some stems have inherently voiceless, others inherently voiced, initial stops. Some stems have initial stops whose voicing alternates, depending on phonological rules that operate in other positions as well. A good many stems (mostly nouns) with an inherently voiceless initial stop may nevertheless appear with a voiced initial stop, to express augmentative meaning. (There are other alternations, but this is the one of concern here). There may also be glottalization (with voiceless stop) to express diminutive meaning. Thus, one can have *i-chikchik* 'truck wagon' : *i-jikjik* 'large truck' : *i-ts'ikst'ik* 'little truck' (change of *sh* to diminutive *s* enters into the picture also).

The occurrence of voicing in a stem-initial stop hence is ambiguous, as a surface feature. It may represent inherent (referential) voicing, or augmentative (stylistic) voicing. The native speaker knows which is which, and indeed, the case is a telling one for the necessity of the kind of relation between grammatical and phonological sectors that transformational generative theory has developed; but what the native speaker knows comprises two kinds of functions, or meanings. He also knows that only some, not all, of the stems of the language are marked for this kind of alternation, and that the diminutive is the more common of the two directions of alternation,

Cases such as the Wasco open up another aspect of the problem of linguistic universals. Sapir (1915; SWES 195) found that "the writer himself feels, or thinks he feels, the intrinsically diminutive or augmentative value of certain consonant changes in Wishram," as do I; glottalization for diminutive, voicing for augmentation, and s for diminutive, sh for augmentation, seem right. For some time, to be sure, modern linguistics has largely avoided the question of a crosscultural basis for the relationship between sounds and meanings, when it did not condemn it. The arbitrariness of the relation between sound and meaning was stressed, to the exclusion of other considerations as "unscientific," "subjective," etc. The case was made from a comparative, "ethnological" perspective, series of words having much the same denotation, but no apparent sameness of shape, being cited, e.g., horse : cheval : Pferd : loshad : misatim : (i)kiutan (English : French : German : Russian : Algonquian : Wasco). The facts of cross-language universals and near-universals, however, have been pressed with increasing vigor in recent years, by Durbin, Friedrich, Jakobson, Samarin, Swadesh and others; there are some earlier references in Hymes (ed.) 1964f: 225, 282. Fischer (1965), for example, has proposed a universal basis for the selection in two related Pacific languages of opposing terms of a morphophonemic alternation as the stylistically unmarked member (relating the choice to contrasting cultural values and attitudes toward language; cf. Fischer 1972).

A language may still surprise us: in Warm Springs Sahaptin, reduplication can be used to mark the diminutive (Virginia Hymes, pers. comm.), where one might think that the opposite, augmentation, would be found. Such cases warn against hasty postulation of universals, and the need for precise inquiry into the cultural norms of each community. Universality may lie a little deeper, and have more complexity, than experience of only a few languages may tempt one to assume. We greatly need to have "phonesthematic" description, as it were, become a standard part of accounts of languages, so that the full range of phenomena of felt phonic appropriateness can be taken into account. The phonological surface of vocabulary is no merely arbitrary representation, from the standpoint of members of a community, who acquire it, not as practitioners of ethnological comparison, but in a milieu of interdependence of shapes and meanings. From an ethnographic standpoint, appropriateness of sound to meaning is a daily, pervasive part of the life of language. Certainly there is abundant reason to believe that patterns for the selection of forms appropriate to meanings can be persistent and pervasive in the history of a language community (cf. Guiraud 1967 with regard to French; Marchand 1959 and Smithers 1954 with regard to English). Languages often differ in the apparent proliferation of such phenomena, and in their direction and location in the system, and we greatly need to develop adequate typologies (cf. Ullmann 1953 for a start) and areal profiles, as well as specific descriptions. It may be that convincing universals can be established in this aspect of language more readily than with regard to formal syntax, and more convincingly explained, in relation to the makeup of the human mind, and, also, body, as well as of the world. Ultimately research in this area must include paralinguistic and kinesic features; here I emphasize what is inescapable within linguistics itself. For a brilliant account of an impasse caused by neglect of phonesthematic relationships, see Bolinger 1950, especially section 14, "Creativity," and the conclusion. Bolinger's analysis of the interplay of productive referential morphology, descriptive etymology (the term is from F. W. Householder, Jr.), and inherited and developing phonesthematic relationships, remains pertinent to the analysis of grammatical formatives today, and, by implication, any attempt to handle all of the detectible patterning in a language from the standpoint of a single function and format.)[3]

In sum, a principled approach to such phenomena cannot restrict itself to cases in which they intrude inescapably into the usual grammatical description, as in Chinookan stem-initials. In Chinookan, indeed, the interdependence of two elementary linguistic functions, the referential and stylistic, is reflected in the fact that a phone type [ae], solely stylistic in most dialects, has become referential in a few names and in color terms in one (Wasco). This instance of sound change is accurately explainable only against a background of description of both kinds of function and element in the language.

Functionally Related Features Generally

The preceding paragraph has expressed a logic that is common in its application to all features of language, and that indeed is a theme of this entire book. We have dealt with it in earlier chapters in relation to forms of speech, code-switching, speech-styles, and speech acts (chs. 2, 4), showing that the analysis of each implicates a general descriptive framework and meanings and relations part of a general theory. Whereas usual practice

3. The preceding two paragraphs draw upon Hymes 1956, the beginning of Hymes 1960, and the conclusion of Hymes 1972e.

treats something social or stylistic, when inescapably intrusive, in an ad hoc way, a principled approach, recognizing that the plurality of functions served by linguistic structures is fundamental to them, would find in the intrusion something requiring to be pursued and generalized to the investigation of all languages, and of the nature of language as a whole.

Consider pronouns briefly. They should be a favored sector for a generalized study of social meanings, particularly of the entailment of roles and characteristics of participants in speech, since their character as "shifters" (Jakobson 1957) makes such roles inescapably part of their analysis, and such characteristics frequently intrude (sex gender, for example). Such has not been the case. In recent formal linguistics some theoreticians have analyzed pronouns almost out of existence, their integrity as factors in speech eviscerated. Even the structural status of the components defining pronouns has tended to remain conventional and ethnocentric to the European tradition. It appears, for example, that the category of personal pronouns must be taken as having, not three, but four basic members, defined by the possible combinations of presence or absence of reference to speaker, and presence or absence of reference to hearer. Our familiar "first person" is of course [+speaker, −hearer], our "second person" [−speaker, +hearer], and our "third person" [−speaker, −hearer]. There is also a "fourth person," the inclusive person, defined as [+speaker, +hearer], and in a language such as Aymara of Bolivia it is explicitly treated the same as the others, taking a plural in exactly the same way (cf. Hymes 1972e). (Such a case shows that there is still a good deal remaining to be explored in the "surface" structures of languages, incidentally, most formal theory recently having tended to take them for granted, or ride roughshod over them).

Sapir's 1915 article on "Abnormal Types of Speech in Nootka" remains a classic introduction to the general subject of person-implication in languages, and Jakobson's invention of a method for specifying person-implication of verbal categories (1957) remains largely undeveloped by others (but cf. Hymes 1961c.) (Sapir's title is unfortunately misleading, in that his article is not restricted to Nootka, and the types of speech are not in themselves abnormal, but expressions of Nootka judgments of the "abnormal" character of various dialect groups and kinds of person).

Let us consider further the component of sex gender. When it appears in personal pronouns (almost always in "third person" pronouns, Tunica being a rare exception in making it in the "second person"), it is treated matter of factly. Our English pronouns ("he," "she" etc.) are that way. When it appears in obligatory elements of word-classes, as in nouns in German, French, Russian, or Wasco, it may attract some interest, and debate as to the extent to which it is referentially active and real, some preferring to stress the arbitrary cases, others insisting on the conversational and poetic realities. When sex gender appears, not as a morphemic component, but as an implicit dimension for the selection of alternate morphemic shapes or word-forms), not themselves marking gender, it is singled out as "men's and women's speech," even though in important part it acts like pronouns and noun-classes, both men and women keeping it straight, and employing both when telling stories, as in Koasati. Invoking the complementary distribution of the alternates, with respect to sex roles, saves the simplicity and referential unity of the description.

To judge from the linguistic literature, then, there are certain languages that have the interesting property of sex-gender in pronouns and even in nouns. (Nineteenth-century classifiers of languages sometimes thought this so impressive a property of language as to divide the world between those languages with it and without it). There are a few languages, mostly American Indian, mostly obsolescent or extinct (Gros Ventre, Koasati, Yana), in which a few or many forms differ according to sex-role of speaker (and sometimes hearer). To leave the matter there is tantamount to postulating that such a fundamental property of social life as sex role has no verbal expression in most of the world.

The mistake is rather like that of nineteenth-century scholars who essentially took the makeup of the verb as the basis for a typology of languages as wholes, or of scholars who would seek to understand case relations on the basis only of languages in which such relationships take the form of nominal affixes. The error is to take a part for the whole, and to identify an underlying function with a particular manifestation. Just as with syntactic relations and meanings, so also with social relations and meanings in languages: one must be able to start with the underlying, universal features and ask *where* and *how* they are expressed. One would start with the assumption that sex role finds verbal expression (as the possibility of mimicry attests), and ask where and how—if not in morphemes, or alternants of morphemes or word-forms, then perhaps in characteristic intonations, lexical selections, initial particles, syntactic choices, discourse structures. Only on the basis of descriptions of this kind can one arrive at a general theory. Some linguists, misled by the cases in which a social meaning, or function, appears as a peculiarity of certain languages or regions, have called such matters "marginal," and marginal they remain, of course, if language continues to be treated as if it were organized only around the function of reference. The fact remains that the range of ways, and the extent to which, meanings such as sex role find verbal expression must be known, if there is to be an accurate inventory of the meanings universal to languages, and explanation of the forms they take in specific cases.

The logic of pursuing what is intrinsic to a given language, so that it opens up a parameter of general linguistics, is complemented by another, the logic of pursuing what is extrinsic to a given language, so that it also opens up a parameter of general linguistics. In this chapter I have concentrated on the first logic, in the hope of making what may appear obvious into something inescapable. A general functional approach on jointly linguistic and ethnographic bases, must nevertheless consider the second, complementary logic of inquiry as well.

The notion of "functions" is often taken to be entirely external. Linguists analyze what language is, structure, so to say, and others may then analyze what language does, i.e., function. There is an important element of truth in this viewpoint. Consider the use of a language to conceal information from parties ignorant of it, as with the use of Navaho interlocutors to transmit military messages in the World Wars, or the decision of immigrant parents not to teach their native language to their children, so that they can retain it for private communications among themselves. Nothing specific to the structure of the language is involved, but only the fact that certain persons know it and others do not. There are many such phenomena, and it is fair to put as a criterion of relevance to linguistic analysis, as does Greenberg (1968: 133), that use be found to have consequences for the content and organization of languages.

There is an important sense, then, in which one might distinguish between functions *of* language (properties extrinsic to the analysis of language itself), and functions *in* language (properties intrinsic to the analysis of language).

Let us call such functions as can be entirely extrinsic to the makeup of a language *uses* of it. The heart of the matter is that we will not be able to understand uses, if we should assume that some uses can be set aside as always extrinsic. There is reason to think that the relation between the makeup of a language and a use is problematic, requiring to be determined. Take concealment. It may be accomplished extrinsically, by use of a language, any language, known to the communicating parties and not to those from whom they wish to conceal what they say. It may be accomplished also by one or another creative aspect of language use that affects language intrinsically. The resources of a language may be *selected* in such a way as to prevent others from comprehending (veiled allusion may become a conventional genre, and even an art; parents often invoke such a method, so that it becomes a recognizable style, in archness of intonation as well as in lexical selection). Or, the resources of a language may be *augmented*, through the invention of a code or form of speech disguise (Conklin 1959), such that operations of substitution, addition, deletion, and permutation give rise to novel word-shapes.

If one is concerned to understand the workings of concealment in language, then, one has to consider a range of cases, from purely extrinsic use to intrinsic uses. Explanation of extrinsic use would involve the availability of a second language known to some and not to others, how such a means of communication was at hand; explanation of intrinsic use would involve the motivation for, but also the mechanism of, specific organizations, and even inventions, of linguistic means. In short, if we are willing to set aside some uses as just (extrinsic) uses, others are associated with what appears to be a creative aspect of language use, quite analogous to the provision of novel sentences for situations requiring them; one has here to do with provision of novel styles and derived codes.

A general type of use, then, such as concealment, is not just a problem to the social scientist or student of modes of communication. Insofar as it involves a creative aspect it becomes a problem in linguistics. The analysis of some languages will require identification of styles or codes made use of for concealment, if only to set them apart. (An English grammar that treated pig-Latin forms indiscriminately with others would be rather awkward.) If linguistic theory is to be more than a theory of the minimal form of grammars, then one will have to consider the factors that cause concealment to take the form of choice of language in some cases, choice of means within a language in other cases, and invention of novel means in yet others.

Again, consider hatred or avoidance, as a social meaning that one language may come to have for users of another. After World War II, German has had that meaning for some in Holland. That in itself is a wholly extrinsic fact. But German and Dutch are of course related languages, and the Dutch attitude may come to have intrinsic consequences, with speakers aware of features of both languages favoring features, and directions of change, in Dutch that make it less like German, rather than more. (Many Dutch speakers take pride in details of pronunciation, such as the fricative sound corresponding to the 'ch' in words spelled like "Scheveringen," the first three letters corresponding to [sx-], not to 'sh-', as a German in wartime trying to pass as a Dutch speaker might think. In Puerto Rico after World War II some speakers began to disfavor the hitherto prestigeful Castilian sound 'th,' because it had become associated with the influx of Americans who had been taught it in the States. Attitudes, in other words, may appear to be an extrinsic factor, and certainly are studied as such by many social scientists. Yet social meanings, even if caused contingently, become a factor in subsequent change within a language —Cf. Labov's important studies on social causes of sound change (1973a, 1973b). Labov's focus on a classic linguistic problem of change unfortunately leads him to underestimate grossly the pervasiveness of social meaning in language; a useful complement is found in Blom and Gumperz 1972, where the focus is on *maintenance* of distinctive phonological features.

Most linguists would probably grant the intrinsic effects of use most readily with regard to such types as standard languages, creoles and pidgins. The available set of categories for types of language in this regard, unfortunately, is too gross and ad hoc to be adequate. It has grown up through recognition of one or another social role, in this or that circumstance, but little has been done to establish a complete and comparable set of categories. The overlap among such categories as koine, lingua franca, creole, literary language, vernacular, etc., from the standpoint of a single language (say, Sranan Tongo) shows that it is necessary to analyze such categories in terms of underlying dimensions, and combinations of features. Moreover, one must generalize these dimensions and features, the processes and functions which they designate, and investigate them with regard to *all* languages, not just the salient representative cases. The processes of simplification and complication of surface structure, for example, and of reduction and expansion of content, and restriction and extension in scope of use, together serve to define the parameters of pidginization and creolization of languages (cf. Hymes 1971e), but they are not limited in occurrence to pidgins and creoles, nor always compresent. They need to be examined in other kinds of case as well, in relation to the needs they serve. Again, the four community functions of separatism, integration, prestige, and frame of reference, postulated for standard languages by some Czech linguists (cf. Garvin 1959) are not limited to standard languages, nor always compresent, and need to be examined in other kinds of case as well (cf. Hymes 1966b).

The generalization of such processes and functions to all languages, investigation of the form they take in languages generally, will help explain past and ongoing change, and present makeup of languages, since, even where the origin of the process

or function is external, there are internal consequences. This
challenge will be welcome, of course, only insofar as the goals of
linguistic theory are taken to include explanation of the makeup
attributable to a generically human mind.

Using Universals

As formulated by Chomsky (1965), the search for universals
is a search for "explanatory adequacy." Adequacy of explanation
consists of justifying the form of particular grammars by what is
universal in language, and, one hopes, innate in the human mind.
The use of universals, then, is to decide among possible alternative grammars, and to shed light on a facet of human nature.

Description and theory of the sort advocated in this chapter
will of course also entail universals, having to do with stylistic
features, elements, and relationships, and social meanings (something of this has just been suggested with regard to phonology).
The universals will have the same uses, constraining choice among
alternative grammars, and shedding light on a facet of human
nature. There will be another use as well. Chomsky's mode of
explanation can be termed "essential"; there is an "existential"
or "experiential" mode of explanation as well. The point of the
first is to explain diverse expressions by finding a unity among,
or behind, them. The point of the second is to explain the existence of diversity.

Notice that the diversity of languages ought to be surprising
to a theory that considers human beings to be "programmed," as
it were, to realize universals involuntarily, and that considers
departure from universals in languages to involve "costs." The
universal acceptance of such "costs" ought to cry out for explanation. There must be powerful forces at work, other than innate
ones, to account for the variety of structures that languages do
display. Discovery of underlying connections does not really
explain the diversity after all. It adds underlying connections, but
it does not (as some seem to assume) erase or make trivial the
specific realities. Put another way: if one is truly interested in the
creative aspect of language use, one ought to take an interest in
what is created. It is rather as if a student of music, having analyzed a synthesizer, satisfied himself that it could produce any
sound wanted or usable in music, and left to others interest in
music itself.

If we are to understand at all the role of language in human
life, we cannot merely postulate it, we must investigate it. To
investigate it, we need to understand the full set of verbal means

available to persons, to members of a speech community. Broadly speaking, a community's verbal means are to be understood as the product of three interacting factors: *provenance*—the historical tradition(s) within which means have been inherited; *human nature*—the universal constraints on means due to the character of mankind as a species, the nature of the human mind being a major, but not exclusive part; the powers and limits of hearing, the capacity of the organs used in speech, noncognitive dimensions of human nature, all play a part; and *use*—the purpose to which verbal means are put.

The interaction of these factors determines the creation and organization of verbal means in terms of functions *in* speech, which is our main concern here. There is a further point to be made, however, and an important one, regarding functions *of* speech. As has been noted with regard to the speech community (ch. 4), a common mistake has been made through much of the course of linguistic theory, in that function has been equated with structure, functional invariance being taken for granted. Thus Whorf's type of linguistic relativity, concerned with the organization of linguistic means into fashions of speaking, took for granted that diverse fashions of speaking had all the same function, namely, to express and shape cognitive orientation. While Whorf's work to develop semantic description and characterization of languages must be applauded, his functional assumption, shared by others, cannot stand. One and the same fashion of speaking may have quite different cognitive consequences, depending on the circumstances of its acquisition, and its place in the linguistic repertoire of a person and a community (cf. Hymes 1966b). Similarly, Chomsky takes for granted that the organization of linguistic means in a formal grammar can be called "competence," and attributed to speakers as knowledge possessed by them. Just as with Whorf's fashions of speaking, however, the relation between an analysis of linguistic data, in and by itself, and actual properties of persons, is problematic. Whether it is world-view, or common competence, inferences from linguistic analysis require ethnography. The plurality of possible functional statuses makes a functional perspective necessarily prior, if we are to say something about persons, as well as languages.

The use of universals, then, is not to extricate language, as abstract mind, from human history, but to enrich our understanding of history. The abstract potentialities of language, the indubitable common properties of all languages, the contingencies of interactions among kinds of provenance, human nature, and kinds of use—one seeks to weave such things into a general theory of language, because people themselves are never abstract mind, but participants in specific communities, changing, and in need of change.

GRAMMAR AGAIN

Most linguists probably regard social and stylistic matters as lying beyond grammar, and as more complex than grammar. I have argued that grammar is perhaps more complex and difficult, when pursued to the point of fine detail. Grammar appears to be the simpler matter only when its abstraction from stylistic and social matters is taken for granted. A "taxonomic" grammar that stops with the patent uniformities of a language can be done on the principles, excluding social factors, of Chomsky (1965), but not a grammar that engages the actual knowledge and abilities of speakers. When the reasons for excluding social factors are critically examined, and when one realizes that such factors cannot be consistently excluded, any attempt to deal with them in a principled way begins to make formal grammar appear to be, not the first, but the last step, in linguistic description and theory.[4] The first step appears as ethnography of speaking, specifically, description of organization of linguistic means in styles of speech in terms of the functional matrix of speaking in a community.

To say this is tantamount to conceiving linguistics itself as sociolinguistic in nature, and this is indeed the conclusion to which I believe one must come. It does not follow that linguistics has no other nature—formal models, psycholinguistic experiments, philological analyses, comparative reconstructions, etc., remain unchallenged, as avenues of insight. I do conclude that linguistics, as a descriptive discipline, as a descriptive, empirical discipline— and no school of thought disputes that it is partly such—finds itself on the threshold of a sociolinguistic conception of itself. I have argued that it is essential to linguistics that it cross over the threshold; that development is equally essential to what is now considered "sociolinguistic" research. Sociolinguistic research cannot develop independently of linguistics. Although some problems require a minimum of linguistic training (studies of alternation between two grossly distinct languages, for example), generality and explanation cannot be achieved on so limited a basis

4. Cf. the still relevant observations of Ferguson (1963: 116): "the successes of the past decades were most spectacular in the treatment of limited corpora of homogeneous data. . . this kind of language material represents only the exceptional situation, the special case, . . . an adequate theory of linguistics . . . must be able to cope with the complex reality of interpenetrating styles, dialects and languages extending out both in social space and time."

(cf. ch. 4 on "code-switching"). A sociolinguistic inquiry must be prepared to identify any feature of speech, for any feature may prove to have relevance to a general dimension of social meaning. Scholars of various backgrounds may master linguistics sufficiently to put it to use, and such mastery should be encouraged; it may indeed contribute additional skills and insights. But there must also be participation of linguists, to provide training, and for training to be effective, the participant linguists must regard it as relevant to linguistics itself. In any case, sociolinguistics cannot be simply a use of the results of linguistic descriptions, but must itself be in part a mode of linguistic description. Its linguistics must not be secondhand or second best.

Some linguists may grant the general argument, yet hold back, from a false impression of what explicit attention to the functional matrix of language entails. In proposing to add something, a new approach is often misunderstood as proposing to add everything imaginable; calling for some change, it may be mistaken as intending to change all. (It may mistake itself in these respects). But though the ultimate consequences of a sociolinguistic approach may be far-reaching, the immediate consequences are to carry forward, and to give a principled basis to, concerns already arising within linguistics itself. Bloomfield's view that the progress of semantics required scientific analysis of everything denotable has been recognized as mistaken (cf. Haugen 1957, Weinreich 1963). It is equally mistaken to think that sociolinguistic description must wait upon, or immediately entail, a complete sociology. Linguistic description does come to need specific knowledge of the natural and social worlds of the users of language, but the relationship is dialectic, not passive. Pursuit of linguistic analysis brings into focus the particular cultural knowledge and social relationships from whose standpoint the organization of linguistic means must be viewed, as much as does ethnography. Speech styles, verbal repertoires, and rules of speaking may appear a vasty deep, but they are in fact finite. Their strangeness (empirically, in a given case, and in nature, for many linguists) should not be confused with absence of structure.

To reiterate: the descriptions we need cannot just make use of the results of independent linguistic descriptions of the ordinary sort. It is a counsel of permanent insolvency to say that sociolinguistic description (or its nominal equivalents) must wait upon the perfection of formal grammatical theory (as in Chomsky 1965) or concern itself with a subset of the output of an ordinary grammar (as in Werner 1966). As we have seen, the structures disclosed by a functional perspective entail novel elements and relationships, an organization of sounds, form, and meanings that partly cuts across, and goes beyond, ordinary grammar. Sociolinguistics must be itself a mode of linguistic description.

Sociolinguistic inquiry will not succeed, will not make its potential contribution to either science or society, if it does not realize itself as a mode of description. What such a mode of description will be like has been adumbrated in earlier chapters (esp. chs. 2 and 4), and earlier in this chapter; more is said in the remaining chapters (chs. 9, 10). As a development out of linguistics, the leading concerns of such a mode of description can be said to be with speech styles, defined by rules of co-occurrence, and with the relations of use underlying their contrast and occurrence with respect to each other, defined by rules of alternation (see further in ch. 10). As a development within ethnography, the leading concern can be said to be to establish the functional matrix of speaking in a community. The two developments merge in rules of alternation, that is, relationships of use.

It is vital to understand and act on this last point. It will never be enough to extend the scope of linguistic description by recognition of stylistic features and elements and patterns, and social meanings, if such recognition amounts only to additions to grammar in the conventional mold. There must be recognition of a new principle of description, a novel fundation for the organization of linguistic means. If I go on about this point, it is because the notion of such a principle, in the sense of a novel mode of organization of linguistic means, has been broached several times in linguistics, and yet has never been carried through. Always the conception of such a principle has stopped short of a break with ordinary grammar, remaining dependent upon it.

From the standpoint of semantic organization, Whorf (1941: 92) wrote:

> They (cognitive orientations mediated by language) do not depend so much upon *any one system* [e.g., tense or nouns— Whorf's italics] within the grammar as upon the ways of analyzing and reporting experience which have become fixed in the language as integrated 'fashions of speaking' and which cut across the typical grammatical classifications, so that such a 'fashion' may include lexical, morphological, syntactic, and otherwise systematically diverse means coordinated in a certain frame of consistency.

Had Whorf lived (he died before publication of the essay), he might have developed his notion of "fashions of speaking" as a mode of description of what can be called "cognitive styles" (cf. Hymes 1961c), although his previous statements of the design of a grammar, from a semantic standpoint, do not themselves show this.

Whorf wrote from within the effort in the Sapir tradition in the 1930s to develop more adequate semantic analyses of basic categories. At the end of a succeeding decade, the major methodological statement of American linguistic description mentioned without regard to cognitive function (Harris 1951: 10):

> . . . differences in style or fashion of speech, in respect to which whole utterances or even discourses are consistent. Although differences of style can be described with the tools of descriptive linguistics, their exact analysis involves so much detailed study that they are generally disregarded.

While there are meritorious exceptions, it is fair to say that Harris' description has remained accurate, across dramatic changes in approach within grammar itself. Stylistic features and their social meanings have been considered only when inescapably intrusive in grammar proper, conceived as based on referential function. It is not, one must add, that the need of "detailed study" has frightened linguists away; it is hard to imagine that stylistic description could be more detailed than ordinary grammar has become. The explanation for neglect of the possibility correctly and fairly stated by Harris must lie in the persistence of an assumption about the nature of organization, of structure, in language that made the possibility seem not a real one, or at least not a relevant one. Pike (1967: 186) presents a telling example:

> Failure to see that meanings can vary non-emically within a morpheme has led to some conclusions different from those reached here. Note Bloch: 'According to our assumptions, if a verb that belongs to a given conjugation differs in meaning or connotation, however slightly, from a verb with a phonemically identical base that belongs to another type, the verbs are different morphemes; the *shine* whose preterit is *shined* is a different verb from the *shine* whose preterit is *shone* and by the same argument the *show* whose participate is *shown* is a different verb from the *show* whose participle is *showed*' [references omitted here]; also: 'The form *n't* is best regarded as a separate morpheme, not as an alternant of the full form *not*. The two forms contrast, at least stylistically and in their connotations, in such phrases as *I cannot go : I can't go*. . . .' [Pike continues:] It is to Nida that we are indebted for the first major suggestion towards the solution of this problem in terms of submorphemic variation in reference to the sociolinguistic environment . . .; he uses the same approach to avoid Bloch's conclusions that /haev, hev, ev, v/ [i.e., variants of *have*] are distinct morphemes. . . .

Notice that sociolinguistic environment is introduced only to avoid the unpalatable results of rigorously carrying through a principle that both parties share, namely, that there is only one, undifferentiated kind of contrastive relevance and basis of linguistic structure. Sociolinguistic considerations are used only as context for treating perceived differences in meaning as variants, conditioned, and *below* the level, or within the level, of referential units (morphemes). The considerations are introduced ad hoc, and are not provided for in principle or systematically investigated. Bloch, moreover, was half right; the forms do contrast. Nida and Pike were half-right too, of course; the contrast is not one between morphemes. Nida and Pike save the referential appearances, the unity and integrity of the morphemes, but neither approach grasps the admitted differences of meaning as evidence of a second kind of contrastive ("emic") relevance, underlying structure too.

This limitation persists to the uttermost threshold of breakthrough into an adequate functional conception. One might expect that Pike's views of the nature of meaning (cf. Pike 1967, section 16.5, p. 609), of the systemic nature of *la parole* (13.81, p. 536), and of a language as a system of systems, as against a "monosystemic nonfield view" (15.336, p. 597) would lead to the kind of conception presented in this chapter. To some extent, such is the case; cf. his treatment of contrastively relevant ways of speaking with regard to phonological features (8.441, p. 311; 8.61, p. 323; 13.81, p. 536; 13.85, p. 543), and his recognition of them in morphology (6.56, p. 160; 15:2, p. 582; 6.91, p. 186—this last having been discussed just above). And in constructing a matrix to show the sectors of language, and the dimensions determining differences in regard to them, Pike does include a fourth column, "Stylistic (Systemic)" among the latter (see Table 3, "Trimodal breakdown of emic classes of syntagmemes", 11.44, pp. 463–64). He does not, however, have a fourth row with the set of sectors determined. There the trimodal schema (phonology, grammar, lexicon) is preserved. (I almost imagine that if only Christian theology and Western culture had conceived of a quadrune God, Pike, to whom the correspondence between trinity and trimodal is significant, would surely have founded a decade or two ago the descriptive approach that is advocated here).

The connection between linguistic organization and social life is broken at this point. Style does not link linguistic features with social life through a novel mode of organization; rather, it encloses linguistic features within grammar. Styles are conceived as "nonsimultaneous congruent systems" (p. 132), their features as "locally-free but systematically-conditioned variants" (8.441, p. 311), i.e., as sources of variation recognized in order to treat phonemes (morphemes, etc.) as unitary on a higher level (that of "hypercongruent system" (8. 6., p. 323). Thus, when meanings in addition to the straightforwardly referential are considered, (16.6, pp. 610ff.), Pike resorts to a dichotomy between "segmental" and "subsegmental" meanings (as seen in discussion of Bloch). The former ("denotational") are explicitly articulated, discussable by speakers; the latter are considered to be vague dispositions, forming the "background unarticulated field within which articulate meaning takes place" (p. 611). The treatment in this regard of the example of Bloomfield's child, who says "I'm hungry" to avoid going to bed, as subsegmental, rather than as an opening into pragmatic analysis of speech acts, is indicative (cf. ch. 1 on this example). The concluding chapter, "The Context of Behavior" (ch. 17), does not carry forward the methodology of the opening chapters, where verbal and nonverbal behavior were to be integrated in the analysis of integral events. It falls back on parallels and analogues between linguistic systems and social systems, analyzed disjointly. The trimodal schema for meanings (subsegmental meanings complementing supra- and plainly segmental meanings), and the trimodal schema for structure (phonology, grammar, lexicon) are preserved, at the expense of articulating the actual relations between linguistic form and social context. The crucial failure, that leads to a conclusion so in contradiction to initial intention, is the failure to find a method of description that actually does lead linguistics into context. And one way to describe the failure is to say that styles are recognized insofar as they are results of rules of co-occurrence, among linguistic features, and even among linguistic features and contextual features, but no further; they are not investigated as themselves a form of organization of language subject to contrast within contexts.

It does not suffice if styles are recognized as an aspect of organization in grammar, but are treated solely as successive modifications of an ordinary grammar, established without reference to ethnographic validation of stylistic relationships. Such an approach invites an a priori and arbitrary interpretation of stylistic relationships, and amounts to a formalization of the view of style as departure and deviation (cf. ch. 4). Thus, Wescott (1962: 61–62) identifies and labels seven styles in the West African language, Bini, in terms of successive additional modifications of the form of words due to speech tempo. The unmodified form is called "ceremonious," followed by "deliberate, slow, ordinary, rapid, hurried, slurred." The modifications may be correctly observed, and the criteria invoked are clear cut, but Wescott remarks:

> By native speakers little note is taken of speech-tempo—except in the oblique sense that ceremonious speech is often said to sound "Ishan" and slurred speech "Yoruba" (two other languages in the region).

In other words, besides the median "ordinary," presumably, speakers appear to discriminate only two poles among the other six postulated levels of style.

Again, Klima (1964) discriminates four English styles in terms of extensional rules accounting for differences in phrase structure and order of transformations that affect the marking of case in pronouns. As with Wescott, the criteria are wholly internal to the grammar; the concern is to find the formally most economical statement of the relations between "systems" or styles.

In each case (Wescott, Klima) one form of grammatical statement in a single domain is taken as a norm, and other phenomena are treated as successive departures. The reality of the styles to speakers of the language is not validated (though it is labelled by Wescott); the social meaning of styles, and rules governing choice among them, are not investigated. To investigate these things, of course, would appropriately test the validity of the postulated styles. The test might confirm them, of course; it might also indicate that the styles present in the community cut across particular domains of grammar and phonology. The net effect of the "successive departures" approach is the same as with Pike's "envelope" analysis of style, the difference being that Pike saves the referential unity of ordinary description by invoking complementary distribution, whereas in these cases it is saved in terms of formal derivation.

The kind of conception of style that is required has been broached, to be sure, by Joos (1959), who makes it the specific condition of stylistic analysis that it crosscut the usual compartments of a grammar. Joos, however, did not follow up his conception with any indication of an empirical approach to the identification and analysis of styles. It has been left for scholars working within a sociolinguistic approach (Gumperz and Ervin-Tripp, see ch. 10) to do this. Much more remains to be done. And if the step into ethnography is essential, the consequences will be carried back into the formal analysis of syntax itself, as the next chapter seeks to demonstrate.

Chapter 9

Syntactic Arguments and Social Roles: Quantifiers, Keys, and Reciprocal vs. Reflexive Relationships

Much recent work in linguistics has recognized the necessity of taking into account characteristics of context, especially of the participants in discourse (e.g., Firth 1935; Gunter 1966; Halliday 1970; Hymes 1964a: 38, 1964b: 3, 1970: 130; Jakobson 1957, 1970; Labov 1970, section 4; R. Lakoff 1969, 1972, 1973; Nida 1945; Pike 1967: sections 1.4, 2.73; Sapir 1933 (SWES 11–2); Tyler 1966; Wheeler 1967; Whiteley 1966).[1] In sociology the work of Harold Garfinkel, Erving Goffman, Harvey Sacks, Emanuel Schegloff and others has shown the necessity of taking in account

---

1. This chapter was first published as "Syntactic Arguments and Role Relationships: Are There Some of the Latter in Any of the Former?" in a book that is being edited by E. Polomé, M. Jazayery, and W. Winter (The Hague: Mouton and Co., n.v., forthcoming). It was also distributed as Working Paper Number 7 in the series, Texas Working Papers in Sociolinguistics (Austin: Department of Anthropology, University of Texas, 1972). The title has been revised here to indicate the main notions dealt with, and the last part of the exposition has been recast. In contributing to this Festschrift for Arch Hill (Professor of English at the University of Texas) I thought of a seminar on literature and linguistics he helped conduct, and in which I sat, as a student in both the Linguistic Institute and School of Letters that summer. I was grateful to him for associating the rigor of linguistics with the richness of language, at a time, some twenty years ago, when application of linguistics to literature seemed frighteningly mechanistic to many literary scholars, and suspiciously unscientific to many linguists.

characteristics of discourse itself. These two directions of research have increasingly converged, but not quite joined. For the
linguist, analysis of social relationships is typically informal, a
matter of ad hoc contexts (but cf. Fought 1972 on Goffman's notion of *with*). For the sociologist, analysis of texts is typically
informal, a matter of ad hoc content (but cf. certain observations
of Schegloff 1968, and Goffman 1971 on remedial interchange).

I shall try to show that more explicit consideration of social
relationships, as an aspect of semantic analysis itself, may contribute to the understanding of both the presuppositions underlying sentences and the values underlying social relationships.

Consider the following four English sentences:
1. If you eat some candy, I'll whip you.
2. If you eat any candy, I'll whip you.
3. If you eat some spinach, I'll give you ten dollars.
4. If you eat any spinach, I'll give you ten dollars.

These sentences are taken from Robin Lakoff's article, "Some
Reasons Why There Can't Be Any *some-any* Rule" (1969: 609–10).
The first pair constitute (4a), the second pair (4b), in her dis-
cussion.

Lakoff abstracts her argument as follows:

> Semantic notions—such as presupposition, speaker's and
> hearer's beliefs about the world, and previous discourse—must be
> taken into account in a complete treatment of the distribution of
> *some* and *any* in conditional, negative, and interrogrative sen-
> tences. Syntactic conditions alone will not account for the fact
> that, in certain sentence types, the two forms occur with
> different meanings. [608]

Lakoff's point is that the two sentences in each of these and
other pairs differ in meaning, yet the only surface difference between the members of each pair is that one has the quantifier
some, and the other *any.* She proceeds to infer that in certain
types of sentences the choice between *some* and *any* depends on
factors other than the superficial syntactic configuration in which
the quantifier is found.

> In questions of certain types, the use of *some* implies that the
> speaker hopes for, or at least anticipates a positive answer; the
> use of *any* implies the expectation of a negative answer, or at least
> a neutral feeling on the part of the speaker. (E.g., "Who wants
> some beans?": "Who wants any beans?") [609]. In conditions . . .
> cases like 4a and 4b . . . are not real conditions; they are, rather,
> threats or promises. In these, again, the emotional bias of the
> speaker comes into play, in the choice between *some* and *any.*
> A threat goes with *any,* since usually someone threatens someone
> else to prevent an undesired action; a promise goes with *some,*
> for a similar reason. [612]

The four sentences of concern here are interpreted in these words:

> In 4a, the first sentence [1] could, I think, only be spoken to someone who wanted to be whipped. The speaker in the second sentence [2], which is much more normal, makes the assumption that the hearer does not want to be whipped: this is a punishment. With *any*, the interpretation of the sentence is that the speaker does not want the hearer to eat the candy. Hence it matches up correctly with the apodosis, a threat of punishment. With *some*, the interpretation is that the speaker wants the hearer to eat the candy; hence the apodosis can't be interpreted as punishment. The sentence can be interpreted as meaningful only if there is an implication of perversion on the part of one of the persons involved.
>
> In 4b, on the other hand, just the opposite is true. The first sentence [3] is the normal one; it assumes that the person addressed wants ten dollars, as most people would, and is offering [sic: being offered?] a reward for doing something the speaker wants him to do. In the second sentence [4] the only possible interpretation is that, for some reason, the person addressed does not want to receive ten dollars, and that this sentence is a threat, parallel to the second sentence of 4a [611].

We have, then, two "normal" sentences and two sentences (1, 4) whose acceptance is taken to strain somewhat the imagination.

To many readers (and hearers) of English, sentence 4 will appear normal quite without strain, not as a threat, but as a promise: It is so unlikely that you will eat spinach that I feel entirely safe in promising you ten dollars if you do. Such sentences are common. We might dub them the "I'll eat my hat" type.

More generally, it is not the case that the meaningfulness of 1 requires an implication of perversion, and that the only possible interpretation of the addressor's assumption about the addressee in 4 is that the latter does not want ten dollars. Beyond the factor of SPEECH ACT PRESUPPOSITION, involving the status of a sentence as something like a *promise* or *threat* (or a guarantee or a warning), there is an additional factor of social meaning, which may be called KEY, involving whether in its conventional intention the sentence is to be taken as *mock* or at *face value*.[2] And the working out of the implication of key as a factor leads to recognition of yet another factor of social meaning, which has to do with the internal role relationships in terms of which a

2. Harvey Sacks has recently stressed the fundamental importance of this factor (cf. Labov 1970: 82, n. 44). I first learned it from Ray Birdwhistell and the writing of Gregory Bateson. As seen below, the notion of "sincerity" itself seems to require further discrimination.

sentence is construed. As we shall see, more than one such construction is possible.

As to key: notice that the contrast does not seem to be quite the same thing as a contrast between *insincere* and *sincere* (Searle 1969:62). The speaker is not taking responsibility for having an intention, in both the insincere and the mock case, but in the latter (unlike the former) the speaker is not purporting to have the intention. The contrast *mock: face value* thus appears to cut across *insincere: sincere*. Further, Searle makes the status of an utterance as promise independent, or neutral, with regard to sincerity or insincerity; the latter contrast is a question of actual intention—of motive, in Skinner's terms (1971). Insincere promises are promises nevertheless, because of what they purport (of their conventional intention, in Skinner's terms). Sincerity conditions, then, as a matter of actual intentions and states, are at a step removed from the essentially cultural analysis in which we, like Lakoff, Searle, and Skinner, are engaged. The interpretation of an utterance as mock or face value, on the other hand, seems inseparable from, and indeed indispensable to, the analysis of speaking as customary behavior. (Cf. Hymes 1967: 24, 1972: 62— although in those papers "serious" was used for conventional intention, and hence ambiguously in retrospect, given specialization of the term "serious" now to motive.)

Notice also that terms such as "promise" and "threat" can only be applied informally here. One might speak instead, or also, of "guarantee" and "warning." (I owe awareness of this point to Bruce Fraser.) In the absence of a fully worked out analysis of the English taxonomy of speech acts in this domain, we cannot be sure whether the availability of a terminological distinction reflects a difference in speech act, as such, or additional aspects of meaning, having to do with topic, context, style level, etc. And of course we should not expect any language, including English, to be a perfect metalanguage for itself, in this or any other respect. This is a principal reason why an independent sociological analysis of conventional acts is essential. Linguistics cannot itself, through analysis of the "folk analysis," or "homemade model," embodied in a language's terminology for speech acts, expect to discover the existence and nature of all the acts performed in a community through speech.

Because of the additional factor of key, the two "nonnormal" sentences (1, 4), then, may be either a threat or a promise, a warning or a guarantee, or the like. Each sentence may have either a mock or a face value and a positive or negative component. In other words, it is not only that sentences differing only in a single quantifier may yet differ in meaning. Sentences that *do not differ at all,* i.e., that have one and the same surface structure, are susceptible of at least two contrasting readings. In keeping with a standard form of argument (e.g., re "Flying planes can be dangerous"), the present case would seem to demonstrate that KEY (as conventional intention, not necessarily actual motive—cf. Skinner 1970, 1971), is a necessary part of the schema of interpretation underlying sentences. The interdependence of two broad types of function, or meaning, would seem to apply here as elsewhere in the analysis of language.

The reasoning behind this conclusion can be presented more clearly if we adopt a format for restating the relevant features of the sentences in question. Let X represent the protasis or condition of a sentence (e.g., "If you eat some candy"), and let Y represent the apodosis or conclusion (e.g., "I'll whip you").

Lakoff's analysis of the four sentences can now be given as the following four interpretations:

1. Addressee wants Y, Addressor wants X.
2. Addressee does not want Y, Addressor does not want X.
3. Addressee wants Y, Addressor wants X.
4. Addressee does not want Y, Addressor does not want X.

In this respect, of course, there are but two types of sentences (1, 3) and (2, 4). The further distinction in terms of "normal" (2, 3) vs. "abnormal" (1, 4) depends on *some* and *any* in relation to the customary wants of the participants and their community.

A somewhat more elaborate description of the interpretation of the sentences will help bring out the implications of key and role:

1. If you do something I want, I'll do something you want.
2. If you do something I don't want, I'll do something you don't want.
3. If you do something I want, I'll do something you want.
4. If you do something I don't want, I'll do something you don't want.

Notice now that the relation between participants (addressor, addressee), here *you, I;* condition and consequence (protasis, apodosis), here X, Y; and distribution of positive and negative evaluation, here *want, not want,* is permutable. In particular, the places of X and Y can be reversed. In terms of the format given first above, one may have, not only interpretations 1–4 above, but an addition.

1'. Addressee wants X, Addressor wants Y.
2'. Addressee does not want X, Addressor does not want Y.
3'. Addressee wants X, Addressor wants Y.
4'. Addressee does not want X, Addressor does not want Y.

In terms of the format given second above, one may have not only (1–4) above, but in addition the interpretations:

1′. If you do something you want, I'll do something I want.
2′. If you do something you don't want, I'll do something I don't want.
3′. If you do something you want, I'll do something I want.
4′. If you do something you don't want, I'll do something I don't want.

For the purpose of this argument it has been assumed that *some* takes only positive senses (excluding "negative") and that *any* takes only negative senses (excluding "positive"), as Lakoff implies. (Nor are possible questions as to the scope of the syntactic analysis itself considered.) Let us assume, as does Lakoff, that the normal cultural assumption or presupposition is that eating candy is positive, eating spinach negative, and that being whipped is negative, receiving ten dollars positive.

We have then two forms of interpretation for each of the sentences. With regard to 1, *If you eat some candy, I'll whip you,* interpretation 1 (If you do something I want, I'll do something you want) yields a *mock promise.* It is contrary to presupposition, as it were. It suggests that the addressee does not like candy and does like being whipped, and/or that the likelihood of either act is slight. In speech the mock promise would require intonation and voice quality suggesting mutual ingratiation. Interpretation 1′ (If you do something you want, I'll do something I want) yields a *face-value threat.* It is in accord with presupposition. If fits the assumption that the addressee likes candy, but not being whipped, and further suggests that the addressor does not want (his?) candy eaten, or does not want the addressee to eat (too much?) candy (sweets?) (before dinner?), and would be willing to punish.

With regard to 2, *If you eat any candy, I'll whip you,* interpretation 2 yields a *face-value threat,* in accord with presupposition just as 1′. Interpretation 2′ yields a *mock threat,* contrary to presupposition, just as 1, that to be carried off in speech would require intonation and voice qualities appropriate to the suggestion of mutual disinclination (of the addressee to eat candy, of the addressor to mind enough to punish for it)—i.e., If you eat candy (but you don't like candy), I'll whip you (but I don't like/wish to whip you).

With regard to 3, *If you eat some spinach, I'll give you ten dollars,* interpretation 3 yields a *face-value promise,* in accord with presupposition. It suggests that the addressee does not like spinach (indeed, some people do, but we are restricting ourself to cultural stereotypes for the moment), but would like to receive ten dollars; it suggests that the addressor wants some spinach eaten (by the addressee?), and, possibly, would not casually part with ten dollars. Interpretation 3' yields a *mock promise*, contrary to presupposition. It suggests that the addressee likes spinach (contrary, at least to stereotype), but would not mind ten dollars; possibly, it suggests also that the addressor is not particularly interested in having the addressee eat spinach, and in any case is eager to seize on any pretext for giving ten dollars (to the addressee?). In speech it could be carried off with intonation and voice qualities suggesting prospective mutual satisfaction.

With regard to 4, *If you eat my spinach, I'll give you ten dollars*, interpretation 4 yields a *mock threat*, contrary to presupposition, that could be carried off in speech with intonation and voice qualities appropriate to mutual disinclination (here, to have spinach eaten, and to receive ten dollars). Interpretation 4' yields a *face-value promise*, in accord with presupposition.

In summary,

1. Mock promise
1'. Face-value threat
2. Face-value threat
2'. Mock threat
3. Face-value promise
3'. Mock promise
4. Mock threat
4.' Face-value promise

Thus, the cases judged a nonnormal promise (1) and a threat (4) respectively, are found instead to be interpretable as instances of the speech act contrary to that to which they were assigned. (Assuming a constant set of presuppositions is preserved—to change the set of presuppositions of course would require us to change the analysis of all the sentences, "normal" as well as nonnormal.)

All this is not to say that each interpretation is equally likely. Indeed, something along the lines of marked and unmarked meanings, or interpretations, can be discerned. This has been indicated in the remarks on intonation, although it must be remembered that normal intonation is itself an ingredient of meaning and interpretation. The key to the marked and unmarked interpretations would seem to involve what can be called a *reciprocal* vs. a *reflexive* construction of the role relationship between participants. Interpretations 1–4, of the type "If you do something I (do/don't) want, I'll do something you (do/don't) want" can be called reciprocal; interpretations 1'–4' of the type "If you do something you (do/don't) want, I'll do something I (do/don't) want" can be called reflexive.

Notice first that reciprocal and reflexive interpretations do not coincide with the status of a sentence as a speech act (threat, promise) or with the key of a sentence (mock, face-value). The two types of interpretation are distributed equally among both types of act and both kinds of key. Thus, threats comprise both 2, 4 and 1', 2' while promises comprise both 1, 3 and 3', 4'. Mock cases comprise both 1, 4 and 2', 3', while face-value cases comprise both 2, 3 and 1', 4'.

The two types are also of course distributed equally overall with regard to the two quantifiers; *any* is found in both 2, 4 and 2', 4', and *some* in both 1, 3 and 1', 3'. There is nevertheless a difference between the two types of interpretation with regard to quantifiers. The reciprocal cases are entirely *any* in the case of threat, and entirely *some* in the case of promise, whereas the reflexive cases are divided, with the mock threat having *any*, the mock promise *some*, but the face value threat *some*, the face value promise *any*.

These relationships can be seen in the following diagram:

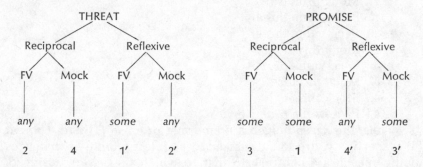

A further difference between the two types of interpretation can also be found in relationships involving the two parts of each sentence. If we consider the two quantifiers to have positive and negative values, following Lakoff (1969: 613), and indicate them with + and −; if we contrast the two types of act themselves, marking threat as − and promise as +; and if we mark the predicates of positive condition (eat candy) and positive consequence (receive ten dollars) with +, and the predicates of negative condition (eat spinach) and negative consequence (be whipped) with −, then the values for the several sentences could be entered at the bottom of the diagram given above, as follows:

2	4	1'	2'	3	1	4'	3'
+ −	− +	+ −	+ −	− +	+ −	− +	− +

A more useful arrangement, for our immediate purpose, is to align the values as follows, giving first culturally assumed values for the predicates of the protasis and apodosis, then the value for the quantifier, then the value for the speech act.

RECIPROCAL

	Protasis	Apodosis	Quantifier	Speech act	
1	+	−	+	+	(Mock promise)
2	+	−	−	−	(Face-value threat)
3	−	+	+	+	(Face-value promise)
4	−	+	−	−	(Mock threat)

REFLEXIVE

	Protasis	Apodosis	Quantifier	Speech act	
1′	+	−	+	−	(Face-value threat)
2′	+	−	−	−	(Mock threat)
3′	−	+	+	+	(Mock promise)
4′	−	+	−	+	(Face-value promise)

With the reciprocal interpretations, the relationships are rather straightforward. The quantifier and the act have invariably the same value (*some* with a promise, *any* with a threat). The quantifier has invariably the same value as the predicate of the apodosis (consequence), when the key value is face value, and the same key as the predicate of the protasis (condition) when the key is mock.

With reflexive interpretation, the relationships are more complex. The quantifier and the act have the same value only when the key is mock (*any* with threat in 2′, *some* with promise in 3′). In these cases the quantifier has the same value as the predicate of the apodosis, in contrast to what obtains with the reciprocal interpretation. When the key is face value, the quantifier and the act have opposite values (*some* with threat in 1′, *any* with promise in 4′). In these cases the quantifier has the same value as the predicate of the protasis, again in contrast to what obtains with the reciprocal interpretation.

The invariant relationships under the two interpretations can be summarized formulaicly, letting Pro = Protasis, Apo = Apodosis, Q = Quantifier, SpA = Speech Act, FV = Face value, and M = Mock. Under the reciprocal interpretation, $Q = SpA$, and $Q = Apo/FV$, $Q = Pro/M$ (or, if $Q = Apo$, then the key is FV, and if $Q = Pro$, then the key is M). Under the reflexive interpretation, it is not the quantifier, but the apodosis that covaries exactly with the speech act, so that $Apo = SpA$, and $Q = SpA/M$, $Q \neq Spa/FV$ (or, if $Q = SpA$, then the key is M, and if $Q \neq SpA$, then the key is FV).

The "paradigmatic" or "field" appproach being followed here (cf. Levi-Strauss 1963: 18)—the approach, really, of all serious structuralism—can be pushed further, as I shall now indicate, but the results approach the uninterpretable, so long as evidence is confined to the manipulation of sentences on a page or in a mind. With just such data, the approach is useful for the generation of

a full set of possibilities, but inadequate to determine their interpretation. For that, observation and analysis of actual conversation in spontaneous settings is required.

With that caution, notice now that the values of the protasis,
and apodosis (condition and consequence) need not be fixed in
opposition, as + −, or − +. One can consider sentences in which
both values are +, and sentences in which both values are −.
Thus, in terms of the reciprocal interpretation, one can have:

[+ +] 5. If you eat some candy, I'll give you ten dollars.
           [If you do what I want (which is conventionally +), I'll
           do what you want (which is conventionally +)]

       6. If you eat any candy, I'll give you ten dollars.
           [If you do what I don't want (conventionally +), I'll do
           what you don't want (conventionally +)]

[− −] 7. If you eat some spinach, I'll whip you.
           [If you do what I want (conventionally −), I'll do what
           you want (conventionally −)].

       8. If you eat any spinach, I'll whip you.
           [If you do what I don't want (conventionally −), I'll do
           what you don't want (conventionally −)]

In terms of the reflexive interpretation, one can have the same
surface sentences, and, as underlying descriptions, the counter-
parts:

[+ +] 5'. [If you do what you want (which is conventionally +),
            I'll do what I want (which is conventionally +)]

       6'. [If you do what you don't want (conventionally +), I'll
            do what I don't want (conventionally +)]

[− −] 7'. [If you do what you want (conventionally −), I'll do
            what I want (conventionally −)]

       8'. [If you do what you don't want (conventionally −), I'll
            do what I don't want (conventionally −)]

Charted along the same lines as before:

RECIPROCAL

	Protasis	Apodosis	Quantifier	Speech Act
5	+	+	+	
6	+	+	−	
7	+	−	+	
8	−	−	−	

REFLEXIVE

	Protasis	Apodosis	Quantifier	Speech Act
5'	+	+	+	
6'	+	+	−	
7'	−	−	+	
8'	−	−	−	

But how to interpret these formal possibilities in terms of speech act and key?

If the invariant relationships previously noted should hold for these sentences, then, under the reciprocal interpretation, where $Q = SpA$, one would take 5 and 7 as Promise, and 6 and 8 as Threat. But no automatic reading of key would be possible. $Q = Apo$, yes, as in cases of FV, but also $Q = Pro$, as in cases of M. (One could have taken $Q = Apo/FV$, but $Q \neq Apo/M$, in which case all these reciprocal cases would be FV, since Q is never not equal to Apo. That seems contrary to interpretations available for certain of the sentences, as suggested below, and contrary to expectations as to the general availability of contrast in key.) Without consideration of other aspects of the message, then, ambiguity results. On the other hand, under the reflexive interpretation, where $Apo = SpA$, one would take 5' and 6' as Promise, and 7' and 8' as Threat. Moreover, key is interpretable. Where $Q = SpA$, as in 5' and 7', the key is M, and where $Q \neq SpA$, as in 6' and 8', the key is FV.

In the cases of reciprocal interpretation, perhaps key can in fact be interpreted in terms of the positive or negative values of the predicates, so that 5 would be a Face-Value Promise in a tone of mutual ingratiation: you like eating candy, and I like giving away ten dollars—recalling lines in W. H. Auden's *For the Time Being; A Christmas Oratorio* (1945: 459) to the effect that "I like committing crimes; God likes forgiving them; Really, the world is admirably arranged." 7 would be a Mock Promise, in a tone of mutual disinclination or arrant improbability: you are as loth to eat spinach, which I do not want you to do, as I am loth to whip you, which you don't want me to do. 6 would be perhaps a Mock Threat, perhaps in a tone such as "If you are so naughty as not to resist the temptation to eat candy (a very likely event, since children such as you like candy), I shall just have to give you ten dollars, whether you like it or not—(ha ha)." 8 is perhaps a Face-Value Threat, perhaps in a tone such as "It may be highly unlikely that you would do something so unpleasant as to eat spinach, but if you do eat any spinach, perhaps just because I've told you not to, I'll whip you, just because I've told you not to." Here we obviously are extending ourselves beyond what the machinery suggested in this paper can take formally into account, although not beyond what, one hopes, further exploration of conversation will make it possible to take formally into account. Let us sum up the status of the additional sentences, 5–8 and 5'–8', letting glossing of the latter go by, and then return to the question of markedness by way of conclusion.

The additional sentences are as follows:
5. Face-Value Promise
6. Mock Threat
7. Mock Promise
8. Face-Value Threat
5'. Mock Promise
6'. Face-Value Promise
7'. Mock Threat
8'. Face-Value Threat

Lakoff's intepretations involved a predisposition to take construal in terms of reciprocal roles as normal and exclusive. A predisposition to take sentences at face value is also reflected. Her normal cases (2, 3) have just these two characteristics. The other two cases (1, 4) cause difficulty because the reciprocal interpretation is imposed upon them without consideration of the possibility of contrast in key.

Predisposition to interpret such sentences in terms of reciprocal roles probably is common in the United States and perhaps throughout English-speaking speech communities. Predisposition to take sentences at face value seems to me less common— the mock interpretation of 4 occurred to me immediately upon suggestion of difficulty with it, and I suspect that the mock : face value contrast is likely to occur readily to many others. I suspect, then, that adequate research would show that the reciprocal role interpretation is the common, unmarked one, but also that interpretation of sentences as mock, as well as at face value, is also likely.

We are dealing, of course, with cultural definitions of situation. Lakoff's point that interpretations depend upon cultural definitions opens up the possibility of different cultural definitions. It seems likely that communities may differ with regard to the likelihood or acceptability of a contrast between mock and face-value interpretation, in general and in regard to types of situation. Perhaps the personal communities of Lakoff and myself differ in this regard, at least within the situation of considering syntactic examples. In any case, her analysis makes clear that interpretation of such sentences depends upon cultural definitions of rewards and punishments, so that what is face value in one group need not be in another. Once the door is opened to contrast in key, one can see the need to determine not only such cultural definitions, but also norms for styles of speech. Mock utterances may be expectable in one group, even stereotyped to the point of losing any special force, and so rare in another group as to be momentarily uninterpretable as such in the flow of ordinary discourse. Much work in the ethnography of speaking is needed on these points.

With regard to the *mock : face value* dimension, then, there is a respect in which the mock cases appear more complex, more marked, if only in the recurrent need to invoke an appropriate intonation or other support of the intended interpretation. Still, vocal features comment upon the relationship between an overt sentence and its presuppositions in all cases, and, as has been suggested, it may be necessary to consider "neutral" intonation as but one choice within a set of appropriate intonations, the entire set being the proper object of analysis. Speech styles in relation to settings have to be considered as well, and in some cases, it may be the face-value interpretation of an utterance that requires special support. In sum, it will not be surprising to conclude that mock interpretations are generally more marked, but it is dangerous to start with that conclusion, and to set them aside as "departures," "deviations," or the like. Much that is normal and natural in speech would then be missed or misperceived.

The second respect in which one kind of interpretation is more complex is far more uncertain. The fact that in cases where the speech act is to be taken at face value, the value of the quantifier is in contrast to that of the act (1′, 4′), whereas in cases where the quantifier does have the same value as the act (2′, 3′), the act is to be taken as mock; the fact that apodosis and face value go together in value under the reciprocal interpretation, but not under the reflexive interpretation—these things suggest that the reflexive interpretation is indeed set off as less likely, requiring more support for its occurrence, and is therefore in a sense marked. A further point in this regard is that Lakoff's initial observation that *any* with a negative sense is appropriate to a threat, *some* with a positive sense to a promise, is sustained insofar as three out of four threats (in cases 1–4, 1′–4′) have *any*, three of four promises *some*. The exceptions help to suggest a scale of "naturalness." Reciprocal appears more "natural" than reflexive (entirely *any* in threats, entirely *some* in promises). Within reflexive interpretations, the mock cases would perhaps be more "natural" than the face value cases (*any* in threat, vs. *some*, and *some* in promise, vs. *any*). A reciprocally interpreted threat or promise would be unmarked; a reflexively interpreted mock threat or promise somewhat marked; a reflexively interpreted face-value threat or promise most marked and most in need of support for its successful interpretation.

Finally, it may say something about the assumptions that users of language make about role relationships to find that threats and promises are naturally construed in terms of reciprocity; but it may also say something to find that a construal in terms of what has been called here reflexivity also does exist. And it would be desirable to investigate the relationship between these two types of construal in other communities.

We are familiar with the type of linguistic relativity that finds in grammar indications of assumptions about the makeup of the world and how it is known. Current work in linguistics and sociolinguistics is beginning to suggest that one may find in grammar evidence of assumptions about the makeup of the social world, and of the rights and duties to be expected and exchanged there.[3] This would be a second type of linguistic relativity, with its universalistic as well as its particularistic side (as was the case with the linguistic relativity of Boas, Sapir, and Whorf), and with a constructive as well as critical role to play.[4]

3. I owe this idea to the stimulation of conversations with Erving Goffman, but he is not responsible for it.

4. In Hymes 1966 I developed the critical role of a second type of linguistic relativity, but did not state the positive role, even though the last section of the paper implicitly exemplified it.

Field research by Elinor O. Keenan and Judith T. Irvine has brought the positive relation between linguistic and social relationships to precise focus (see their contributions in Bauman and Sherzer 1974). Comparative study of a relation between speech styles and types of society was advocated by Jacobs (1945: 6–7). Recent work with Regna Darnell, Joel Sherzer and others on a guide to research has brought the idea into view on a more general basis (see Darnell 1972, ch. 2). Of current models of grammar, the functional approach of Halliday (1970, 1973) would seem to have the most to contribute.

Chapter 10

The Scope of Sociolinguistics

The term "sociolinguistics" began to gain currency about ten years ago.[1] The subsequent decade has seen a great deal of activity. There have been general symposia (e.g. Bright 1966, Lieberson 1966, Istituto Luigi Sturzo 1970, Ardener 1971, Smith and Shuy 1972); symposia on major topics (e.g. Gumperz and Hymes 1964, Macnamara 1967, Fishman, Ferguson and Das Gupta 1968, Hymes 1971, Whiteley 1971, Rubin and Jernudd 1972, Cazden, John and Hymes 1972); notable major research efforts (e.g. Fishman 1966, Labov 1966, the several surveys of East African countries, Le Page's survey in British Honduras, Labov's U. S. Regional Survey); the launching of working papers (e.g. Berkeley's Language and

1. This chapter was presented as the concluding address of the 23rd Annual Round Table at Georgetown University in March 1972, and published in *Sociolinguistics: Current Trends and Prospects,* Report of the 23rd Annual Round Table, ed. by Roger W. Shuy (Monograph Series on Languages and Linguistics, 25) (Washington, D.C.: Georgetown University Press, 1972), pp. 313–33. It was also distributed as Working Paper Number 9 in the series, Texas Working Papers in Sociolinguistics (Austin: Department of Anthropology, University of Texas, 1972). The relation of the work of Ervin-Tripp to that of John Gumperz was unfortunately omitted from the published text, but is noted here; a few minor revisions have been made.

Behavior Laboratory series, and now the series out of Texas, and
the Georgetown series); books of readings, increasingly specific
to the field (e.g. Hymes 1964, Fishman 1968, Giglioli 1972, Gumperz and Hymes 1972, Fishman 1972b); textbooks (e.g. Burling
1969, Pride 1970, Fishman 1970, Fishman 1972a); even a series of
collected papers of middle-aged men who find themselves senior
scholars (Greenberg 1971, Ferguson 1971, Gumperz 1971, Haugen
1972, Fishman 1972b, Lambert 1972, Ervin-Tripp 1973), as well as
Bernstein (1972); and specific journals, one more applied in orientation (*La Mundo Lingvo-Problemo*), one more theoretical (*Language in Society*).

Where do we now stand? To what point have we gotten? In
some ways, very far. In one fundamental regard, I think, simply
to a threshold.

Energetic activity and prolific publication need not warrant
confidence in the scientific worth of what is done. We are all
familiar with the gap that can exist between public concerns and
the competence of scientists. Sociolinguistics is nourished in
important part by the obvious relevance of much of its subject-
matter, joining other academic fields in which concern for education, children, ethnic relations, governmental policies, find expression. But the importance of the questions is no guarantee of the
value of the answer. Indeed, one can wonder if research funds are
not commonly ways of finding employment for sons and daughters
of the middle class, while avoiding confrontation of the real problems; perhaps what is needed is not research but substantial doses
of money, love, and democratic participation. In a society which
expects to organize bureaucracies and to retain scholars to minister to whatever is defined as a national need, sociolinguistics
might drift indefinitely, profuse and shallow, "a mile wide and an
inch deep."

I take it that most of us aim higher than that. We see a scientific as well as a practical need. If relevance to social problems
were not recognized, sociolinguistics research would still be
needed for the sake of an adequate theory of language. Some of
what is done under the heading of "sociolinguistics" may be justified only in the sense that something is better than nothing, when
need is great. But in the present state of sociolinguistics, I would
maintain three things: (1) the scientific as well as the practical side
of linguistics stands in need; (2) the scientific and practical needs
converge; and (3) the past decade has seen steps taken which do
bring us to the threshold of an integrated approach to linguistic
description. As to (1), witness the current disarray with regard to
arguments in syntax and semantics, and with regard to the place
of semantics, intonation, and indeed phonology and lexicon in a

model of grammar itself, as issues of empirical adequ
validity are pressed against the dominant "intuitionist" a
and as other, contextually-oriented traditions of work ar
ally reinvented or grudgingly rediscovered. As to (2), n
findings as to the organization of variation and the stru
speech acts, both issues central to linguistic theory, contribute to
the scientific basis of which successful practice stands in need,
while patent facts of practical experience (e.g., the organization of
linguistic features in terms of verbal repertoires, the role of social
meaning as a determinant of acceptability and the "creative aspect
of language use," the effects of personal identity, role, and setting
as constraints on competence) point to severe limitations of present linguistic theory and motivate efforts to overcome them. As
to (3), if we take "integrated" to encompass the structure of sentences within the structure of discourse, of referential meaning
within the meanings of speech acts, and of dialects and languages
within the organization of verbal repertoires and speech communities, then we can both see a convergence implicit in much of the
best recent work and envisage a unity to which it can arrive.

To explain this view of the state of sociolinguistic research,
I must say something about its goals.

GOALS OF SOCIOLINGUISTICS

The term "sociolinguistics" means many things to many people, and of course no one has a patent on its definition. Indeed not
everyone whose work is called "sociolinguistic" is ready to accept
the label, and those who do not use the term include and emphasize different things. Nevertheless, three main orientations can be
singled out, orientations that can be labelled: (1) the social as well
as the linguistic; (2) socially realistic linguistics; (3) socially constituted linguistics. Let me characterize each of these orientations
in relation to conventional linguistic theory.

1. *The social as well as the linguistic.* Here may be placed
ventures into social problems involving language and the use of
language, which are not seen as involving a challenge to existing
linguistics. American linguistics does have a tradition of practical
concerns—one can mention Sapir's semantic research for an international auxiliary language, Bloomfield's work in the teaching of
reading, Swadesh's literacy work, the "Army method" of teaching
foreign languages. The salient examples today involve American
cities and developing nations, and concern problems of education,
minority groups, and language policies. For the most part this
work is conceived as an application, lacking theoretical goals, or
else as pursuing theoretical goals that are in addition to those of

normal linguistics, or perhaps even wholly unrelated to them. When "sociolinguistics" serves as a legitimizing label for such activity, it is, as said, not conceived as a challenge to normal linguistics; linguists who perceive such a challenge in the label tend to echew it.

2. *Socially realistic linguistics.* This term is apt[2] for work that extends and challenges existing linguistics with data from the speech community. The challenge, and indeed the accomplishment, might be summed up in the two words, "variation" and "validity." A salient example is the work of William Labov, whose orientation toward linguistics is represented in such papers as "The Study of Language in its Social Context" (1970) and "Methodology" (1971) (see now Labov 1973a, b). The expressed theoretical goals are not distinct from those of normal linguistics, e.g., the nature of linguistic rules, the nature of sound change, but the method of work, and the findings, differ sharply. Here might also be put work which recognizes dependence of the analysis of meaning and speech acts on social context (e.g., R. Lakoff 1972, 1973).

Both of these orientations are thriving, here at this meeting and elsewhere. Less developed, but representing, I think, the fundamental challenge to whose threshold we have come, is socially constituted linguistics.

3. *Socially constituted linguistics.*[3] The phrase "socially constituted" is intended to express the view that social function gives form to the ways in which linguistic features are encountered in actual life. This being so, an adequate approach must begin by identifying social functions, and discover the ways in which linguistic features are selected and grouped together to serve them. Such a point of view cannot leave normal linguistic theory unchallenged as does the first orientation, nor limits challenge to reform, because its own goals are not allowed for by normal theory, and cannot be achieved by "working within the system." A "socially constituted" linguistics shares the practical concerns of other orientations; it shares concern for social realism and validity; but even if it could wait for the perfection of a "linguistic theory" of the normal sort, it could not then use it. Many of the features and relationships with which it must deal would never have been taken up in a "theory" of the normal sort. (That is why, indeed, "linguistic theory" of the normal sort is not a "theory of language," but only a theory of grammar.) A "socially constituted" linguistics is concerned with social as well as referential meaning, and with

2. I owe this term to Maxine Bernstein, in whose dissertation in progress I encountered it.

3. Or, as heard and repeated by one linguist at Georgetown, socially reconstituted linguistics.

language as part of communicative conduct and social action. Its
task is the thoroughgoing critique of received notions and practices, from the standpoint of social meaning, that is, from a functional perspective. Such a conception reverses the structuralist
tendency of most of the twentieth century, toward the isolation of
referential structure, and the posing of questions about social
functions from that standpoint. The goals of social relevance and
social realism can indeed be fully accomplished only from the
standpoint of the new conception, for much of what must be taken
into account, much of what is there, organized and used, in actual
speech, can only be seen, let alone understood, when one starts
from function and looks for the structure that serves it.

I have given examples to support this thesis in other chapters
(chs. 4, 6, 8) and will offer only a few. Let me merely mention that
from a comprehensive functional standpoint, a phonetic feature
such as aspiration appears a true phonological universal, specialized to referential function in some languages, and to stylistic
function in others, hence not of indifference to general theory in
its role in English, as Chomsky and Halle (1968:viii) would have
it; recognition of a social-identifying function motivates an independently controllable articulation otherwise left unintelligible
(Chomsky and Halle 1968:298; cf. ch. 8; the status of a sentence as
a speech act depends upon the rights and obligations, roles and
statuses, of the participants; unless one extends the rules governing a verbal summons in English to include nonverbal acts (a
knock, a telephone ring), a significant generalization is lost (Schegloff 1968); similarly, the function of deixis in San Blas Cuna is
served by a set of forms that includes lip-pointing (Sherzer 1973);
speech probably serves to mark sex-role and status in every community, but linguists have hitherto discovered it only when intrusive in a normal grammatical description; some consistent ways of
speaking make use of the resources of more than one language,
e.g. the Dutch of Surinam blacks, which should be grammatically
and lexically standard, and phonologically creole (Eersel 1971); in
some communities distinct languages can be described as lexically
distinct with a common grammar and phonology—Kupwar approaches this, according to Gumperz and Wilson (1971); the
semantic structure represented by a choice of pronoun in one
community may be expressed by a choice of dialect in another,
and choice of language in still a third, so that analysis of function
from a universal standpoint cannot stay with one part of language,
or even within the category, language. In sum, if our concern is
social relevance and social realism, we must recognize that there
is more to the relationship between sound and meaning than is
dreamt of in normal linguistic theory. In sound there are stylistic

as well as referential features and contrasts; in meaning there is social as well as referential import; in between there are relationships not given in ordinary grammar but there for the finding in social life.

From this standpoint, what there is to be described and accounted for is not in the first instance a language (say, English), but *means of speech,* and, inseparably, their meanings *for those who use them.* The set of conventional resources available to a competent member of a community can be so described. As we have seen, this set of resources is more extensive than a single norm, grammar, or language; nor can the nature of its organization be given in those terms. Yet it is *this* set of resources with which one must deal, if "linguistic theory" is to become synonymous with "theory of language."

It is not that phenomena pointing to a more general conception of the relationship between sound and meaning have not long been noted, and often enough studied with insight and care. Expressive language, speech levels, social dialects, registers, functional varieties, code- and style-switching, are familiar and essential concepts; the interlocked subjects of stylistics, poetics, and rhetoric have flourished in recent years. Anything that can be accomplished in theory and method for a socially constituted linguistics must incorporate and build on that work, which has done much to shape what I say here. But the tendency has been to treat such phenomena and such studies as marginal or as supplementary to grammar (cf. ch. 8). (Certainly that has been the tendency of grammarians.) The hegemony of grammar as a genre, and of the referential function as its organizing basis, has been preserved. Whereas the essence of a functional approach is not to take function for granted, but as problematic; to assume as part of a universal theory of language that a plurality of functions are served by linguistic features in any act and community; to require validation of the relationships between features and functions, and of their organization into varieties, registers, ways of speaking, ethnographically within the community; and to take functional questions, a functional perspective, as having priority, that is, as being fundamental, both in general theory and in specific accounts, to whatever can be validly said as to structure, competence, universals, etc. (cf. Hymes 1964a).

Such a perspective was present in the structuralism of the period before World War II (cf. Jakobson 1963, Firth 1935, and below), and has never been wholly lost. In Anglo-American circles it has begun to come to the fore in work under the aegis of sociolinguistics in recent years. Salient examples include the work of Labov (1966, 1970, sect. 3) on "sociolinguistic structure," of Gumperz (1964) on verbal repertoire, of Bernstein (1972) on codes, of Fishman on domains (1966), of Denison (1970) and Le Page (1969) on multilingualism, and of Ervin-Tripp (1972) on sociolinguistic rules.[4] What is important here is the element in each work that contributes to a general methodological perspective. Such work goes beyond the recognition and analysis of particular cases to suggest *a mode of organization of linguistic features other than that of a grammar*. The common implication, which I want to draw, emphasize, and elaborate, is, in its weaker form, that such alternative modes of organization exist; and, in its stronger form, that one or more such alternative modes of organization may be fundamental.

There is a second point, linked to the first, and owing its full recognition to much the same body of work: *a conception of the speech community not in terms of language alone* (especially not just one language, and a fortiori, not just one homogeneous language).

Although they would find the wording odd, many linguists might accept a definition of the object of linguistic description as: the organization of features within a community. From the present standpoint, the wording is not odd, but vital. The two points just stated in negative terms can now be put positively.

1. The organization of linguistic features within a speech community is in terms of ways of speaking within a verbal repertoire.

2. Membership in a speech community consists in sharing one (or more) ways of speaking.

From this standpoint, the usual linguistic description identifies a part (not the whole) of the linguistic features, resources, verbal means, of a community, and says little or nothing about their actual organization. Grammar indeed originated as a pedagogical and literary genre, and has been revitalized as a logical one; neither its traditional nor its mathematical pedigree is much warrant for taking it for granted that it is the form in which speech comes organized in use. Psychologists and psycholinguists have recently discovered and begun to build on recognition of this fact, with regard to the organization of language for production, reception, and acquisition. Those of us interested in the existence of social facts and customary behavior must build on it too. Classical antiquity did not stop with grammar, but went on to rhetoric— cf. Marrou (1965) 1964, part two, chs. VII, X, and part three, chs.

---

4. Note also the relevance of the multifunctional approach to grammar itself being developed by Halliday (1970:336, 1971). The development of my own understanding of these questions can be traced in papers of 1961, 1962, 1964, 1967, 1970b, 1970c, 1971a, 1971b.

V, VI. So should we, but without the normative, exclusionary bias
that has dogged the genre of grammar throughout its history, and
in a thoroughgoing, reconstructing way.

What is the nature of such a reconstruction, of a method of
description adequate to the goals of a socially constituted linguistics, as just stated? Briefly and broadly put, "the task is to identify
and analyze the ways of speaking in a community, together with
the conditions and meanings of their use. In sociolinguistic
description, the first application of the commutation test is to ways
of speaking" (ch. 8). In what way is a person speaking? What is
the set of such ways? And the contrastive as well as identifica-
tional meaning of each? Within ways of speaking, commutation
will further discover two mutually implicated modes of meaning,
the "referential" and "social." There is the systemic invariance
in terms of which two utterances of "fourth floor" are repetitions,
the same utterance, and there is the contrast in virtue of which
they may be different (see Labov 1966 on style-shifting in New
York City department stores with respect to "repetitions" of utterances with post-vocalic constriction). Conversely, there is the
contrast by which utterances of "third floor" and "fourth floor"
may differ in what they convey (as to location), and there is the
systemic invariance in terms of which they are repetitions, conveying the same meaning (as to social position and speech community identification). It is not obvious, is it, after all, that the
energies of linguistics should be devoted entirely to the signals
that tell where things can be bought in department stores, and not
at all to the signals that tell where the people in department
stores have come from, are now, and aspire to be?

The principle of mutually implicated modes of meaning holds
for underlying relationships as well as overt utterances—sentences
the same in "referential" basic structures may be contrastive in
social/stylistic meaning, and conversely, as any reflective writer has
occasion to know.[5] In sum, the often stated foundation of linguistic

5. Notice that to attempt to handle all modes of meaning on one grammatical framework ends by dissolving structure and making the actual
organization of both kinds of meaning difficult and even impossible to
discern (cf. Jacobs and Rosenbaum 1971:viii–ix): "the importance of expressing semantic insights has come to overshadow the criterion of expressibility
within a formalizable rule." The very point of discovering the organization
of linguistic features in the service of stylistic and social meaning is an
argument for keeping distinct and precise the ways in which language is
not organized for such a function. For some linguists it may be sufficient to
express semantic insights, rather than to maintain "the initially indispensable
desire for explicit precision that Chomsky inherited from structuralism"
(Jacobs and Rosenbaum 1971:viii), but it would be a fatal disservice to the
standpoint advocated here if the expression of social and stylistic semantic

theory, that in a speech community some utterances are the same, differing only in "free" variation, that the goal of theoretical explanation is to account for what counts as contrast, what does not, has perhaps served the development of linguistics well in its purely "referential" interpretation. One bird of function in the hand, so to speak, may have been preferable to entering the bush to cope with two. But, to elaborate the figure, it appears that neither bird will fly without the other, even that neither is itself a whole bird. To pursue the figure no doubt too far, the bird in the hand proves to be a featherless monopter, to be restored only out of the ashes of conventional grammar. The true foundation of theory and method is that in a speech community some *ways of speaking* are the same, that some of the persons talk the same way (see Hymes 1973, 1974).

A community, then, is to be characterized in terms of a repertoire of ways of speaking. Ways of speaking are to be characterized in terms of a relationship between styles, on the one hand, and contexts of discourse, on the other. The formal concept underlying speech styles is what Ervin-Tripp (1972), building on work of John Gumperz, has called rules of *co-occurrence*. The formal concept of relating speech styles to contexts of discourse is called by her *rules of alternation*. The speech styles defined by rules of co-occurrence draw on the linguistic varieties present in a community, from whose resources they select and group features in sometimes complex ways. The relationships dubbed "rules of alternation" are in the first instance considerations of appropriateness, and of marked and unmarked usage.

Ervin-Tripp's delineation of these two concepts is a culmina-

---

insights were regarded as warrant for scrapping structuralist inheritance and explicit precision. In this regard the grammatical analyses of Harris, Hiz, Chomsky and some others are more useful than recent attempts that in effect dissolve the many purely syntactic regularities that do exist. The transformationalists are right to reject the extreme to which some American structuralists went, such that one exception could disprove a universal. But have they not fallen into the same fallacy with the principle that one exception can disprove a level? The fact would seem to be that Chomsky is right that there are many syntactic regularities which are independent of the exceptions which motivate generative semantics, and which appear unmotivated from the latter standpoint. It is also true that others are right that there are many phonological regularities that are independent of the exceptions that motivated "systematic phonemics," and that appear unmotivated from the latter point of view (witness the awkward efforts to recapture an understanding of canonical forms by "conspiracies"). The very plain truth is, as Sapir said, that "grammars leak," and that the major sectors of a language (grammar): phonology, lexis, syntax, comprise patterns and habits which can have rather autonomous histories—in chronological and social time and space.

tion of the quest in linguistics throughout this century for adequate descriptive concepts, concepts that would be formal and universal to all languages, yet concretely valid in application to each. This history can be traced in American linguistics from discussion early in the century as to grammatical categories (e.g., incorporation, compounding, inflection) by Boas, Sapir, and Kroeber, through the generalization of the terms "phoneme," "morpheme," and "distinctive features," to the discovery of transformational relationships. The notion of speech style, as a mode of organization of features cutting across the standard sectors of phonology, grammar, and lexicon, has indeed been advanced a number of times (Whorf 1942:92, Harris 1951:10, Joos 1959, Pike 1967:463–4), but not really generalized as a perspective for the analysis of a speech community, and always stopping short of the decisive step taken by Ervin-Tripp, which is to recognize speech styles themselves as the elements of a further system of rules. The recognition of this fact is comparable in nature and importance to the recognition of transformations (as rules operating on rules). The study of the structure of relationships among speech styles opens up the possibility of a generative approach; and it makes the study of social meaning as embodied in roles, activities and situations integral to the explanation of the meanings of the speech styles themselves. What Friedrich (1972) had shown with regard to "pronominal breakthrough," meaning emergent from the interaction of pronominal and contextual meanings, is here generalized as a methodology.

Many of you will be quick to note that linguistics does not itself command analysis of social role, activities, and situations. Of this, two things can be said. First, such analysis is necessary. There really is no way that linguistic theory can become a theory of language without encompassing social meaning, and that means becoming a part of the general study of communicative conduct and social action (see ch. 9). Second, this step is dictated by the development of linguistics itself. Having begun its structural course at the far side of meaning, with a focus on phonology, linguistics has proceeded through successive foci on morphology, syntax, semantics, and now performative and speech acts. There is no way to analyze speech acts adequately without ethnography; no language is a perfect metalanguage for the acts that can be performed with it. The study of speech acts can indeed be a center of a socially constituted linguistics; but its own logic broaches the general study of the vocabulary of action, in communities and in social science. Again, if we take seriously Chomsky's implicit call for linguistics to concern itself with the "creative aspect" of language use, and with the basis of the ability to generate novel, yet appropriate sentences, we again are forced into analysis of setting as well as syntax. For appropriateness is not a property of sentences, but of a relationship between sentences and contexts. This holds a fortiori for the property of "creativity," whether saying something new in a familiar setting, or something familiar in a setting that is new. At every turn, it almost would seem, linguistics is wrestling with phenoma, and concepts, that turn out to entail relationships, only one pole of which is within linguistics' usual domain. The true generalizations can never be captured except from a perspective that encompasses both poles.

One way to bring out this point is to say that a socially constituted linguistics has as a goal a kind of explanatory adequacy complementary to that proposed by Chomsky. Chomsky's type of explanatory adequacy leads away from speech, and from languages, to relationships possibly universal to all languages, and possibly inherent in human nature. It is an exciting and worthwhile prospect. The complementary type of explanatory adequacy leads from what is common to all human beings and all languages toward what particular communities and persons have made of their means of speech. It is comparative and evolutionary in a sociocultural, rather than a biological, sense. It sees as in need of explanation the differential elaboration of means of speech, and of speech itself. At a surface level it notices gross contrasts in speech activity, from great volubility to great taciturnity; gross contrasts in elaboration of message-form; gross contrasts in the predominance of traditional and of spontaneously encoded utterance; gross contrasts in the complication, or simplification, of the obligatory surface structure of languages themselves. These contrasts, and the typologies to which they point, no doubt find their explanation at a deeper level. Rules of conduct in relation to roles and settings; the role of a language—variety in socialization or in boundary-maintenance; values, conceptions of the self, and beliefs as to the rights and duties one owes to others as fellow members of a community, all will be found to have a place. The general problem, then, is to identify the means of speech and ways of speaking of communities; to find, indeed, where are the real communities, for language boundaries do not give them, and a person or a group may belong to more than one—to characterize communities in terms of their repertoires of these; and through ethnography, comparative ethnology, historical, and evolutionary considerations, become able to explain something of the origin, development, maintenance, obsolescence, and loss of ways of speaking and types of speech community—of the face speech wears for human

re they learn that it is language, a thing apart, and the
linguists.[6]

omplementary goal of explanatory adequacy comes not,
admitted, from the internal logic of linguistics, but from
al aspiration. Chomsky's goal of explanatory adequacy,
to be sure, would seem to owe much to his own concern to understand the human mind and to revitalize rationalist philosophy. He
has made his concern an effective goal for many in linguistics,
philosophy, and psychology (cf. Dingwall 1971). The concern that
motivates explanation directed toward ways of speaking and
speech communities may or may not find a similar response. This
concern, put simply, is with human liberation. The goal of a second type of explanatory adequacy is necessary if linguistic
research is to serve that human goal.

Consider the present stance of linguistics, as reflected perhaps
in the response of many members of the Linguistics Society of
America to suggestions of racial inferiority. Many linguists, like
many anthropologists, believe that no group of human beings is
innately incapable of the highest achievements of civilization.
They have much reason so to believe. And they speak out. What
they can speak to is the potential equality of all human groups.
Neither their theory, nor their liberalism, quite prepares them to
speak concretely to actual inequalities. Difference itself is offensive. The scientific equality of all languages was declared early in
the century, and for most scientists, that continues to suffice. But
means of speech are what their users make of them; they have
been put to different ends, in differing circumstances, and sometimes been caught up in the ends and circumstances of others. No
minister of education in a developing nation is of the view that
anything can be said and read in any language. That it could be,
were there time, money, and intent, does not speak to the actual
situation. And quite apart from situations that suggest judgments
of inferiority, it is simply the case that a certain language, or
speech itself, has meant and been made to mean different things
in different communities. The general observations on the functions of language, typically on the manifold marvelousness of language, found in texts are trash. We hardly know in any systematic
way what communities have made of language.

If linguistic research is to help as it could in transcending the
many inequalities in language and competence in the world today,
it must be able to analyze these inequalities. In particular, a practical linguistics so motivated would have to go beyond means of
speech and types of speech community to a concern with persons,

6. I am thinking here of "The Fetishism of Commodities and the Secret
Thereof," section 4, ch. I, part I, book I, of Das Kapital.

and social structure. If competence is to mean anything useful (we do not really need a synonym for grammar), it must refer to the abilities actually held by persons. A salient fact about a speech community, realistically viewed, is the unequal distribution of abilities, on the one hand, and of opportunities for their use, on the other. This indeed appears to be an old story in mankind, and even a cursory look at the globe discloses definition of women as communicatively second-class citizens to be widespread. When, where, and what they may speak, the conceptions of themselves as speakers with which they are socialized, show again and again that from the community point of view, they at least are not "ideal speakers," though they may on occasion be ideal hearers.

Beyond the structure of ways of speaking, then, is the question of explanation, and beyond that, the question of liberation. This is not a simple matter, and I cannot say much about it now except to observe that some seemingly attractive views have hidden pitfalls. Simply to overcome restrictions is not enough, for a community in which everyone could say anything might have no one listening. To overcome "restricted," context-dependent codes is not enough, for, as the German sociologist Habermas has been pointing out (and as Sapir did before him), human life needs some areas of symbolic interaction and communication in which much can be taken for granted. Simply defending "restricted" codes is not enough, for the explicitness of the "elaborated," context-independent code may be needed to analyze publicly and so transform the existing order. (See "A Critique of Compensatory Education" in Bernstein 1972.)

The goal of explanatory adequacy with regard to speech communities as comprising ways of speaking, will, I suppose, be quite enough for most linguists to consider, let alone to accept. Yet, I believe, if linguistics is to realize its potential for the well-being of mankind, it must go even further, and consider speech communities as comprising not only rules, but also sometimes oppression, sometimes freedom, in the relation between personal abilities and their occasions of use.

THEMES OF SOCOLINGUISTICS

If we associate "sociolinguistics" with "socially constituted linguistics," then there are a number of themes, or indeed slogans, for a sociolinguistics of the scope just sketched. There are of course the seven points made earlier (in chs. 1 and 3). We can partly generalize, partly elaborate them with another seven here. (If this were a political movement, or a Chinese banquet, we might put them on banners about the walls).

1. Linguistic theory as theory of language, entailing the organization of speech (not just of grammar).

2. Foundations of theory and methodology as entailing questions of function (not just of structure).

3. Speech communities as organizations of ways of speaking (not just equivalent to the distribution of the grammar of a language).

4. Competence as personal ability (not just grammatical knowledge, systemic potential of a grammar, superorganic property of a society, or, indeed, irrelevant to persons in any other way).

5. Performance as accomplishment and responsibility, investiture and emergence (not just psycholinguistic processing and impediment).

6. Languages as what their users have made of them (not just what human nature has given).

7. *Liberté, Egalité, Fraternité* of speech as something achieved in social life (not just postulated as given as a consequence of language).

THE SCOPE OF SOCIOLINGUISTICS

What, then, is the scope of sociolinguistics? Not all I have just described, but rather, that part of it which linguists and social scientists leave unattended. The final goal of sociolinguistics, I think, must be to preside over its own liquidation. The flourishing of a hybrid term such as sociolinguistics reflects a gap in the disposition of established disciplines with respect to reality. Sometimes new disciplines do grow from such a state of affairs, but the recent history of the study of language has seen the disciplines adjacent to a gap themselves grow to encompass it. Some can recall a generation ago when proper American linguists did not study meaning, and ethnographers had little linguistic method. A study of meaning in another language or culture (say, grammatical categories or kinship terms) could qualify as "ethnolinguistic" then. Today, of course, semantics is actually pursued in both linguistics and ethnography, and a mediating interdisciplinary label is unnecessary; "semantics" itself will usually suffice.

Let us hope for a similar history for "sociolinguistics." In one sense, the issue again is the study of meaning, only now, social meaning.[7]

7. The two main facets of "social" meaning can be identified as "interpersonal" and "textual," following Halliday 1970. That is, the facets of meaning involved with nonlinguistic context (the participants in the speech act and their interaction in that setting), on the one hand, the facets involved with the linguistic context, on the other. I put "social" in quotes because it, like some other common terms for this aspect of language, seems to me to apply to all of meaning. All of meaning is social in basis and may take part

What are the chances for such a history to be written, say, from the vantage point of the year 2000 A.D.? To see, in retrospect, the flourishing of "sociolinguistics" as a transitional stage in the transformation of linguistics and adjacent social science disciplines to encompass what I have called "socially constituted linguistics"? The chances, I think, are quite uncertain.

Clearly recognition of the gap, and advocacy of a perspective to overcome it, are not enough. The future historian will notice that there were "efforts towards a means–end model of language" between the two world wars (Jakobson 1963). And in the literature of that period, he will find in the writings of another of the five or six great linguists of the century such statements as the following:

The true locus of culture is in the interaction of specific individuals and, on the subjective side, in the world of meaning which each one of these individuals may unconsciously abstract for himself from his participation in these interactions. [1932, SWES 515]

For it is only through an analysis of variation that the reality and meaning of a norm can be established at all, and it is only through a minute and sympathetic study of individual behavior in the state in which normal human beings find themselves, namely in a state of society, that it will ultimately be possible to say things about society itself and culture that are more than fairly convenient abstractions. [1938, SWES 576]

It is not really difficult, then, to see why anyone brought up on the austerities of a well-defined science must, if he is to maintain his symbolic self-respect, become more and more estranged from man himself. [1939, SWES 580]

The very terminology which is used by the many kinds of segmental sciences of man indicates how remote man himself has become as a necessary concept in the methodology of the respective sciences. . . . In linguistics, abstracted speech sounds, words, and the arrangement of words have come to have so authentic a vitality that one can speak of 'regular sound change' . . . without knowing or caring who opened their mouths, at what time, to communicate what to whom. [1939, SWES 578, 579]

As we follow tangible problems of behavior rather than selected problems of behavior rather than selected problems set by recognized disciplines, we discover the field of social psychology. [1939, SWES 513]

The social psychology into which the conventional cultural and psychological disciplines must eventually be resolved is re-

---

in stylistic effect as well. Similarly, "cognition" and "ideational," for what is often called "referential," should not imply that no cognition or thought is involved in expression of social identity, attitude, stylistic consistency or verbal art. Still, "social" often will conveniently identify Halliday's "interpersonal," and "stylistic" either his "textual," or simply nonreferential status of features.

lated to these paradigmatic studies as an investigation into living speech is related to grammar. I think few cultural disciplines are as exact, as rigorously configurated, as self-contained as grammar, but if it is desired to have grammar contribute a significant share to our understanding of human behavior, its definitions, meanings, and classifications must be capable of a significant restatement in terms of a social psychology which . . . boldly essays to bring every cultural pattern back to the living context from which it has been abstracted in the first place . . . back to its social matrix. [1934, SWES 592–93, 592]

These quotations are from the writings of Sapir's last years, when he began to rethink the nature of language, culture, and society from a standpoint he sometimes called "psychiatric," or "social psychology," and which today we might more readily label the standpoint of social interaction, or communicative conduct; the standpoint, as I would see it, of sociolinguistics.

Obviously Sapir's intellectual lead did not prevail, after his death in 1939, although its influence can be traced in many quarters. Such a fact must humble expectation. A decade ago (when the introduction to my book of readings was written) I did venture to predict:

It may be that the development of these foci of interest (semantic description, sociolinguistic variation) will lead historians of twentieth-century linguistics to say that whereas the first half of the century was distinguished by a drive for the autonomy of language as an object of study and a focus upon description of structure, the second half was distinguished by a concern for the integration of language in sociocultural context and a focus upon the analysis of function. (1964b:11)

Ten years later, we are, I think, only at a threshold. Whether we pass over and occupy the land will depend crucially upon the commitment of those who have the essential skills, especially linguists. For a criterion of the field I envisage is that it is a linguistics, a functionally oriented, more adequate linguistics, that has at last realized itself as a social science. Perhaps in this respect there will be in the year 2000 A.D. three main branches of linguistic science: psychological, sociological (these two answering to the two directions of explanatory adequacy), and the traditional and indispensable work oriented toward specific languages, language families, and language areas. With regard to the sociological branch of the three, there are many reasons within theoretical linguistics today why it appears a necessary step. But holes in a scientific pattern, like those in a phonological one, may go long unfilled. Perhaps as much or more will depend on practical as on scientific concern. It may not have been accidental that it was the

1930s that saw Sapir's concern with personal meaning and social
interaction. Perhaps socially concerned linguists in the coming
decade will discover wisdom in Chairman Mao Tse-tung's remark
(1952:7):

> If you want to know a certain thing or a certain class of
> things directly, you must personally participate in the practical
> struggle to change reality, to change that thing or class of things,
> for only thus can you come into contact with them as phenomena;
> only through personal participation can you uncover the essence
> of that thing or class of things and comprehend them.

Certainly it is a sociolinguistic perspective, uniting theory and
practice, that is most appropriate to a vision of the future of mankind as one in a world at peace. There are three ways of seeking
unity in the phenomena of language. One has been to seek a unity
of origin in the past. Comparative-historical linguistics, linguistics
oriented toward individual languages and language families, can
discover and maintain such unities; indeed, it has had positive
effect in that regard (Matthew Arnold pointed to the Indoeuropean
unity of the English and Irish, Sir Henry Maine to that of England
and India, as warrant for overcoming prejudice and accepting
brotherhood). A second way has been to seek a unity of underlying structure, a timeless or continuing origin, so to speak, in
the present. Structural and psychologically-oriented linguistics
can point to this. A third way is to seek the origins of a unity in
the future—to see the processes of sociolinguistic change that
envelop our objects of study as underlain by the emergence of a
world society. It is a sociolinguistic perspective that naturally and
inevitably considers mankind, not only as what it has been, and
is, but also as what it is becoming. Linguistics as sociolinguistics,
if it will, can envisage and work toward a unity that is yet to come.

Bibliography

Abrahams, R. D. 1968. Introductory remarks to a rhetorical theory of folklore. *Journal of American Folklore* 81: 143-158.

———. 1970. Rapping and capping: black talk as art. In *Black America*, ed. J. F. Szwed. New York: Basic Books.

———. 1972. The training of the man of words in talking sweet. *Language in Society* 1: 15-30.

Abrahams, R. D., and Bauman, R. 1971. Sense and non-sense in St. Vincent: speech behavior in a Caribbean community. *American Anthropologist* 73: 762-772.

Albert, E. 1972. Culture patterning of speech behavior in Burundi. (with special attention to 'rhetoric,' 'logic,' and 'poetics.') In *Directions in sociolinguistics*, eds. J. J. Gumperz and D. Hymes, pp. 73-105. New York: Holt, Rinehart and Winston.

Alisjahbana, S. T. 1965. *The failure of modern linguistics in the face of linguistic problems of the twentieth century.* Kuala Lumpur: University of Malaya.

Ardener, E. C., ed. 1971. *Social anthropology and language.* ASA monographs, 10. London: Tavistock.

Arewa, E. O., and Dundes, A. 1964. Proverbs and the ethnography of speaking folklore. In *The ethnography of communication*, eds. J. J. Gumperz and D. Hymes. pp. 70-85. (*American Anthropologist* 66 (no. 6, part 2).) Washington, D.C.: American Anthropological Association.

Barker, L. M., ed. 1968-69. *Pears cyclopedia.* 77th edn. London: Pelham Books.

Barnard, F. M. 1965. *Herder's social and political thought. From enlightenment to nationalism.* Oxford: Clarendon Press.

Barth, F. 1969. Ethnic groups and boundaries. In *The social organization of culture difference*, ed. F. Barth. London: Allen and Unwin.

Barthes, R. 1953. *Le degré zéro de l'écriture.* Paris: Le Seuil.

Bartholomew, G. A. Jr., and Birdsell, J. 1953. Ecology and the proto-hominids. *American Anthropologist* 55: 481-498.

211

Basso, K. 1970. To give up on words: silence in the Western Apache culture. *Southwestern Journal of Anthropology* 26: 213-230.

Bateson, G. 1949. Bali: the value system of a steady state. In *Social Structure: Studies presented to A. R. Radcliffe-Brown*, ed. Meyer Fortes. New York: Oxford University Press.

———. 1958. *Naven*. 2nd edition. Stanford: Stanford University Press.

———. 1960. Minimal requirements for a theory of schizophrenia. *A.M.A. Archives of General Psychiatry* 2: 477-491.

———. 1963. Exchange of information about patterns of human behavior. In *Information storage and neural control*, eds. W. Fields and W. Abbott. Springfield: Charles C. Thomas.

Bauman, R. 1972. The La Have Island general store. Sociability and verbal art in a Nova Scotia community. *Journal of American Folklore* 85: 330-343.

Bauman, R. and Sherzer, J., eds. 1974. *Explorations in the ethnography of speaking*. New York and London: Cambridge University Press.

Ben-Amos, D. 1967. Folklore: the definition game once again. Paper read at the meeting of the American Folklore Society, Toronto, 1967. (Revised and published as Ben Amos, 1971.)

Ben-Amos, D. 1969. Analytical categories and ethnic genres. *Genre* 2: 275-301.

———. 1971. Towards a definition of folklore in context. *Journal of American Folklore* 84: 3-15.

Berger, P. 1967. *The sacred canopy*. New York: Doubleday.

Bernstein, B. 1964. Elaborated and restricted codes: Their social origins and some consequences. In *The ethnography of communication*, ed. J. J. Gumperz and D. Hymes, pp. 55-69. Washington, D.C.: American Anthropological Association.

———. 1972. *Class, codes and social control, I: Theoretical papers*. London: Routeledge, Kegan Paul.

Birdwhistell, R. 1960. A look at evolutionary theory in the light of recent developments in communication research. In *Report of the 9th round table meeting*, ed. W. A. Austin, pp. 149-155. Washington, D.C.: Georgetown University Press.

Blom, J-P., and Gumperz, J. 1966. Some social determinants of verbal behavior. ms.

———. 1972. Social meaning in linguistic structures: code-switching in Norway. In *Directions in sociolinguistics*, eds. J. J. Gumperz and D. Hymes, pp. 404-434. New York: Holt, Rinehart and Winston.

Bloomfield, L. 1927. Literate and illiterate speech. *American Speech* 2: 423-439. (Reprinted in *Language in culture and society*, ed. D. Hymes, pp. 391-396. New York: Harper and Row.)

———. 1933. *Language*. New York: Holt.

Bloomfield, M. W., and Newmark, L. 1963. *A linguistic introduction to the history of English*. New York: Knopf.

Boas, F. 1911. *Introduction*. In *Handbook of American Indian languages*, ed. F. Boas, pp. 1-83. Washington, D.C.: Smithsonian Institution.

Bolinger, D. 1950. Rime, assonance, and morpheme analysis. *Word* 6: 117-136.

Bricker, V. 1973. Three genres of Tzotzil insult. In *Meaning in Mayan languages*, ed. M. S. Edmonson, pp. 183-203. The Hague: Mouton.

———. 1974a. The ethnographic context of some traditional Mayan speech genres. In *Explorations in the ethnography of speaking*, ed. R. Bauman and J. Sherzer. New York: Cambridge University Press.

———. 1974b. Some cognitive implications of informant variability. *Language in Society* 3(1).

Bright, W., ed. 1966. *Sociolinguistics*. The Hague: Mouton.

Brown, R. 1958. *Words and things*. Glencoe: The Free Press.

Brown, R., and Gilman, A. 1960. The pronouns of power and solidarity. In *Style in language*, ed. T. A. Sebeok, pp. 253-276. Cambridge, Mass.: The Technology Press.

Buchanan, C. O. 1968. *Modern Anglican liturgies*. London: Oxford University Press.

Burke, K. 1931. *Counterstatement*. New York: Harcourt Brace. (Reprinted, Chicago: Phoenix Book P14, 1957.)

———. 1932. *Towards a better life*. New York: Harcourt Brace. (Reprinted, Berkeley: University of California Press, 1966.)

———. 1935. *Permanence and change: an analysis of purpose*. New York: New Republic.

———. 1937. *Attitudes toward history*. New York: Editorial Publications.

Burke, K. 1941. *The philosophy of literary form: studies in symbolic action*. Baton Rouge: Louisiana State University Press. (Revised, New York: Vintage, 1957.)

———. 1945. *A grammar of motives*. New York: Prentice-Hall. (Reissued by University of California Press.)

———. 1950. *A rhetoric of motives*. New York: Prentice-Hall. (Reissued by University of California Press.)

———. 1951a. Three definitions. *Kenyon Review* 13: 173-192.

———. 1951b. Othello: an essay to illustrate a method. *Hudson Review* 4: 165-203. (Also in Hyman 1964a: 152-195.)

———. 1954. Fact, inference and proof in the analysis of literary symbolism. In *Symbols and values: an initial study* (Thirteenth Symposium of the Conference on Science, Philosophy and Religion), pp. 283-306. New York: Harper. (Also in Hyman 1964b: 145-172.)

———. 1955. Linguistic approach to problems of education. *Fifty-fourth Yearbook of the National Society for the study of education*, part I, pp. 259-303. Chicago.

———. 1957. *The philosophy of literary form*. Revised ed. New York: Vintage.

———. 1958. The poetic motive. *Hudson Review* 11: 54-63.

———. 1961. *The rhetoric of religion: studies in logology.* Boston: Beacon. (Reprinted, University of California Press, 1970.)

———. 1968. Dramatism. *International encyclopedia of the social sciences* 7: 445-452. New York: Macmillan.

Burling, R. 1969. *Man's many voices.* New York: Holt, Rinehart and Winston.

Calame-Griaule, G. 1965. *Ethnologie et langage. La parole chez les Dogon.* Paris: Gallimard.

Carneiro, R. L. 1964. The Amahuaca and the spirit world. *Ethnology* 3: 6-12.

Carpenter, E., and McLuhan, M. 1960. *Explorations in communication. An anthology.* Boston: Beacon Press.

Cassirer, E. 1944. *An essay on man. An introduction to a philosophy of human culture.* New Haven: Yale University Press. (Doubleday Anchor Book, 1953.)

———. 1950. *The problem of knowledge. Philosophy, science and history since Hegel.* New Haven: Yale University Press.

———. 1955. *The philosophy of the enlightenment.* Boston: Beacon Press. (Princeton University Press, 1955; German original, Tübingen, 1932.)

———. 1961. *The logic of the humanities.* New Haven: Yale University Press. (German original, Goteborg, 1942.)

Cazden, C., John-Steiner, V., and Hymes, D., eds. 1972. *Functions of language in the classroom.* New York: Teachers College Press.

Chatman, S., ed. 1970. *Literary style: a symposium.* London: Oxford University Press.

Chatman, S. and Levin, S., eds. 1966. *Essays on the language of literature.* Boston: Houghton Mifflin.

Cherry, E. C. 1961. *On human communication. A review, a survey and a criticism.* New York: Science Editions.

Chomsky, N. 1957. *Syntactic structures.* The Hague: Mouton.

———. 1965. *Aspects of the theory of syntax.* Cambridge, Mass.: MIT Press.

———. 1966. *Cartesian linguistics.* New York: Harper and Row.

———. 1968. *Language and Mind.* New York: Harcourt, Brace and World.

———. 1973. *For reasons of state.* New York: Pantheon.

Chomsky, N., and Halle, M. 1968. *Sound pattern of English.* New York: Harper and Row.

Cohen, P. S. 1968. *Modern social theory.* London: Heinemann.

Conant, F. P. 1961. Jarawa kin systems of reference and address. *Anthropological Linguistics* 3 (2): 1-33.

Conklin, H. 1955. Hanunoó color categories. *Southwestern Journal of Anthropology* 11: 339-344.

———. 1959. Linguistic play in its cultural context. *Language* 35:

631-636. (Reprinted in *Language in culture and society*, ed. D. Hymes. New York: Harper and Row.)

——. 1962. Lexicographical treatment of folk taxonomies. In *Problems of lexicography*, eds. F. W. Householder and S. Saporta, pp. 119-141. (Publication 21 of the Indiana University Research Center in Anthropology, Folklore and Linguistics.)

——. 1964. Ethnogenealogical method. In *Explorations in cultural anthropology*, ed. W. Goodenough, pp. 22-55. New York: McGraw-Hill.

Cowan, G. 1948. Mazateco whistle speech. *Language* 24: 280-286.

Craig, D. 1971. Education and Creole English in the West Indies: Some sociolinguistic factors. In *Pidginization and Creolization of Languages*, ed. D. Hymes, pp. 371-392. London: Cambridge University Press.

Currie, H. 1932. A projection of socio-linguistics: The relationships of speech to social status. *Southern Speech Journal* 18: 28-37.

Daneš, R. 1964. A three-level approach to syntax. *Travaux linguistiques de Prague* 1: 225-240.

Darnell, R., ed. 1972. *Prolegomena to typologies of speech use.* (Texas Working Papers in Sociolinguistics, Special Number) Austin: Department of Anthropology, University of Texas.

Darnell, R., and Sherzer, J. 1972. A field guide to the study of speech use. In *Directions in sociolinguistics*, eds. J. Gumperz and D. Hymes, pp. 548-554. New York: Holt, Rinehart and Winston.

DeCamp, D. 1969. Toward a formal theory of sociolinguistics. Unpublished ms.

——. 1970. Is a sociolingustic theory possible? In *Report of the 20th round table meeting*, ed. J. E. Alatis, pp. 157-168. (Monograph series on language and linguistics 22.) Washington, D.C.: Georgetown University Press.

——. 1972. Toward a generative analysis of a post-creole speech continuum. In *Pidginization and creolization of languages*, ed. D. Hymes, pp. 349-370. London: Cambridge University Press.

Denison, N. 1968. Sauris: a trilingual community in diatypic perspective. *Man* (n.s.) 3 (4): 578-592.

——. 1970. Sociolinguistic aspects of plurilingualism. *Proceedings of the International Days of Sociolinguistics*, pp. 255-278. Rome: Istituto Luigi Sturzo.

Dennis, W. 1940. *The Hopi child.* Charlottesville: University of Virginia Press.

Devereux, G. 1949. Mohave voice and speech mannerisms. *Word* 5: 268-272.

——. 1951. Mohave Indian verbal and motor profanity. In *Psychoanalysis and the social sciences.* Vol. 3, ed. Geza Roheim. New York: International Universities Press.

Dillard, J. 1968. The creolist and the study of Negro non-standard dialects in the United States. In *Pidginization and creolization of languages*, ed. D. Hymes, pp. 393-408. London: Cambridge University Press.

Dong, Q. P. ms. A note on conjoined noun phrases.

Duncan, H. D. 1968. *Symbols in society*. New York: Oxford University Press.

Easton, L., and Guddat, K. H., eds. 1967. *Writings of the young Marx on philosophy and society*. Garden City, New York: Doubleday.

Ebeling, G. 1966. *Theology and proclamation: a discussion with Rudolf Bultmann*. London: Collins.

Eersel, C. 1971. Prestige in choice of language and linguistic form. In *Pidginizaton and creolization of languages*, ed. D. Hymes, pp. 317-322. London: Cambridge University Press.

Eggan, D. 1943. The general problem of Hopi adjustment. *American Anthropologist* 45: 357-373.

Ervin-Tripp, S. 1964. An analysis of the interaction of language, topic and listener. In *The ethnography of communication*, eds. J. J. Gumperz and D. Hymes, pp. 86-102. Washington, D.C.: American Anthropological Association.

————. 1972. On sociolinguistic rules: alternation and co-occurence. In *Directions in sociolinguistics*, eds. J. J. Gumperz and D. Hymes, pp. 213-250. New York: Holt, Rinehart and Winston.

————. 1973. *Language acquisition and language choice*. Selected and introduced by A. S. Dil. Stanford: Stanford University Press.

Faris, J. 1966. The dynamics of verbal exchange; a Newfoundland example. *Anthropologica* 8: 235-248.

————. 1968. The lexicon of 'occasions' in Cat Harbour: some comments on the cultural validation of ethnographic descriptions. *Man* (n.s.) 3: 112-124.

Ferguson, C. A. 1963. Linguistic theory and language learning. In *Report of the 14th Round Table*, ed. R. J. DiPietro, pp. 115-124. (Monograph Series in Languages and Linguistics, 16.) Washington, D.C.: Georgetown University Press.

————. 1966. National sociolinguistic profile formulas. In *Sociolinguistics*, ed. W. Bright, pp. 309-315. The Hague: Mouton.

————. 1971. *Language structure and language use*. Selected and introduced by A. S. Dil. Stanford: Stanford University Press.

Ferguson, C. A., and Gumperz, J. J., eds. 1960. *Linguistic diversity in South Asia: studies in regional, social and functional variation*. (Research Center in Anthropology, Folklore, and Linguistics, Publication 13; International Journal of American Linguistics 26 [3], part III.) Bloomington: Indiana University Research Center.

Fillmore, C. 1968. The case for case. In *Universals in linguistic theory*, eds. E. Bach and R. Harms, pp. 1-88. New York: Holt, Rinehart and Winston.

Firth, J. R. 1935. The technique of semantics. *Transactions of the philological society*, pp. 36-72. London.

Fischer, J. L. 1964. Words for self and other in some Japanese families. in *The ethnography of communication,* eds. J. J. Gumperz and D. Hymes, pp. 115-126.

———. 1972. The stylistic significance of consonantal sandhi in Trukese and Ponapean. In *Directions in sociolinguistics: The ethnography of communication,* eds. J. J. Gumperz and D. Hymes, pp. 500-511.

Fishman, J. 1966. *Language loyalty in the United States.* The Hague: Mouton.

———., ed. 1968. *Readings in the sociology of language.* The Hague: Mouton.

———. 1970. *Sociolinguistics.* Rowley, Mass.: Newbury House.

———. 1972a. *The sociology of language.* Rowley, Mass.: Newbury House.

———. ed. 1972b. *Advances in the sociology of language.* 2 vols. The Hague: Mouton.

Fishman, J., Ferguson, C., and Das Gupta, J., eds. 1968. *Language problems of developing nations.* New York: Wiley.

Fock, N. 1965. Cultural aspects of the "oho" institution among the Waiwai. *Proceedings of the 36th International Congress of Americanists* (1964), pp. 136-140. Copenhagen: Munksgaard.

Fontana, B. 1968. Savage anthropologists and unvanishing Indians in the American Southwest. Paper read before the 67th annual meeting of the American Anthropological Association. Seattle, Washington.

Frake, C. O. 1961. The diagnosis of disease among the Subanun of Mindanao. *American Anthropologist* 63: 113-132.

———. 1962a. Cultural ecology and ethnography. *American Anthropologist* 64: 53-59.

———. 1962b. The ethnographic study of cognitive systems. In *Anthropology and human behavior,* eds. R. Gladwin and W. C. Sturdevant, pp. 72-85. Washington, D.C.: Anthropological Society of Washington.

———. 1964. A structural description of Subanun 'religious behavior.' In *Explorations in cultural anthropology,* ed. W. H. Goodenough, pp. 111-129. New York: McGraw-Hill.

———. 1972. Struck by speech: The Yakan concept of litigation. In *Directions in sociolinguistics: The ethnography of communication,* eds. J. J. Gumperz and D. Hymes, pp. 109-129.

Franklin, K. 1967. Names and aliases in Kewa. *Journal of the Polynesian Society* 76: 76-81.

Friedrich, P. 1966. Structural implications of Russian pronominal usage. In *Sociolinguistics,* ed. W. Bright, pp. 214-253. The Hague: Mouton.

———. 1972. Social context and semantic feature: the Russan pronominal usage. In *Directions in sociolinguistics,* eds. J. J. Gumperz and D. Hymes, pp. 272-300. New York: Holt, Rinehart and Winston.

Gardner, P. 1966. Symmetric respect and memorate knowledge: the structure and ecology of individualistic culture. *Southwestern Journal of Anthropology* 22: 389-415.

Garfinkel, H. 1972. Remarks on ethnomethodology. In *Directions in sociolinguistics*, eds. J. J. Gumperz and D. Hymes, pp. 309-324.

Gayton, A. and Newman, S. 1940. *Yokuts and Western Mono myths*. (University of California Publications, Anthropological Records, 5). Berkeley and Los Angeles.

Giglioli, P. P., ed. 1972. *Language and social context*. London: Penguin.

Gluckman, M. 1959. The technical vocabulary of Barotse jurisprudence. *American Anthropologist* 61: 743-759.

———. 1963. Gossip and scandal. *Current Anthropology* 4: 307-315.

Goodenough, W. 1956. Residence rules. *Southwestern Journal of Anthropology* 12: 22-37.

———. 1957a. Cultural anthropology and linguistics. *Report of the 7th round table meeting*, ed. P. Garvin, pp. 167-173. Washington, D.C.: Georgetown University Press.

———. 1957b. Review of Keesing and Keesing 1956. *Language* 34: 24-29.

———. 1961. Formal properties of status relationships. Paper read at the annual meeting of the American Anthropological Association, November 16. Philadelphia. (Published in *The relevance of models for social anthropology*, ed. M. Banton. London: Tavistock publications and Praeger, 1965.)

———. 1965. Personal names and modes of address in two Oceanic societies. In *Context and meaning in cultural anthropology*, ed. M. Spiro, pp. 265-276. New York: Free Press.

Goody, J., and Watt, I. 1963. The consequences of literacy. *Comparative Studies in Society and History*, 5: 304-345.

Greenberg, J. 1948. Linguistics and ethnology. *Southwestern Journal of Anthropology* 4: 140-148.

———. 1968. *Anthropological linguistics*. New York: Random House.

———. 1971. *Language, culture and communication*. Selected and introduced by A. S. Dil. Stanford: Stanford University Press.

Gross, L. P. 1973a. Modes of communication and the acquisition of symbolic competence. In *Communications, technology, and social policy*, eds. G. Gerbner, L. Gross, and W. Melody. New York: Wiley.

———. 1973b. Art as the communication of competence. *Social Science Information*. The Hague: Mouton.

Guiraud, P. 1961. *La stylistique*. Third edition. Paris: Presses Universitaires de France.

———. 1967. *Structures étymologiques du lexique français*. Paris: Librairie Larousse.

Gumperz, J. J. 1962. Types of linguistic communities. *Anthropological Linguistics* 4(1): 28-40.

———. 1971. *Language in social groups.* Selected and introduced by A. S. Dil. Stanford: Stanford University Press.

Gumperz, J. J. and Hymes, D., eds. 1964. *The ethnography of communication.* Washington, D.C.: American Anthropological Association. (First issued as *American Anthropologist* 66(6), part 2).

———, eds. 1972. *Directions in sociolinguistics: The ethnography of communication.* New York: Holt, Rinehart and Winston.

Gumperz, J. J., and Wilson, R. 1971. Convergence and creolization. In *Pidginization and creolization,* ed. D. Hymes, pp. 151-167. London: Cambridge University Press.

Gunter, R. 1966. On the placement of accent in dialogue: a feature of context grammar. *Journal of Linguistics* 2: 159-179.

———. 1972. Intonation and relevance. In *Intonation,* ed. D. Bolinger, pp. 194-215. Harmondsworth, England: Penguin Books.

Haas, M. 1944. Men's and women's speech in Koasati. In *Language in culture and society,* ed. D. Hymes. New York: Harper and Row.

Habermas, J. 1970. Toward a theory of communicative competence. In *Recent Sociology no. 2: Patterns of communicative behavior,* ed. H. P. Dreitzel, pp. 114-148. New York: Macmillan.

Hall, E. 1959. *The silent language.* New York: Doubleday.

Halliday, M. A. K. 1967-68. Notes on transitivity and theme in English. *Journal of Linguistics* 3: 37-81, 199-244; 4: 179-215.

———. 1970. Functional diversity in language as seen from a consideration of modality and mood in English. *Foundations of Language* 6: 322-361.

———. 1971. Linguistic function and literary style: an inquiry into the language of William Golding's *The inheritors.* In *Literary style: A symposium,* ed. S. Chatman. London: Oxford University Press. (Also in Halliday 1973: 103-140).

———. 1973. *Explorations in the functions of language.* London: Edward Arnold.

Hallowell, A. I. 1964. Ojibwa ontology, behavior and world view. *Primitive views of the world,* ed. S. Diamond, pp. 49-82. New York: Columbia University Press.

Harrah, D. 1963. *Communication: a logical model.* Cambridge, Mass.: MIT Press.

Harris, Z. 1951. *Methods in structural linguistics.* Chicago: University of Chicago Press.

Hasan, R. 1968. *Grammatical cohesion in spoken and written English.* London: Longmans.

Hattori, S. 1964. A special language of the older generations among the Ainu. *Linguistics* 6: 43-58.

Haugen, E. 1957. The semantics of Icelandic orientation. *Word* 13: 447-460.

———. 1972. *The ecology of language.* Selected and introduced by A. S. Dil. Stanford: Stanford University Press.

Hertzler, J. O. 1965. *A sociology of language.* New York: Random House.

Herzog, G. 1945. Drum-signalling in a West African tribe. *Word* 1: 217-238.

Hilger, Sister I. 1957. *Araucanian child life and its cultural background.* (Smithsonian miscellaneous collections 135. Public 4297.) Washington, D.C.

Hockett, C. 1955. *A manual of phonology.* (Indiana University Publications in Anthropology and Linguistics; Memoir 11 of the International Journal of American Linguistics.) Bloomington.

————. 1958. *A course in modern linguistics.* New York: Macmillan.

————. 1960. Ethno-linguistic implications of studies in linguistics and psychiatry. *Report of the 9th round table meeting,* ed. W. Austin, pp. 175-193. Washington, D.C.: Georgetown University Press.

Hockett, C., and Ascher, R. 1964. The human revolution. *Current Anthropology* 5 (3): 135-168.

Hogan, H. 1967. *An ethnography of communication of the Ashanti.* Master's thesis. University of Pennsylvania. (Issued as Working Papers in Sociolinguistics, 1; Austin: University of Texas, Department of Anthropology).

Hunter, A. M. 1964. *Interpreting the parables.* London: SCM Press.

Hymes, D. 1956. The supposed Spanish loanword in Hopi for jaybird. *International Journal of American Linguistics* 22: 186.

————. 1960. Phonological aspects of style: some English sonnets. In *Style in Language,* ed. T. A. Sebeok, pp. 109-151. Cambridge, Mass.: MIT Press.

————. 1961a. Functions of speech: the evolutionary approach. In *Anthropology and education,* ed. F. C. Gruber, pp. 55-83. Philadelphia: University of Pennsylvania.

————. 1961b. Linguistic aspects of cross-cultural personality study. In *Studying personality cross-culturally,* ed. B. Kaplan, pp. 313-359. Evanston: Row, Peterson.

————. 1961c. On typology of cognitive styles in language (with examples from Chinookan). *Anthropological Linguistics* 3 (1): 22-54.

————. 1961d. Abstract of Vachek, The London Group of Linguists. *International Journal of American Linguistics* 27: 166-167.

————. 1962. The ethnography of speaking. *Anthropology and human behavior,* eds. T. Gladwin and W. Sturtevant, pp. 15-53. Washington, D.C.: Anthropological Society of Washington.

————. 1964a. Directions in (ethno) linguistic theory. *Transcultural studies of cognition,* eds. A. K. Romney and R. G. D'Andrade, pp. 6-56. (Special publication, *American Anthropologist* 66 (3), part 2.) Washington, D.C.: American Anthropological Association.

————. 1964b. Introduction: toward ethnographies of communication. In *The ethnography of communication,* eds. J. J. Gumperz and D. Hymes, pp. 1-34. (Special publication, *American Anthropologist*

66 (6), part 2.) Washington, D.C.: American Anthropological Association.

———. 1964c. Introduction. In *Language in culture and society*, ed. D. Hymes. New York: Harper and Row.

———. 1964d. A perspective for linguistic anthropology. In *Horizons of anthropology*, ed. S. Tax, pp.. 92-107. Chicago: Aldine.

———. 1964e. Formal comment. In *The acquisition of language*, ed. U. Bellugi and R. Brown, pp. 107-112. Lafayette: Child Development Publications.

———., ed. 1964f. *Language in culture and society.* New York: Harper and Row.

———. 1966a. On anthropological linguistics and congeners. *American Anthropologist* 68: 143-153.

———. 1966b. Two types of linguistic relativity. In *Sociolnguistics,* ed. W. Bright, pp. 114-158. The Hague: Mouton.

———. 1966c. Some points of Suislaw phonology. *International Journal of American Linguistics.* 32: 328-342.

———. 1966 ms. Sociolinguistic determination of knowledge: notes on the history of its treatment in American anthropology. Prepared for Research Committee on the Sociology of Knowledge, International Sociological Association.

———. 1967a. Why linguistics needs the sociologist. *Social Research* 34 (4): 632-647.

———. 1967b. Models of the interaction of language and social setting. (*Problems of bilingualism,* ed. J. Macnamara.) *Journal of social issues* 23 (2): 8-28.

———. 1967c. The anthropology of communication. In *Human communication theory,* ed. F. Dance, pp. 1-39. New York: Holt, Rinehart and Winston.

———. 1967 ms. On communicative competence.

———. 1968a. Review of Burke, Language as symbolic action. *Language* 44: 664-669.

———. 1968b. Linguistic problems in defining the concept of the 'tribe.' In *Essays on the Problem of Tribe,* ed. J. Helm, pp. 23-48. (Proceedings of the American Ethnological Society, 1967.) Seattle: University of Washington Press.

———. 1968c. Linguistics — the field. *International encyclopedia of the social sciences* 9: 351-371. New York: Macmillan.

———. 1968d. The 'wife' who 'goes out' like a 'man': reinterpretation of a Clackamas Chinook myth. *Social Science Information* 7 (3): 173-199.

———. 1969. Ends and meanings. Review of *Symbols in society* by H. D. Duncan. *Science* (9 May) 1964: 695-696.

———. 1970a. Linguistic aspects of comparative political research. In *Methodology of comparative* research, eds. R. T. Holt and J. Turner, pp. 295-341. New York: The Free Press.

————. 1970b. Linguistic method of ethnography. In *Method and theory in linguistics,* ed. P. Garvin, pp. 249-325. The Hague: Mouton.

————. 1970c. Linguistic theory and the functions of speech. In Proceedings of International Days of Sociolinguistics, pp. 111-144. Rome: Istituto Luigi Sturzo.

————. 1971a. Sociolinguistics and the ethnography of speaking. In *Social anthropology and language,* ed. E. Ardener, pp. 47-93. (ASA monographs 10.) London: Tavistock.

————. 1971b. Competence and performance in linguistic theory. In *Acquisition of language: models and methods,* eds. R. Huxley and E. Ingram, pp. 3-28. London: Tavistock.

————. 1971c. On linguistic theory, communicative competence and the education of disadvantaged children. In *Anthropological perspectives on education,* eds. M. L. Wax, S. A. Diamond, and F. O. Gearing, pp. 51-66. New York: Basic Books.

————. 1971d. Foreword. In *The origin and diversification of languages,* by M. Sawdesh; ed. J. Sherzer, pp. v-x. Chicago: Aldine.

————. 1971e. Introduction, Part III. In *Pidginization and creolization of languages,* ed. D. Hymes, pp. 65-90. London: Cambridge University Press.

————. 1972a. Models of the interaction of language and social life. In *Directions in sociolinguistics,* eds. J. J. Gumperz and D. Hymes, pp. 35-71. New York: Holt, Rinehart and Winston.

————. 1972b. Introduction. In *Functions of language in the classroom,* eds. C. Cazden, V. John-Steiner, and D. Hymes, pp. xi-lvii. New York: Teachers College Press.

————. 1972c. The use of anthropology: critical, political, personal. In *Reinventing anthropology,* ed. D. Hymes, pp. 3-79. New York: Pantheon Books.

————. 1972d. Formal comment. In *Sociolinguistics in cross-cultural analysis,* eds. D. M. Smith and R. W. Shuy, pp. 103-115. Washington, D.C.: Georgetown University Press.

————. 1972e. On personal pronouns: 'fourth' person and phonesthematic aspects. In *Studies in linguistics in honor of George L. Trager,* ed. M. E. Smith, pp. 100-121. The Hague: Mouton.

————. 1973a. *Toward linguistic competence.* (Working papers in sociolinguistics, 16.) Austin: University of Texas, Department of Anthropology.

————. 1973b. Speech and language: on the origins and foundations of inequality in speaking. *Daedalus* (Summer): 59-86. (Proceedings of the American Academy of Arts and Sciences 102 (3).)

————. 1974. Ways of speaking. In *Explorations in the ethnography of speaking,* ed. R. Baumann and J. Sherzer. New York and London: Cambridge University Press.

Irvine, J. 1968. Speech and music in two cultures. ms.

Jacobs, M. 1940. Coos myth texts. (University of Washington Publications in Anthropology 8 (2): 127-260.) Seattle: University of Washington Press.

———. 1945. Kalapuya texts. (University of Washington Publications in Anthropology, 11.) Seattle: University of Washington Press.

———. 1958. *The content and style of an oral literature.* Chicago: University of Chicago Press.

———. 1959. *Clackamas Chinook texts,* part 2. (Research Center in Anthropology, Folklore and Linguistics, Publication 11.) Bloomington, Indiana.

Jacobs, R. and Rosenbaum, P. 1971. *Transformations, style and meaning.* Waltham, Mass.: Xerox College Publishing.

Jain, D. K. 1969. Verbalization of respect in Hindi. *Anthropological Linguistics* 11 (3): 79-97.

Jakobson, R. 1953. Chapter 2. In *Result of the conference of anthropologists and linguists,* C. Lévi-Strauss, R. Jakobson, C. F. Voegelin and T. Sebeok, pp. 11-21. (Memoir 8 of the International Journal of American linguistics, Indiana University Publications in Anthropology and Linguistics.) Bloomington. (Reprinted in his *Selected Writings,* 2: 554-567. The Hague: Mouton.)

———. 1957. *Shifters, verbal categories, and the Russian verb.* Cambridge, Mass.: Harvard University, Russian language project. (Reprinted in his *Selected Writings,* 2: 130-147. The Hague: Mouton.)

———. 1960. Concluding statement: linguistics and poetics. In *Style in Language,* ed. T. Sebeok, pp. 350-373. Cambridge, Mass.: MIT Press.

———. 1963. Efforts towards a means-ends model of language in interwar continental linguistics. In *Trends in modern linguistics,* eds. C. Mohrmann, F. Norman and A. Sommerfelt, pp. 104-108. Utrecht: Spectrum Publishers. (Reprinted in his *Selected Writings,* 2: 522-526. The Hague: Mouton, 1971.)

———. 1965. Quest for the essence of language. *Diogenes* 51: 21-37. (Reprinted in his *Selected Writings,* 2: 345-359. The Hague: Mouton.)

———. 1969. Linguistics in relation to other sciences. In *Actes du X congres international des linguistes,* pp. 75-122. Bucharest: Editions de l'Académie de la République Socialiste du Roumanie. (Reprinted in his *Selected Writings,* 2: 655-696. The Hague: Mouton, 1971.)

Jeremias, J. 1963. *The parables of Jesus.* London: SCM Press.

Jespersen, O. 1924. *The philosophy of grammar.* London: Allen and Unwin.

John, V. 1963. The intellectual development of slum children: some preliminary findings. *American Journal of Orthopsychiatry* 33: 813-822.

———. 1964. The social context of language acquisition. *Merrill-Palmer Quarterly* 10: 265-275.

Joos, M. 1959. The isolation of styles. In *Report of the 10th round table meeting*, ed. R. Harrell, pp. 107-113. Washington, D.C.: Georgetown University Press.

Joseph, Sister M. 1962. *Rhetoric in Shakespeare's time. Literary theory in Renaissance Europe*. New York: Harcourt, Brace and World. (Abridged from *Shakespeare's use of the arts of language*. New York: Columbia University Press, 1947.)

Kasper, W. 1969. *The methods of dogmatic theology*. Shannon: Ecclesia Press.

Katz, J. J. 1967. Recent issues in semantic theory. *Foundations of Language* 3: 124-194.

Katz, J., and Fodor, J. 1963. The structure of a semantic theory. *Language* 39: 170-210.

Keesing, F. M., and Keesing, M. M. 1956. *Elite communication in Samoa: a study in leadership*. Stanford: Stanford University Press.

Kenyon, J. S. 1948. Cultural levels and functional varieties in English. *College English* 10: 31-36.

Kiparsky, P. 1968. Tense and mood in Indo-European syntax. *Foundations of Language* 4: 30-57.

Kjolseth, R. 1972. Making sense: natural language and shared knowledge in understanding. In *Advances in the sociology of language*, ed. J. Fishman, Vol. 2, pp. 50-76. The Hague: Mouton.

Klima, E. 1964. Relatedness between grammatical systems. *Language* 40: 1-20.

Kluckhohn, C. 1961. Notes on some anthropological aspects of communication. *American Anthropologist* 63: 895-910.

Kroeber, A. 1911. Incorporation as a linguistic process. *American Anthropologist* 13: 577-584.

―――. 1916. Arapaho dialects. *University of California Publications in American Archaeology and Ethnology* 12: 71-138.

―――. 1960. Evolution, history and culture. In *Evolution after Darwin*, ed. Sol Tax, pp. 1-16. Chicago: University of Chicago Press.

Labov, W. 1965. On the mechanism of linguistic change. In *Report of the 16th round table meeting*, ed. C. Kreidler, pp. 91-114. (Monograph Series in Languages and Linguistics, 18.) Washington, D.C.: Georgetown University Press.

―――. 1966. *The social stratification of English in New York City*. Washington, D.C.: Center for Applied Linguistics.

―――. 1970. The study of language in its social context. *Studium Generale* 20: 30-87.

―――. 1971. Methodology. In *A survey of linguistic science*, ed. W. O. Dingwall, pp. 412-491. College Park, Maryland: University of Maryland, Linguistics Program.

―――. 1973a. *Language in the inner city*. Philadelphia: University of Pennsylvania.

———. 1973b. *Sociolinguistic Patterns.* Philadelphia: University of Pennsylvania.

Ladefoged, P. 1964. *A phonetic study of West African languages.* Cambridge: At the University Press.

Lakoff, R. 1972. Language in context. *Language* 48: 907-927.

———. 1973. Language and woman's place. *Language in society* 2 (1): 45-80.

Lambert, W. 1967a. A psychology of bilingualism. (*Problems of bilingualism,* ed. J. Macnamara.) *Journal of social issues* 23 (2): 91-109.

———. 1967b. The use of *tu* and *vous* as forms of address in French Canada: a pilot study. *Journal of Verbal Learning and Verbal Behavior* 6: 614-617.

———. 1972. *Language, psychology and culture.* Selected and introduced by A. S. Dil. Stanford: Stanford University Press.

Lamb, S. 1964. The sememic approach to structural semantics. *American Anthropologist* 66 (3): 57-78.

Lammers, W. 1936. *Wilhelm von Humboldts weg zur Sprachforschung 1785-1801.* Berlin.

Lanham, R. 1968. *A handlist of rhetorical terms.* Berkeley and Los Angeles: University of California Press.

Lee, D. 1959. *Freedom and culture.* Englewood-Cliffs, N.J.: Prentice-Hall, Spectrum Books.

Lefebvre, H. 1966. *Le Langage et la société.* Paris. Gallimard.

———. 1968. *The sociology of Marx.* London: Allen Lane, The Penguin Press.

Le Page, R. 1969. Problems of description in multilingual communities. *Transactions of the Philological Society* (1968), pp. 189-212. London.

Leroux, R. 1958. *L'Anthropologie comparée de Guillaume de Humboldt.* (Publications de la Faculté des lettres de l'Université de Strasbourg, Fascicule 135.) Paris: Société d'éditions.

Lévi-Strauss, C. 1953. Social structure. In *Anthropology today,* by A. L. Kroeber et al., 524-553. Chicago: University of Chicago Press.

———. 1958. *La pensee sauvage.* Paris: Plon.

———. 1960. L'Anthropologie sociale devant l'historie. *Annales* 15 (4): 625-737.

Lieberson, S., ed. 1966. *Explorations in sociolinguistics.* Sociological Inquiry 36 (2).

Lisker, L., Cooper, F., and Liberman, A. 1962. The uses of experiment in language description. *Word* 18: 82-106.

Lomax, A. 1959. Folk song style. *American Anthropologist* 61: 927-954.

Lonsbury, F. 1955. The varieties of meaning. In *Report of the 6th round table meeting,* ed. R. Weinstein. pp. 158-164. (Monograph Series on Languages and Linguistics 8.) Washington, D.C.: Georgetown University Press.

———. 1956. A semantic analysis of the Pawnee kinship usage. *Language* 32: 158-194.

Lowie, R. 1917. Notes on the social organization of the Mandan, Hidatsa, and Crow Indians. *American Museum of Natural History*, Anthropological Papers 21 (I).

———. 1937. *A history of ethnological theory.* New York: Rinehart.

Macnamara, J., ed. 1967. *Problems of bilingualism.* (*Journal of Social Issues* 23 (2).)

McAwley, J. 1968. The role of semantics in a grammar. In *Universals in linguistic theory*, eds. E. Bach and R. Harms, pp. 125-170. New York: Holt, Rinehart and Winston.

McIlwraith, T. 1948. *The Bella Coola Indians.* Toronto: University of Toronto Press.

McLuhan, M. 1962. *The Gutenberg Galaxy. The making of typographic man.* Toronto: University of Toronto Press.

———. 1964. *Understanding media. The extensions of man.* New York: McGraw-Hill.

Mair, L. 1935. Linguistics without sociology: some notes on the Standard Luganda dictionary. *Bulletin of the School of Oriental Studies, London* 7: 913-921.

Malinowski, B. 1935. *Coral gardens and their magic*, Vol. 2. London: Allen and Unwin.

Mandelbaum, D., ed. 1949. *Selected writings of Edward Sapir.* Berkeley and Los Angeles: University of California Press.

Mao Tze-Tung. 1964. *On practice.* Peking: Foreign Language Press.

Marchand, H. 1959. Phonetic symbolism in English word-formation. *Indogermanische Forschungen* 64: 146-168, 256-277.

Marrou, H. 1965. *A history of education in antiquity.* New York: Sheed and Ward.

May, L. C. 1956. A survey of glossolalia and related phenomena in non-Christian religions. *American Anthropologist* 58: 75-96.

Mead, M. 1937. Public opinion mechanisms among primitive peoples. *Public Opinion Quarterly* 1: 5-16.

———. 1948. Some cultural approaches to communication problems. In *The communication of ideas*, ed. L. Bryson, pp. 9-26. New York: Harper.

———. 1964. *Continuities in cultural evolution.* New Haven: Yale.

Mehan, H. 1972. Language using abilities. *Language Sciences* 22:1-10.

Meillet, A. 1906. Comment les mots changent de sens. *L'année sociologique* (1905-1906). (Reprinted in *Linguistique historique et linguistique générale*, Vol. 1: 230-271.) Paris: Klincksieck.

Merleau-Ponty, M. 1967. Introduction a la prose du monde. *La Revue de Metaphysique et de Morale* 2: 139-153. (Published in English in *Prose of the world.* Evanston: Northwestern University Press, 1970.)

Merriam, A. 1964. The arts and anthropology. In *Horizons of anthropology*, ed. S. Tax. Chicago: Aldine Press.

Messenger, J. Jr. Anang proverb riddles. *Journal of American Folklore* 73: 225-235.

Metcalf, G. 1938. *Forms of address in German* (1500-1800). (Washington University Studies, n.s., Language and Literature, 7.) St. Louis.

Metzger, D., and Williams, G. 1963. Tenejapa medicine I: the cure. *Southwestern Journal of Anthropology* 19: 216-234.

Miller, G. 1956. The magical number seven, plus or minus two: some limits to our capacity for processing information. *The Psychological Review* 63: 81-97.

Mills, C. W. 1959. *The sociological imagination*. New York: Oxford University Press.

Morris, C. 1946. *Signs, language and behavior*. Englewood-Cliffs: Prentice Hall.

Moule, C. 1966. *The birth of the New Testament*. London: Adam and Charles Black.

Murphy, R. 1967. Tuareg kinship. *American Anthropologist* 69: 163-170.

Newman, S. 1955. Vocabulary levels: Zuni sacred and slang usage. *Southwestern Journal of Anthropology* 11: 345-354. (Reprinted in Hymes 1964).

Nida, E. 1945. Linguistics and ethnology in translation problems. *Word* 1: 194-208.

Parain, B. 1969. *Petite métaphysique de la parole*. Paris: Gallimard.

Petrovic, G. 1967. *Marx in the mid-twentieth century*. Garden City, New York: Doubleday, Anchor Books.

Philips, S. 1970. Acquisition of rules for appropriate speech usage. In *Report of the 21st round table meeting*, ed. J. Alatis, pp. 77-96. (Monograph Series in Languages and Linguistics, 23.) Washington, D.C.: Georgetown University Press.

————. 1972. Participant structure and communicative competence: Warm Springs children in community and classroom. In *Functions of language in the classroom*, eds. C. Cazden, V. John, and D. Hymes, pp. 370-394. New York: Teachers College Press.

Pike, K. 1967. *Language in relation to a unified theory of the structure of human behavior*. The Hague: Mouton. [Preliminary edition in three parts, 1954, 1955, 1960 from Santa Ana, California: Summer Institute of linguistics, with essentially same numbering but different pagination; pagination here is to the 1967 edition.)

Pittenger, R., Hockett, C., and Danehy, J. 1960. *The first five minutes*. Ithaca: Paul Martineau.

Postal, P. 1964. Underlying and superficial linguistic structure. *Harvard Educational Review* 34: 246-266.

————. 1968. *Aspects of the theory of phonology*. New York: Harper and Row.

Pride, J. 1970. *Social meaning and language.* London: Oxford University Press.

Quirk, R. 1968. *Essays on the English language, medieval and modern.* London: Longmans.

Reichling, A. 1947. What is general linguistics? *Lingua* 1 (1): 8-24.

Reichel-Dolmatoff, G. and A. 1961. *The people of Aritama.* Chicago: University of Chicago Press.

Revill, P. 1966. Preliminary report on paralinguistics in Mbembe (E. Nigeria). In *Tagmemic and matrix linguistics applied to selected African languages,* by K. Pike, pp. 245-254. Appendix VIII. Final Report, Contract no. OE-5-14-065. Washington, D.C.: U.S. Dept. of Health, Education and Welfare, Office of Education, Bureau of Research.

Richardson, A. 1961. *The Bible in the age of science.* London: SCM Press.

Roberts, J. ms. *Four southwestern men.*

Rubin, J. 1968. *National bilingualism in Paraguay.* The Hague: Mouton.

Rubin, J., and Jernudd, R., eds. 1972. *Can language be planned?* Honolulu: University Press of Hawaii.

Ruesch, J. 1961. *Therapeutic communication.* New York: W. W. Norton.

Ruesch, J., and Kees, W. 1956. *Nonverbal communication. Notes on the visual perception of human relations.* Berkeley and Los Angeles: University of California Press.

Sacks, H. 1972. On the analyzability of stores by children. In *Directions in sociolinguistics,* eds. J. J. Gumperz and D. Hymes, pp. 329-345. New York: Holt, Rinehart and Winston.

Salisbury, R. 1962. Notes on bilingualism and linguistic change in New Guinea. *Anthropological Linguistics* 4 (7): 1-13.

Samarin, W. 1965. The language of silence. *Practical Anthropology* 12: 115-119.

————. 1969. The art of Gbeya insults. *International Journal of American Linguistics* 35: 323-329.

Sandys, Sir J. E. 1920. *A history of classical scholarship.* Vol. 1. Cambridge: Cambridge University Press.

Sankoff, G. 1974. A quantitative approach to the study of communicative competence. In *Explorations in the ethnography of speaking,* eds. R. Bauman and J. Sherzer. New York: Cambridge University Press.

Sapir, E. [Papers by Sapir reprinted in Mandelbaum (ed.), *Selected writings of Edward Sapir* (Berkeley and Los Angeles: University of California Press, 1949) are indicated by "SWES," together with their pages in that collection.]

————. 1911. The problem of noun incorporation in American languages. *American Anthropologist* 13: 250-282.

————. 1912. Language and environment. *American Anthropologist* 14: 226-242. (SWES 89-103.)

————. 1915. Abnormal types of speech in Nootka. (Canada, Dept. of Mines, Geological Survey, Memoir 62; Anthropological Series, no. 5). Ottawa: Government Printing Bureau. (SWES 179-196.)

————. 1916. *Time perspective in aboriginal American culture: a study in method.* (Canada, Dept. of Mines, Geological Survey, Memoir 90; Anthropological Series, No. 13) Ottawa: Government Printing Bureau.) (SWES 389-462.)

————. 1921. *Language.* New York: Harcourt, Brace.

————. 1922. Takelma. In *Handbook of American Indian Languages,* Part II, ed. F. Boas, pp. 7-296. (Bureau of American Ethnology, Bulletin 40.) Washington, D.C.

————. 1924. Culture, genuine and spurious. *American Journal of Sociology* 29: 401-492. (SWES 308-331.)

————. 1925. Sound patterns in language. *Language* 1: 37-51. (SWES 33-45.)

————. 1927a. Speech as a personality trait. *American Journal of Sociology* 32: 892-905. (SWES 533-543.)

————. 1927b. The unconscious patterning of behavior in society. In *The unconscious,* ed. E. S. Dummer, pp. 114-142. New York: Knopf. (SWES 544-559.)

————. 1929. The status of linguistics as a science. *Language* 5: 207-214. (SWES 160-166.)

————. 1932. Cultural anthropology and psychiatry. *Journal of Abnormal and Social Psychology* 27: 229-242. (SWES 509-521.)

————. 1933a. Language. *Encyclopedia of the Social Sciences* 9: 155-169. (SWES 7-32.)

————. 1933b. Communication. *Encyclopedia of the Social Sciences* 4: 78-81. (SWES 104-109.)

————. 1934. The emergence of the concept of personality in a study of cultures. *Journal of Social Psychology* 5: 408-415. (SWES 590-597.)

————. 1938. Why cultural anthropology needs the psychiatrist. *Psychiatry* 1: 7-12. (SWES 569-577.)

————. 1939. Psychiatric and cultural pitfalls in the business of getting a living. *Mental Health, Publication No. 9,* 237-244. (American Association for the Advancement of Science.) (SWES 578-589.)

Saussure, F. de. 1916. *Cours de linguistique générale.* Paris: Payot.

Schaff, A. 1962. *Introduction to semantics.* London: Pergamon Press.

Schegloff, E. 1968. Sequencing in conversational openings. *American Anthropologist* 70: 1075-1095.

Schneider, D. 1969. Componential analysis—a state of the art review. Prepared for Wenner-Gren symposium on cognitive studies and artificial intelligence research. Chicago.

Searle, J. 1962. Meaning and speech acts. *The Philosophical Review* 71: 423-432.

————. ms. How to promise. (Revised in Searle, 1969.)

————. 1969. *Speech acts*. Cambridge: Cambridge University Press.

Sebeok, T. 1962. Coding in the evolution of signalling behavior. *Behavioral Science* 7: 430-442.

Sebeok, T., Hayes, A. S., and Bateson, M. C., eds. 1964. *Approaches to semiotics: cultural anthropology, education, linguistics, psychiatry, psychology*. 's-Gravenhage: Mouton.

Service, E. 1960. Kinship terminology and evolution. *American Anthropologist* 62: 747-763.

Sherzer, D., and J. 1972. Literature in San Blas: discovering the Cuna *Ikala. Semiotica* 6 (2): 182-199.

Sherzer, J. 1967. *An exploration into the ethnography of speaking of the Abipones*. M.A. dissertation. Department of linguistics. University of Pennsylvania.

————. 1970. La parole chez les Abipones. *L'Homme* 10: 42-76.

————. 1973. Verbal and non-verbal terms: the pointed-lip gesture in San Blas Cuna. *Language in Society* 2 (1): 117-132.

Sherzer, J. and Darnell, R. 1972. Outline guide for the ethnographic study of speech use. In *Directions in sociolinguistics*, eds. J. J. Gumperz and D. Hymes, 548-554. New York: Holt, Rinehart and Winston.

Skinner, Q. 1970. Conventions and the understanding of speech acts. *The Philosophical Quarterly* 20: 118-138.

————. 1971. On performing and explaining linguistic actions. *The Philosophical Quarterly* 21: 1-21.

Slobin, D., ed. 1967. *A field manual for cross-cultural study of the acquisition of communicative competence*. Berkeley, Dept. of Psychology. University of California.

Smith, D. M., and Shuy, R., eds. 1972. *Sociolinguistics in cross-cultural analysis*. Washington, D.C.: Georgetown University Press.

Smith, K. D. 1969. The phonology of Sedang personal names. *Anthropological Linguistics* 11 (6): 187-198.

Smith, M. G. 1957. The social functions and meaning of Hausa praise singing. *Africa* 27: 26-44.

Smithers, C. V. 1954. Some English ideophones. *Archivum Linguisticum* 6: 73-111.

Snyder, G. 1969. *Earth house hold: technical notes and queries to fellow dharma revolutionaries*. New York: New Directions.

Sonnino, L. A. 1968. *A handbook to sixteenth century rhetoric*. London: Routledge and Kegan Paul.

Spier, L., and Sapir, E. 1930. *Wishram ethnography*. (University of Washington Publications in Anthropology 3 (3): 151-300.) Seattle: Washington University Press.

Ssukung, T. 1963. The twenty four modes of poetry. *Chinese Literature* 7: 65-83. Peking Foreign Languages Press.

Steinmann, M. Jr., ed. 1967. *New rhetorics*. New York: Scribners.

Stern, G. 1931. *Meaning and change of meaning.* (Göteborg Högskolas Arsskrift, 1932, 38 (1).) Goteborg. (Reprinted, Bloomington: Indiana University Press, n.d. [1963]).

Stern, T. 1957. Drum and whistle languages: an analysis of speech surrogates. *American Anthropologist* 59: 487-506.

Swadesh, M. 1933. Chitimacha verbs of derogatory or abusive connotation with parallels from European languages. *Language* 9: 192-201.

Taber, C. R. 1966. The structure of Sango narrative. (Hartford studies in Linguistics, 17.) 2 Vols. Hartford, Connecticut: Hartford Seminary Foundation.

Tambiah, S. J. 1968. The magical power of words. *Man* 3: 175-208.

Tedlock, D. 1971. On the translation of style in oral poetry. *Journal of American Folklore* 84: 114-133.

———. ms. From prayer to reprimand: The inversion of stress and pitch in Zuni.

Thorne, J. P. 1969. The grammar of jealousy. *Edinburgh studies in English and Scots.* London: Longmans.

Tillich, P. 1964. *Theology of culture.* New York: Oxford University Press.

Titles and forms of address: a guide to their correct use. 1967. 13th edition. London: Adam and Charles Black.

Trager, G. T. 1949. *The field of linguistics.* (Studies in Linguistics; Occasional papers, 1.) Norman, Oklahoma: Battenburg Press.

Trueblood, D. E. 1960. Robert Barclay and Joseph John Gurney. In *Then and now: Quaker essays.* Philadelphia: University of Pennsylvania.

Tulisano, R., and Cole, J. 1965. Is terminology enough? *American Anthropologist* 67: 747-748.

Turner, R. 1969. Words, utterances and activities. *Existential sociology,* ed. J. Douglas. New York: Appleton-Century-Crofts.

Tyler, S. A. 1965. Koya language morphology and patterns of kinship terminology. *American Anthropologist* 67: 1428-1440.

———. 1966. Context and variation in Koya kinship terminology. *American Anthropologist* 68: 693-708.

Tylor, E. 1871. *Primitive culture.* London: John Murray.

Uldall, H. 1957. *Outline of glossematics.* Part I. (Travaux du cercle linguistique de Copenhague, Vol. 11.) Copenhagen.

Ullmann, S. 1953. Descriptive semantics and linguistic typology. *Word* 9: 225-240.

Urban, W. 1939. *Language and reality.* New York: Macmillan.

Vachek, J. 1959. The London school of linguists. *Sbornik Praci Filosoficke Fakulty Brenske University, Recnik* 8: 106-113.

Van Holk, A. 1962. Referential and attitudinal construction. *Lingua* 11: 165-181.

Wallace, A. F. C. 1961. *Culture and personality.* New York: Random House.

Wallis, E. 1956. Sociolinguistics in relation to Mezquital Otomi transition education. *Estudios Anthropologicos Publicados en Homenaje al Doctor Manual Gamco,* pp. 523-535. Mexico, D. F.: Sociedad Mexicana de Antrópologia.

Waterhouse, V. 1963. Independent and dependent sentences. *International Journal of American Linguistics* 29: 45-54.

Watson, O. M., and Graves, T. D. 1966. Quantitative research in proxemic behavior. *American Anthropologist* 68: 971-985.

Weinreich, U. 1953. *Languages in contact.* New York: Linguistic Circle of New York.

————. 1963. On the semantic structure of language. In *Universals of Language,* ed. J. H. Greenberg, pp. 114-171. Cambridge, Mass.: MIT Press.

Weinreich, U. 1966. Explorations in semantic theory. *Current trends in linguistics 3: Theoretical foundations,* ed. T. A. Sebeok. The Hague: Mouton.

Weinreich, U., Labov, W., and Herzog, M. 1968. Empirical foundations for a theory of language change. In *Directions for historical linguistics: a symposium,* ed. W. Lehman and Y. Malkiel, pp. 97-195. Austin: University of Texas Press.

Werner, O. 1966. Pragmatics and ethnoscience. *Anthropological Linguistics* 8 (8): 42-65.

Wescott, R. 1962. *A Bini grammar. Part I: Phonology.* East Lansing: Michigan State University, African Language and Area Center.

Wheeler, A. 1967. Grammatical structure in Siona discourse. *Lingua* 19: 60-77.

Whiteley, W. H., ed. 1971. *Language use and social change.* London: Oxford University Press for the International African Institute.

Whiting, J., and Child, I. 1953. *Child training and personality: a cross-cultural study.* New Haven: Yale University Press.

Whorf, B. L. 1940. Linguistics as an exact science. *Technological review* 43: 61-63, 80-83. (Reprinted in *Language, thought and reality: selected writings of Benjamin L. Whorf,* ed. J. Carroll. New York: John Wiley, pp. 220-232.)

————. 1941. The relations of habitual thought and behavior to language. In *Language, culture and personality, Essays in memory of Edward Sapir,* eds. L. Spier, A. I. Hallowell, and S. S. Newman. Menasha, Wisconsin: Banta Books. (Reprinted in *Language, thought and reality,* pp. 134-159.)

Williams, R. 1960. *Culture and society 1780-1950.* Garden City, New York: Anchor Books.

Index

LANGUAGES AND GROUPS

PERSONS

TOPICS

sociolinguistics, status of, Ch.
10, 194, 206
sociolinguistics, the term, 3, 8,
32, 83f., 86, 193, 195
sociology, 6, 44, 65 n. 6, 69f., 74,
76, 79f., 81, 82, 84, 116, 173,
179-180, 208
some-any distinction, semantics,
180
Sound and meaning, 163, 197f.,
198
sound change, 76, 169
sound patterns, 159f.
speaker-hearer, ideal, 46, 54,
132, 205
SPEAKING (mnemonic), 62
speech activity, patterning of, 3
speech acts, 4, 26, 49, 52, 53, 81,
101f., 114, 181, 202
speech community, 34-35, 47-51,
72-73, 102, 120, 123, 132, 200,
202, 206. See also linguistic
community
speech, cultural role of, 33f.,
35f., 108f., 116, 127. See also
functional   relativity;   language, functions of
speech disguise, 8, 168
speech economy, 46. See also
communicative economy
speech event, 4, 23, 52, 109-110.
See also communicative event
speech field, 50
speech levels, 111
speech network, 50. See also
communicative network
speech situation, 26, 51ff.
speech styles, 59, 102, 105, 190,
202
speech styles, dimensions of,
36-40, 41, 174; discursive disclosure, 37; elaborate, 38; laconic, 36; pithy, 36; reticent,
36, 37; sparse, 38; taciturn,

36, 37; verbose, 36, voluble,
36, 37
speech surrogates, 25, 48
speech varieties, 77
Sprachbund, 49
Sprechbund, 49
storytelling, 127
strategies, 57, 100 n. 17, 138
"structural" linguistics, 70f., 78,
79, 92, 100
structuralism, pre-World War I,
5-6
structure, 8-9, 89, 100, 102, 171
style, analysis of, 16, 17, 45f.,
105f., 131, 174f., 178. See also
speech styles
style shifting, 200
stylistic perspective, as ethnography of speaking, 58, 66, 67-
69, 146, 149, 159f., 174f., 198
surface structure, value, 149
symbolic action, 80, 135f., 139
symbolic competence, 139
symbolic form, speech as, 31,
46, 66, 81, 109, 139
syntactic structure, scope of, 91,
98, 180
syntagmatic, 97, 150, 153
systemic potential, 95

taxonomies of speaking, need
for, 34-35, 41, 182
terms, key, 138
texts, analysis of, 98f., 100, 137
theory, 87
topic, 13, 23, 53, 55, 57, 60, 103
traditional control, 40
translation, 108
typologies, 17, 41ff., 164, 203

universals, 33, 35, 41ff., 43, 60,
74, 77, 122, 134, 159f., 163,
169, 170f.